CRITICAL INSIGHTS

Beloved

CRITICAL

INSIGHTS

Beloved

Editor

Maureen N. Eke

Central Michigan University

SALEM PRESS

A Division of EBSCO Information Services, Inc.

Ipswich, Massachusetts

GREY HOUSE PUBLISHING

Publisher's Cataloging-In-Publication Data
(Prepared by The Donohue Group, Inc.)

Beloved / editor, Maureen N. Eke, Central Michigan University. -- [First edition].

  pages ; cm. -- (Critical insights)

Edition statement supplied by publisher.
Includes bibliographical references and index.
ISBN: 978-1-61925-828-0 (hardcover)

  1. Morrison, Toni. Beloved. 2. Morrison, Toni--Criticism and interpretation. 3. Slavery in literature. 4. Infanticide in literature. 5. Spirituality in literature. I. Eke, Maureen N. II. Series: Critical insights.

PS3563.O8749 B436 2015
813/.54

First Printing

PRINTED IN THE UNITED STATES OF AMERICA

Contents

Resources

About This Volume

Maureen N. Eke

This volume brings together fourteen original essays which offer new ways of exploring Toni Morrison's Pulitzer award-winning novel, *Beloved*. Because scholars in the same field belong to a discourse community, it is not uncommon to notice that they have used the same sources or arrived at similar interpretations or conclusions. The essays in this volume may have some commonalities because they focus on one subject, the novel, *Beloved* and one author, Toni Morrison. While much has been written about the novel, the aim here is to offer innovative (and needed) new perspectives.

In order to provide a historical background for Morrison's novel, Kristine Yohe returns to the informing story of Margaret Garner, the fugitive slave woman who murdered her infant daughter to "save" her from being returned to slavery. Yohe argues that Morrison's novel "demonstrates a deep concern with the legacy of slavery in the United States" by making "comprehensible for readers the dehumanizing personal experiences of enslaved individuals." Through an extensive survey of several essays and reviews of Morrison's novel, Touria Khannous then looks at the reception of *Beloved* over several eras and across several disciplines, arguing that the "critical readings constitute a literary theoretical discourse" on *Beloved* that is still unfolding.

Anne Herbert deploys an eclectic literary reading of *Beloved*, demonstrating how the novel can serve as a model for bringing together black feminist criticism and feminist archetypal theory through the use of cultural semiotics. Herbert draws attention to the ways in which the novel connects Jungian universal archetypes and West African female archetypes, such as the Great Mother and mother-daughter dyads, through Morrison's characters and semiotic representation. In so doing, maintains Herbert, the novel serves as Morrison's way of preserving African American cultural memory.

Beloved certainly does not exist in a vacuum. And it is well known that Morrison has been compared to other American and international writers of her generation and earlier ones. So, it is no wonder that Herman Beavers sees parallels between *Beloved* (1987) and Harriet Beecher Stowe's *Uncle Tom's Cabin* (1852). Beavers argues that the former revises scenes from the latter, "in order to foreground the anxieties that occur at the intersection of race and masculinity, for both white male characters like Mr. Garner and black male characters like Paul D and Stamp Paid."

The next set of essays read *Beloved* from various critical perspectives. Joseph McLaren claims that *Beloved* is a neo-slave narrative that retells the history of the "peculiar institution of slavery" using the historical Margaret Garner incident as the foundation for constructing Sethe's character. As a neo-slave narrative, McLaren suggests, *Beloved* presents "modes of escape" through the Underground Railroad exemplified by Stamp Paid in the novel.

Beloved also reminds us of the African presence in America not only through references to the Middle Passage, but also through Morrison's invoking of a range of African folkloric, spiritual, healing, mythic, and performance forms—storytelling, songs—as when Baby Suggs gathers her people and performs before them in the woodland Clearing. Africans who were brought to the New World also brought their cultures with them and scholars such as Joseph Holloway, for example, have pointed to these African retentions, including some burial practices, healing arts, foods, musical forms, folktales, and religious practices.

African spirituality also serves as the foundational structure of syncretic religions such as Candomblé and Ubanda, Santeria, and Voodoo (Hoodoo). Consequently, it is to be expected that African spirituality and performance forms find their way into *Beloved*, for after all, the novel is a story about the experiences of people of African descent and their survival in the New World.

Both Kokahvah Zauditu-Salessie and Sarah Berry underscore the presence of African spirituality and healing practices in *Beloved*. Zauditu-Salessie's reading from an African spirituality perspective connects Sethe's chokecherry tree to the tree of life and the Yoruba and West African spirituality through communion with the natural world. Zauditu-Selassie asserts that Morrison performs what the Yoruba describe as ashé to enable Sethe and the characters to recuperate from the trauma. Sarah Berry examines the African presence in the novel from a pan-Africanist perspective, suggesting that the novel "privileges the worldview of Sethe and her family" and in so doing, "preserves the folkways" that enable "the survival of individuals, families, and communities under slavery" and afterwards.

Writers are storytellers and visionaries, who often serve as critics or truth-tellers in their societies. It is in this context that Khalilah T. Watson sees *Beloved*, arguing that the novel represents "a manifestation of Morrison's prophetic utterances to the literary world and her intense study of history." Lynne Simpson builds on this theme, pointing to the problems arising when history of slavery is studied through numbers. This history, she says, becomes alienating because "numbers remove the real human impact of slavery." She proposes a study of history through literature—*Beloved* in particular—for it is a powerful tool for teaching slavery as it "delves into the real psychological warfare of slavery that lasted beyond captivity."

While Simpson reminds us of how slavery rendered individuals into numbers, Sandy Alexandre believes that Toni Morrison's work "attempts to persuade readers to adopt a history that may not necessarily belong *directly* to them" by presenting them slavery through the body of Beloved. In other words, when Sethe welcomed the physical manifestation, the embodied Beloved, into her home at 124 Bluestone Road, it is as if she were adopting slavery embodied (as a person). Alexandre asks the reader to consider the following: What kind of reminder regarding slavery does Beloved represent as a character?

Blessing Diala-Ogamba addresses *Beloved* from the perspective of genre studies, focusing on the gothic, fantastic, and supernatural elements in the novel. She perceives the character of *Beloved* as a ghost, an aspect of the supernatural, which Morrison uses "to explore the evil effects of slavery on the characters." The ghost enables the characters to confront their traumatic experiences under slavery, thus helping them move towards healing.

The last two essays focus on ways in which to engage in close readings of *Beloved*. One of the inspirations for this volume is a comment I have heard several times over the years from teachers and/or students and friends who confess that they have difficulty understanding the book; they cannot finish reading it because it overwhelms and resists them. For teachers, the problem is finding ways to teach the novel and/or its subject. Some students have told me that the novel has drained them of emotions. Indeed, *Beloved* is a complex work, full of questions, but rich with compelling stories. Durthy A. Washington encourages a "culturally responsive approach" to literary studies through the LIST paradigm, which explores four keys to culture: Language, Identity, Space, and Time. Washington suggests that using a LIST Paradigm approach will "unlock a text for deeper learning and foster critical reading from multiple perspectives" as it "encourages students to explore unique aspects of multicultural literatures often overlooked by mainstream scholars and critics."

Lastly, Nicole M. Coonradt closes the volume with an essay on literary analysis, focusing on the ways in which readers enter a discourse community through a close reading of *Beloved*. Coonradt elucidates the techniques used in literary analysis—such as annotation, identification, and examination of motif—designed to encourage a close reading of the text and help students develop critical thinking skills.

Taken together, the essays presented in this volume give special attention to the traumatic horrors of slavery. Indeed, although their authors examine Sethe's act of infanticide from various perspectives, it is evident that the recurring theme throughout the volume is not the question of the rightness or the wrongness of the act itself, but the ways in which the characters contend with and survive a dehumanizing and absurd historical moment. *Beloved*, the narrative, and Beloved, the character, become Morrison's conduits for confronting a story that is impossible to tell but needs to be told.

THE BOOK AND THE AUTHOR

Mapping Toni Morrison's *Beloved*: Of Love, History, Trauma, and Healing_____

Maureen N. Eke

According to Nellie Y. McKay, of all of Toni Morrison's novels, *Beloved* "is the one most often taught and the one most written about across the world" (4). Not only is the novel "recognized for outstanding literary worth" and "a signal achievement in African American and American letters" (McKay 4), *Beloved* also stands as a monumental engagement with the legacy of slavery. It can easily be described as the most traumatizing of Morrison's works. What could be worse than the theme of a mother killing her own child in order to save it?

Beloved was published in 1987, several years after Morrison's discovery of the real story of Margaret Garner, a "young mother who, having escaped slavery, was arrested for killing one of her children (and trying to kill the others) rather than let them be returned to the owner's plantation" in "a newspaper clipping in *The Black Book*," which Morrison had published (Morrison xvii). According to Morrison, *Beloved* "entered" into her narrative consciousness or presented itself "a few days after [her] last day at work" (xvi) in 1983. For Morrison, the story provided an opportunity to creatively flesh out Margaret Garner, "invent her thoughts, plumb them for subtext that was historically true in essence" so as to "relate her history to contemporary issues about freedom, responsibility, and women's 'place'" (xvii).

Although set in 1873, almost a decade after the end of slavery in 1863, the novel serves as a vehicle for examining slavery as a traumatizing historical event at various levels: individual, group, and national. Morrison asks the reader to consider the unthinkable, that which cannot be narrated, retold, forgotten, or even remembered. In this story, we enter a landscape of ambiguities, of spaces in-between, spaces that open and close, where Sethe says, "Some things go. Pass on. Some things just stay... out there in the world" (Morrison 43), even when they are gone. The narrative also compels us to ask: What does freedom mean within the context of Margaret Garner's or Sethe's life? What does it mean to be a slave mother? How does one recover from such trauma?

Indeed, the novel challenges the reader to reconsider what it means to be simply human. In many ways, that, too, is the significance of Margaret Garner's act, which serves as the informing historical narrative for Morrison's text. Certainly, while *Beloved* deals with slavery and its effects, it confronts us with what it means to lose or to be threatened with the loss of our humanity. Slavery represents the totalizing negation of personhood. To be enslaved is to not own one's self, not to claim ownership of anything, to be subject to another's will, to be an object, disposable. The accompanying trauma of slavery which *Beloved* addresses announces itself in the book's opening line in a few words: "124 WAS SPITEFUL. Full of a baby's venom" (Morrison 3, capitalization in original). Like the opening chapter of Frederick Douglass' autobiography, *The Narrative of the Life of Frederick Douglass an American Slave* (1845), which presents the reader with the various ways in which slavery dehumanized those who experienced it, Toni Morrison's *Beloved* throws its audience into a house of alienation, a place of fear, pain, and death, whose origin is slavery. How can a house be spiteful and a baby be venomous? What factors enable such conditions, victimizing the occupants of the house and forcing others to flee?

The novel's attempt to address the questions raised by its opening sentences becomes a tour de force in the exploration of the traumatic history of slavery and its impact on the lives of those who experienced it. The wounds persist, even after slavery. In the words of Barbara Schapiro, the novel:

> reveals how the condition of enslavement in the external world, particularly the denial of one's status as a human subject has deep repercussions in the individual's internal world. These internal resonances are so profound that even if one is eventually freed from external bondage, the self will still be trapped in an inner world that prevents a genuine experience of freedom. (194)

As the essays in this volume suggest, there are various approaches to reading and/or teaching Morrison's *Beloved*. A historical approach, which connects the novel to its informing story—the Margaret Garner incident (1856) and the Fugitive Slave Act (1850), to which Garner was responding—would expose the challenges of achieving freedom or claiming it for blacks, free or fugitive, at the time. Because black people in the United States at the time were perceived as not "full" human beings and citizens, they had no rights. The American Constitution classified a slave as one-fifth of a person for congressional appointment in 1787. Ultimately, without rights or citizenship, enslaved blacks could not seek justice or any protection by the law. Indeed, it was the very law of the land that denied them dignity and rights.

Black people were simply considered "disposable" property, and as slaves, they could be willed to anyone, while black women could be raped and bred whenever a master wished to increase his slave property. These experiences are perennial themes in slave narratives, such as Olaudah Equiano's *The Interesting Narrative of the Life of Olaudah Equiano the African* (1789), Frederick Douglass's *Narrative of the Life of Frederick Douglass an American Slave* (1845), William Wells Brown's *The Narrative of William Wells Brown Fugitive Slave* (1847), Solomon Northup's *12 Years a Slave* (1853), William and Ellen Craft's *Running a Thousand Miles for Freedom* (1860), and Harriet Jacobs' *Incidents in the Life of a Slave Girl* (1861). All these narratives point to their authors' quests for human rights and dignity.

One response for these Africans was to succumb and simply accept their social conditions, but, as each of these slave narratives informs us, the idea of freedom—real or imagined—is so powerful that many slaves would sacrifice their lives to attain it. The various slave rebellions represent the exercise of agency, the will to act on behalf of oneself, to free oneself by those whose humanity, rights and dignity have been trampled.[1] Article 1 of the Universal Declaration of Human Rights (1948) asserts that "All human beings are born free and equal in dignity and rights" and while the subjects of the slave narratives and *Beloved* may not belong to the twentieth century, their struggles were attempts to claim their humanity and rights as human beings, the same rights embedded in the language of the US Declaration of Independence back in 1776: "all men are created equal…they are endowed by their Creator with certain unalienable Rights…among these are Life, Liberty and the pursuit of Happiness." Of course, excluded from these rights were blacks (free and enslaved), Native Americans, and women, although white women had more rights than blacks and Native Americans.

For blacks, the Fugitive Slave Acts (1793 and 1850), therefore, worsened their status by further ensuring the continuation of slavery through laws that upheld that system even within the so-called free states. Ohio, to which Sethe had escaped with her family, was a free state. Thus, after twenty-eight days of freedom in Ohio, Sethe knew, when she saw schoolteacher, one nephew, one slave catcher, and a sheriff approach her house, that neither she nor her children were safe. She would either surrender herself to them for re-enslavement or she would die. In choosing death, Sethe believed that she was securing freedom for her children. "I took and put my babies where they'd be safe," she tells Paul D (Morrison 193). Her response to the "Fugitive Bill," as Stamp Paid calls it (201), thus represents her assertion of agency, as a mother, a human being with rights, and a declarative defiance of schoolteacher's mutilation of her body. It is also a defiance of a national law and the systemic violence that has been used to objectify her. Sethe killed her child, Stamp Paid says, because "She was trying to out-hurt the hurter" (276).

As a book that introduces us to a historical event and laws that denied the humanity and dignity of those affected, *Beloved* links us to urgent contemporary social justice issues, in this case, modern-day forms of slavery and/or human trafficking. Although individuals may no longer be in chains (publicly) and defined as slaves, as in the antebellum era, slavery exists globally today. According to the UN *Protocol to Prevent, Suppress and Punish Trafficking in Persons, especially Women and Children* of 2000[2], human trafficking—which generally involves forced servitude and sexual exploitation—is a form of modern-day slavery. So a discussion of *Beloved* can certainly include an exploration of how past slavery intersects with its various permutations today. According to UNICEF, "Cases of human trafficking have been reported in all 50 US States; anyone can be trafficked regardless of race, class, education, gender, age, or citizenship..." In other words, slavery still exists today, even if the demographics of those affected may have changed.

In her autobiography *Incidents in the Life of a Slave Girl*, Harriet Jacobs describes her anguish at the possibility of losing her children or leaving them behind and fleeing Dr. Flint, who was harassing her with sexual overtures. Instead of fleeing, Jacobs chose to spend seven years in hiding in an attic or crawl space above her grandmother's house in order to be close to her children. Unlike Sethe, she did not kill her children, but she was alienated from them. However, unlike Jacobs, Sethe did not have the protection of a respected grandmother. Even then, Jacobs' grandmother could not protect her granddaughter from her powerful master. Jacobs, like Sethe, asserted her will by fleeing to the North. According to Morrison, Margaret Garner, on whom Sethe's character is based,

> became a cause célèbre in the fight against the Fugitive Slave laws, which mandated the return of escapees to their owners. Her sanity and lack of repentance caught the attention of Abolitionists as well as newspapers. She was certainly single-minded and, judging by her comments, she had the intellect, the ferocity, and the willingness to risk everything for what was to her the necessity of freedom. (Morrison xvii)

Earlier, Sethe sums up her feeling and exercise of agency to Paul D in an eloquent self-empowering description of how she alone, and without her husband, managed to shepherd her children to safety: "I did it. I got us all out. Without Halle too. Up till then it was the only thing I ever did on my own. Decided. And it came off right like it was supposed to. We was here. Each and every one of my babies and me too..." (Morrison 190). This speech reveals the emergence of Sethe as an intentional being, a Sethe who claims ownership of her body and of her children—of the rights and desires that slavery denied her. She recreates herself as a thinking and acting human because she "decided" to free herself and her children from Sweet Home and from the clutches of schoolteacher. Like Margaret Garner, she is unrepentant. Sethe confirms her "new" self when she adds, "…it was me doing it; me saying, *Go on*, and *Now*. Me having to look out. Me using my own head" (190). Moreover, Sethe narrates for Paul D what and how it feels to love and, thus to be human, especially to be a mother—an emotion and relationship which under slavery were alien to her. "It was a kind of selfishness I never knew nothing about before. It felt good. Good and right… Look like I loved em more after I got here. Or maybe I couldn't love em proper in Kentucky because they wasn't mine to love" (190), she tells him.

It is within this context of a protective motherly love that Sethe's murder of her infant child could be considered. According to Barbara Schapiro, for "African-Americans in a racist, slave society, there is no reliable other to recognize and affirm their existence" (194). For Sethe, it seems, to love one has to be free, claim freedom, or even steal it. Her flight to Ohio freed her to love herself and her children as she tells Paul D. Indeed, Paul D confirms Sethe's transformative theorizing of her understanding of love when he thinks of Sethe's love as "risky," adding that

> for a used-to-be-slave woman to love anything that much was dangerous, especially if it was her children she had settled on to love. The best thing, he knew, was to love just a little bit; everything, just a little bit, so when they broke its back, or shoved it in a croaker sack, well, maybe you'd have a little love left over for the next one. (Morrison 54)

In effect, Sethe's decision to murder her children was also her articulation of her love for them, her only way to protect them, and ironically to grant them the humanity that slavery had denied them. She claims that she "Collected every bit of life she had made, all the parts of her that were precious and fine and beautiful, and carried, pushed, dragged them through the veil, out, away, over there where no one could hurt them. Over there. Outside this place, where they would be safe" (192). Indeed, her description of her actions underscores Morrison's comments in her interview with Bill Moyers that some of the love her women characters express is "very fierce, powerful, distorted even, because the duress they work under is overwhelming" (Moyers).

In the case of Margaret Garner, her "fierce" response was heightened not only by the physical and psychological torture that she had experienced at the hands of schoolteacher and his nephews, but her realization that her children would suffer a similar fate. In her struggle to persuade Beloved that "what she had done was right because it came from true love" (Morrison 296), Sethe declares that under slavery, "…anybody white could take your whole self for anything that came to mind. Not just work, kill, or maim you, but dirty you. Dirty you so bad you couldn't like yourself anymore. Dirty you so bad you forgot who you were and couldn't think it up" (Morrison 295). For Sethe, her action was right because "she could never let it happen to her children… And no one, nobody on this earth would list her daughter's characteristics on the animal side of the paper" (295–96). Sethe, therefore, saw her love as protest against schoolteacher's characterizing of her parts earlier in bestial terms, and above all, Sethe's declaration of children's humanity.

In her poem, "The Slave Mother" (1856), Frances Ellen Watkins Harper describes a slave mother's life as a conundrum—she is present yet absent, and she cannot protect her child from the violence of slavery. Harper writes, "He is not hers, although she bore / For him a mother's pains; He is not hers, although her blood / Is coursing through his veins!" (n.p.). While Harper's poem was published before the Garner incident, it anticipates it.[3] The alienated relationship between mother and child, which the poem describes, was familiar to enslaved blacks, hence, Paul D's alarm when Sethe describes her love for her children to him. Baby Suggs also knows the pain of a slave mother, for "seven times she had done that: held a little foot" only to lose the child to slavery (Morrison 163), except Halle. Moreover, Frederick Douglass in his 1845 autobiography describes how slavery made his mother a stranger to him. So, Garner's or Sethe's open defiance of the law was a declaration of rights of ownership, not in material terms as property, but in relational terms: My child is mine! Yet, while Sethe or Margaret Garner's action was not common, it was not unusual since slave women sometimes smothered their babies to save them from slavery, but, explained the deaths as a form of infant sudden death or still birth.

Trauma and Healing

In one of the poignant scenes in the novel, Morrison demonstrates the power of love to heal through Baby Suggs, Sethe's mother-in-law, who functions as a woodland healer, a *griotte*, a reservoir of community memory and general knowledge. Leading her people to the woodland Clearing, Baby Suggs administers healing to her people, whose bodies, psyches, and spirits have been traumatized.

As a healer or shaman, Baby Suggs recognizes that she and her people have been wounded and that she must help them reconcile their bodies with themselves. Thus, she guides their healing process, returning to them parts of their bodies which had been commodified or dismembered under slavery. "She did not tell them to clean up their lives or to go and sin no more... She only told them that the only grace they could have was the grace they could imagine" (Morrison 103). In gathering them together in the Clearing, she offered them their humanity by granting them permission to do all those things that they had been denied. "Let your wives and your children see you dance," she instructed "the grown men," who could neither claim their children nor their wives while enslaved. Here as an ancient mother-goddess, she would slowly guide their recovery, telling them:

> '[I]n this here place, we flesh; flesh that weeps, laughs; flesh that dances on bare feet in grass. Love it. Love it hard. Yonder they do not love your flesh. They despise it. They don't love your eyes; they'd just as soon pick em out. No more do they love the skin on your back. Yonder they flay it. And O my people they do not love your hands. Those they only use, tie, bind, chop off and leave empty. Love your hands! Love them. Raise them up and kiss them.' (Morrison 103)

In her healing incantation, Baby Suggs catalogs the various ways in which her people's bodies have been wounded, recognizing that to love their bodies, her people must first acknowledge their wounding, face it, mourn the loss of their bodies and themselves, work through their wounding, and finally love their bodies. This will be their path to recovering from both their individual and collective traumas and to reclaiming themselves. Indeed, through Baby Suggs, Morrison also catalogs the ways in which slavery dismembered her people's bodies, almost in a process similar to Frederick Douglass's and Harriet Jacobs's cataloging of the injustices and horrors of slavery in their narratives.

According to Cathy Caruth, trauma is inaccessible (10). "It is the fundamental dislocation implied by all traumatic experience that is both its testimony to the event and to the impossibility of its direct access" (Caruth 9). Clearly, all the black characters in Morrison's *Beloved* have been dislocated—psychically, physically, emotionally, spiritually. Thus, Baby Suggs's woodland Clearing healing ritual becomes necessary as a celebration of life and self. Caruth's comments are also significant as they suggest that a traumatic experience or even working through it is a double-edged sword. On the one hand, one wants to leave it behind; but, on the other, one must access it and own it in order to work through it. Baby Suggs' healing in the Clearing performs a similar function. It is organic therapy, holistic spiritual healing, whose purpose is to connect the wounded to their pains in order to facilitate catharsis.

Morrison is also engaged in a similar process through Baby Suggs. Beloved the character and *Beloved* the novel serve as conduits through which Morrison addresses what Jeffrey C. Alexander refers to as collective trauma, "wounds to social identity" (2). As a narrative about trauma, *Beloved*, therefore, is a "[representation] of social suffering" (Alexander 2). In this case, the affected group has experienced tremendous shock to its sense of collective identity because the trauma has shattered "the individual or collective actor's sense of well-being" (7). Alexander sees this type of wounding as "cultural trauma," which he states occurs when "members of a collective feel they have been subjected to [an event so] horrendous…that [it] leaves indelible marks upon their group consciousness, marking their memories forever and changing their future identity in fundamental and irrevocable ways" (6). Morrison would agree. Slavery was a horrendous event, an ailment, and the

Margaret Garner fugitive slave incident was only its symptom. In *Beloved*, the memory of the experience continues, and one may say that it returns to haunt Sethe and the community. So, enter *Beloved*, enter trauma, enter the past, and the future.

Coda

Beloved resurrects a ghost from the past. It is a ghost of memories and narratives, which have been buried, but which needed to be unearthed in order to make comprehensible the present and to secure the future. Among many African groups, the memory of the past is linked to the future; hence, many Africans believe that one cannot fully comprehend one's present and future without an understanding of, or reconciliation of oneself and one's past. One needs to know where one has been in order to understand where one is going. Often, people will visit local shamans, healers, and spiritual guides to investigate the past, consult the ancestors, obtain explanations for the present, advice, and direction that will help them move forward. Baby Suggs fulfills several of these functions in Morrison's novel as *griotte*, healer, guide, and holder of community wisdom.

In writing *Beloved*, Morrison also serves a similar function. It is not only Margaret Garner's or Sethe's past that lies buried, but also the past(s) of the entire community, African and African Diaspora peoples, and the nation. In unearthing Sethe's story or the historical narrative of Margaret Garner, Toni Morrison, like Baby Suggs, helps her people to confront their own ghosts and to recuperate themselves, to face the past in all its ugliness, pain, and beauty, and eventually to heal. The community begins to heal itself when it gathers as a collective to exorcise the ghost of Beloved from 124 Bluestone Road. In doing so, the community also recovers its humanity and expiates its own guilt in causing the death of Sethe's daughter, when it failed to warn Baby Suggs and Sethe of schoolteacher's arrival in town with the sheriff, slave catcher, and one nephew.

As individuals, some of the members begin to reach out to Sethe through Denver after they find out that Sethe has been ill. They offer food to Denver for her family, and some of them remember that her grandmother Baby Suggs was kind to them when she healed them in the past. Stamp Paid, for instance, visits Ella to solicit her help in rescuing Sethe and her family. But, it is only when Denver fully "[inaugurates] her life in the world as a woman" (Morrison 292) by finding work in the community and telling Janey Wagon how ill Sethe had become since the arrival of the enlarging Beloved that the community goes into a frenzy about rescuing Sethe, thus, initiating communal catharsis.

"The news that Janey got hold of she spread among the other colored women. Sethe's dead daughter, the one whose throat she cut had come back to fix her. Sethe was worn down, speckled, dying, spinning, changing shapes and generally bedeviled" (Morrison 302). It is after this that Ella "convinced the others that a rescue was in order. She was a practical woman who believed there was a root either to chew or avoid for every ailment" (301). Ella forgives Sethe, because she "didn't like the idea of past errors taking possession of the present" (302). Saving Sethe from Beloved also means securing their community's safety. "So, thirty women," armed with "what they could bring and what they believed would work," marched to 124 Bluestone Road to do battle with the demon, Beloved.

Although Sethe does not recover immediately after the women exorcise Beloved, it is Paul D, another wounded figure from Sethe's past, who enables her recovery by telling her "You your best thing, Sethe" after she tells him her baby "She left me....'She was my best thing'" (Morrison 321). Morrison has said that Beloved is about "exorcising ghosts," but it is also about raising them to confront them. In Beloved, therefore, Morrison enables the "we" of black people and of America in general to symbolically confront the trauma of the past and the attendant violence of racism whose ghosts continue to haunt us. We cannot truthfully recover from the violence of slavery without acknowledging its history. Its repression, erasure, or silencing binds all of us to an unending cycle of guilt, repression, and violence.

The trauma which Morrison's Beloved excavates is encompassing. What compels a mother or anyone to kill the person s/he loves the most as an act of love and in order to protect it? "It is not a story to pass on" (324), Morrison says, because "they forgot her. Like an unpleasant dream during a troubling sleep" (324), yet, the memory of it is present, refusing to submerge, thus, demanding to be acknowledged, to be passed on. Indeed, the story of the traumatic experience of African and African American slavery represented by Margaret Garner's act in 1856 is one of "acute discomfort entering into the core of [our collective] sense of our…identity…one of fundamental threat to [our] sense of who [we] are, where [we] come from, and where [we] are going" (Alexander 15). In her often cited speech, "A Bench by the Road," Morrison explains the reasons for writing *Beloved*:

> There is no place you or I can go, to think about or not think about, to summon the presences of, or recollect the absences of slaves; nothing that reminds us of the ones who made the journey and of those who did not make it. There is no suitable memorial, or plaque, or wreath, or wall, or park, or skyscraper lobby. There's no 300 foot tower. There's no small bench by the road. There is not even a tree scored, an initial that I can visit or you can visit in Charleston or Savannah or New York or Providence or, better still, on the banks of the Mississippi. And because such a place does not exist (that I know of) the book had to. (qtd. *Toni Morrison's Beloved: A Casebook* 3)

Beloved, therefore, represents Morrison's historical and cultural recuperative act, a memorialization of that past which must be activated so that the future can emerge. It is a story about what Primo Levi describes as the "demolition of man" (*Survival in Auschwitz* 26), a story where language fails us, but which we must tell. It is simultaneously a story to pass on and not to pass on.

Notes

1. The history of black people's resistance to slavery is extensive and ranges from escapes to bloody revolts and written protests and small acts, such as sabotage. Some of the notable revolts and revolutionary leaders include: the Stono Rebellion (also called Cato's Rebellion), South Carolina (1739); Gabriel Prosser and Jack Bowler in Richmond, Virginia (1800); François-Dominique Toussaint Louverture in Haiti (1802); Charles Deslondes in Louisiana (1811); Denmark Vesey in

Charleston, South Carolina (1822); and Nat Turner in Southampton County, Virginia (1831).

2. *The UN Protocol to Prevent, Suppress and Punish Trafficking in Persons, Especially Women and Children, Supplementing the United Nations Convention against Transnational Organized Crime* was adopted and opened for signature and ratification by the UN General Assembly resolution 55/25 on November 15, 2000.

3. In 1874, Frances E. W. Harper published another poem under the title: "The Slave Mother, a Tale of the Ohio" in her collection *Poems and Miscellaneous Subjects*. This 1874 poem was informed by the Margaret Garner incident. See: https://apece.pbworks.com/f/The+Slave+Mother-poem.doc.

Works Cited

Alexander, Jeffrey C. *Trauma: A Social Theory*. Cambridge, UK: Polity, 2012.

Caruth, Cathy. *Unclaimed Experience: Trauma, Narrative, and History*. Baltimore, MD: Johns Hopkins UP, 1996.

UNICEF. "Child Trafficking." *UNICEF United States Fund*. US Fund for UNICEF, 2015 Web. 29 Sept. 2015. <http://www.unicefusa.org/mission/protect/trafficking>.

"The Declaration of Independence: A Transcription." *National Archives and Records Administration*. National Archives and Records Administration, 2015. Web. 29 Sept. 2015.

Harper, Frances Ellen Watkins. "The Slave Mother." *Poetry Foundation*. Poetry Foundation, n.d. Web. 06 Oct. 2015. <http://www.poetryfoundation.org/poem/182614>.

Levi, Primo. *Survival in Auschwitz*. New York: Touchstone, 1996.

McKay, Nellie Y. "Introduction." *Toni Morrison's Beloved: A Casebook*. Eds. William L. Andrews & Nellie Y. McKay. New York: Oxford UP, 1999. 3–19.

Morrison, Toni. *Beloved*. New York: Vintage, 2004.

Moyers, Bill. "Interview with Toni Morrison." *A World of Ideas*. Youtube, 16 Dec. 2014. Web. 9 Sept. 2015. <https://www.youtube.com/watch?v=Gcr5v5DHqMg>.

Schapiro, Barbara. "The Bonds of Love and the Boundaries of Self in Toni Morrison's *Beloved*" *Contemporary Literature* 32.2 (1991): 194–210. *JSTOR*. Web. 06 Oct. 2015.

United Nations. *Protocol to Prevent, Suppress and Punish Trafficking in Persons*. RefWorld, 15 Nov. 2000. Web. 28 Oct. 2015. <http://www.refworld.org/docid/4720706c0.html>.

_____. *The Universal Declaration of Human Rights*. United Nations, 2015. Web. 29 Sept. 2015. <http://www.un.org/en/documents/udhr/>.

Biography of Toni Morrison

Maureen N. Eke

Nobel Laureate Chloe Toni (Anthony) Morrison is one of the most recognized woman writers today. Her works are taught in literature courses across the globe, from the Americas to Europe, and from Africa to Asia. A simple web search on Google using her name culled about 9,700,000 results in 0.44 seconds. The number of doctoral dissertations, book chapters, and journal articles on Morrison continues to grow every year. In short, Morrison is the representative of African American literature today.

Morrison was born as Chloe Wofford on February 18, 1931 in Lorain, OH, to George and Ella Ramah Wofford. Lorain, OH, is a small town on the edge of Lake Erie with a complex history, where according to Toni Morrison, during her childhood, "Everybody was somebody from the South or an immigrant from east Europe or from Mexico. And there was one church and there were four elementary schools" (Gross). Lorain was an integrated, working-class community with no black neighborhoods.

Morrison has indicated in interviews and conversations that her parents, particularly the women in her family, instilled in her the love of stories because they told folktales and stories about African American culture and heritage. "The grown-ups told stories, the same stories, over and over again....," she told *Fresh Air* host Terry Gross.

The second of four girls, she learned to read at an early age, and her love of reading and storytelling was encouraged by the stories that she heard from her mother and aunts. She attended Lorain High School, where she read and studied the works of great European writers such as Jane Austen, Dostoyevsky, and Tolstoy, whose writing she admired. She graduated with honors from Lorain High School in 1949 and went to Howard University, from which she graduated in 1953 with BA in English and minor in classics. While at Howard, she developed interest in theatre and joined a Howard University theatre group. Morrison would be the first woman in her family to earn a college degree. After graduating from Howard, she attended Cornell University where she earned a master of arts degree from Cornell University in 1955 and wrote a thesis comparing Virginia Woolf and William Faulkner.

Between 1955 and 1957, she taught at Texas Southern University but returned to Howard University in 1957 to teach English. It was there that she met Jamaican-born architect, Harold Morrison, whom she married in 1958 and with whom she had two sons, Slade Morrison, an artist who died of pancreatic cancer in 2010, and Harold Ford Morrison. She and Harold Morrison were divorced in 1964.

Morrison returned to Howard University in 1963 to teach, and there, she joined a writers' group and began writing a short story, which she "later incorporated into a novel"—*The Bluest Eye* (1970)—the story of a young black girl who wished she had blue eyes, so that she could be loved. *The Bluest Eye* was published in 1970. After the end of her marriage to Harold Morrison, Toni Morrison moved with her two sons to Syracuse, NY, in 1965, to serve as a senior editor with L.W. Singer, the textbook subsidiary of Random House. It was in Syracuse where she would transform her short story into a novel because she "did not have anyone to talk to" (Harris 7). In 1968, she moved to New York City as a trade book editor with Random House. She would eventually become a senior editor at Random House, and one of only a few blacks (male or female) in that position at that time. While at Random House, she published the works of several emerging black writers. "My list was to me spectacular" she states. The list included "Toni Cade Bambara, June Jordan, Gayle Jones, Lucille Clifton, Henry Dumas, Leon Forrest," as well as "scholars with original ideas and hands-on research" (*Beloved* xv), such as William H. Hinton, Ivan van Sertima, Karen DeCrow, Angela Davis, and Muhammad Ali to mention a few.

The publication of *The Bluest Eye* (1970), her first novel, garnered Morrison some attention. In this novel, she examines black people's perceptions of beauty and of themselves through the psychosis of Pecola, her young black female protagonist who desperately desires love and believes that only blue eyes would make her beautiful enough to be loved. In her essay "Behind the Making of *The Black Book*, Morrison says, "When the strength of a race depends on its beauty, when the focus is turned to how one looks as opposed to what one is, we are in trouble" (38).

Morrison's second novel, *Sula* (1973), received a mixed critical reception. Here, Morrison focuses on the tensions between Sula Peace, a rebellious, independent, young black woman and the residents of her community, the Bottom, a predominantly black community in Ohio. *Sula* earned Morrison new accolades, particularly because of its daring and innovative exploration of gender identity in the black community, centering on the relationship between two women: Sula and her childhood friend Nel Wright. *Sula* was nominated for the American Book Award and received the Ohioana Book Award in 1974.

In her next novel, *Song of Solomon* (1977), Morrison shifts her attention to a young black male protagonist Milkman Dead, whose quest for "a cache of gold hidden in the Virginia mountains" (Giddings 11) leads him also to self-discovery and better understanding of his origins. Milkman's journey takes him from an unnamed town in Michigan (critics suggest maybe Detroit) to Shalimar in the South (Virginia), where he discovers that his great grandfather Solomon was the flying African in the children's song he heard on his route. The book was chosen as "a main selection of the Book-of-the Month-Club," and "the first" by an African American author "since Richard Wright's *Native Son*" in 1940 (Giddings 10). *Song of Solomon* is also the first of Morrison's novels to focus on a male protagonist. In this novel, Morrison returns to the myth of the flying Africans, who resisted slavery by flying back to Africa. At the end of the novel, Milkman takes flight like his great ancestor Solomon, the flying African. The myth is not unfamiliar to Morrison who says in an interview that "'Everybody told me, my grandmother, all of them...' They'd say, 'You know, during the days when Black people could fly...'" (Charles 21).

Song of Solomon also connects Morrison's work to those of other writers including Virginia Hamilton's *The People Could Fly* and the stories of those resistant Igbos of the Igbo Landing. Paula Giddings claims that "*Solomon* also represented a part of [Morrison's] own personal history. There was such a song about her family, and the myth of the flying African is a part of her folklore" (12). Even then, Morrison states that she had difficulty writing the novel, because she had "to get excited about things that were alien to [her]—like being excited in the presence of women or relishing the male sense of dominion" (Giddings 12). *Song of Solomon* received other awards, including the National Book Critics Circle Award. Morrison was also named distinguished writer by the American Academy of Arts and Letters.

In 1980, Toni Morrison was appointed to National the Council on the Arts and in 1981, she published *Tar Baby*, a book about African diaspora connections using an African/Caribbean folktale of the tar baby as its source. Morrison was elected to the American Academy and Institute of Arts and Letters, and she appeared on cover of the March issue of *Newsweek Magazine*.

In 1983, Morrison's short story, "Recitatif," appeared in *Confirmations: An Anthology of African American Women Writers* edited by African American playwright Amiri Baraka and Amina Baraka. In the same year, she resigned from Random House after eighteen years. The following year, she was named the Albert Schweitzer Professor of the Humanities at the College of the Humanities and Fine Arts, State University of New York, Albany.

Beloved (1987), Toni Morrison's fifth novel, is by many considered to be her masterpiece. The novel is based on the case of the historical Margaret Garner, a nineteenth-century Kentucky slave woman who fled into Ohio with her children, only to kill one when threatened with the possibility of being captured and re-enslaved. In the year *Beloved* came out, Morrison received the Anisfield-Wolf Book Award, which recognizes literary works that contribute to the understanding of race relations; the Pulitzer; and several other awards, and she was inducted into the American Academy of Arts and Letters. Morrison uncovered the story of Margaret Garner in a "newspaper clipping in *The Black Book*" (1974), which she helped to publish while at Random House. She has said that she wanted to "relate [Garner's] history to contemporary issues about freedom, responsibility, and women's 'place'" (Morrison, "Behind the Making" xvii). So in writing *Beloved*, Morrison grants her twentieth-century readers access to the real experiences of black people under slavery. While the novel may be a recasting of Margaret Garner's real story, it is also about the exclusion and silencing of the voices of blacks and some whites as well as about how these groups intersect in a system as absurd as slavery.

Morrison will immortalize Margaret Garner again in *Margaret Garner*, a libretto (2002), an opera co-commissioned by the Michigan Opera Theatre, Cincinnati Opera, and Opera Company of Philadelphia, with Richard Danielpour as the composer. The opera has since been performed in Detroit, Cincinnati, Philadelphia, Charlotte, and New York. In 1998, *Beloved* was also adapted into a movie directed by Jonathan Demme and starring Oprah Winfrey as Sethe, the fictionalized Margaret Garner. The film was nominated for a Grammy for the Best Spoken Word Album for that year.

In 1993, Morrison received the Nobel Prize in Literature. According to the Nobel Committee, the award was given to Toni Morrison "*who in novels characterized by visionary force and poetic import, gives life to an essential aspect of American reality*" ("The Nobel Prize"). In the same year, Morrison was also awarded Commander of the Order of Arts and Letters (Paris, France). Indeed, the list of Morrison's awards is extensive and includes several from American and international organizations and institutions, among them the Modern Language Association of America Commonwealth Award in Literature, the Chianti Ruffino Antico Fattore International Literary Prize, and the Chubb Fellowship at Yale University.

Today, Morrison is courted by universities all over the world and has delivered speeches and lectures at American and international institutions, including the Massey Lectures at Harvard University in 1990; the Clark Lectures at Trinity College, Cambridge, England in 1990; the National Endowment for the Humanities Jefferson Lecture in 1996; the United Nations Secretary General's Lecture Series in

2002; and beginning in March 2016, six lectures as the Charles Eliot Norton Professor of Poetry at The Mahindra Humanities Center, Harvard University.

Morrison has also received honorary degrees from American and international universities and colleges. In 2003, for example, she received the Docteur Honoris Causa from École Normale Supérieure, Paris, France. In 2005, she was awarded a Doctor of Letters Degree by Oxford University, England, and, in 2006, an Honorary Doctorate of Letters by the Sorbonne in Paris, France. In 2009, Morrison received the Norman Mailer Prize for Lifetime Achievement, and in 2012, she received the Presidential Medal of Freedom, awarded by President Barack Obama.

On October 17, 2014, Princeton University announced that the Toni Morrison papers will become part of Princeton University Libraries' permanent collection ("Toni Morrison Papers"). Clearly, as Princeton's President Christopher L. Eisgruber said during his announcement of the acquisition, "Toni Morrison's place among the giants of American literature is firmly entrenched." That position was secured by the overwhelming support Morrison receives from readers and scholars alike, and especially from African American women.

At the center of Morrison's creative life are the experiences of African Americans from slavery to the present. She remains fiercely committed to the recuperation of African American history and heritage. In helping to produce *The Black Book*, a collaborative work with several authors and artists, she said she wanted to create something "that got close to the way we were" (Morrison, "Behind the Making" 38) before it all disappeared or we forgot. Throughout much of her career, Morrison has endeavored to serve as the *griotte*, the archivist, the cultural critic, and the historian of her people. In her essay "Rootedness: The Ancestors as Foundation," Morrison indicates that she wants to combine "both print and oral literature . . . so that stories can be read in silence" (59). This has been her task all along, from her first novel (*The Bluest Eye*, 1970) to her most recent work (*God Save the Child*, 2015): to challenge us to sit in silence and contemplate who we are, where we have been, and where we might be going.

Works Cited

Charles, Pepsi. "An Interview with Toni Morrison." *Toni Morrison: Conversations*. Ed. Carolyn C. Denard. Jackson: UP of Mississippi, 2008. 17–23. Literary Conversations Ser.

Giddings, Paula. "The Triumphant of Song." *Toni Morrison: Conversations*. Ed. Carolyn C. Denard. Jackson: UP of Mississippi, 2008. 10–16. Literary Conversations Ser.

Gross, Terry. "'I Regret Everything:' Toni Morrison Looks Back on Her Personal Life." Interview with Terry Gross. *Fresh Air*. NPR, 20 Apr. 2015. Transcript.

Harris, Jessica. "'I Will Always Be a Writer.'" *Toni Morrison: Conversations*. Ed. Carolyn C. Denard. Jackson: UP of Mississippi, 2008. 3–9. Literary Conversations Ser.

Morrison, Toni. "Behind the Making of *The Black Book*." *Toni Morrison What Moves at the Margin*. Ed. Carolyn Denard. Jackson: UP of Mississippi, 2008. 34–38.

_____. "Rootedness: The Ancestors." *Toni Morrison What Moves at the Margin*. Ed. Carolyn C. Denard. Jackson: UP of Mississippi, 2008. 56–64.

_____. "A Slow Walk of Trees." *Toni Morrison: What Moves at the Margin*. Ed. Carolyn C. Denard. Jackson: UP of Mississippi, 2008. 3–14.

"The Nobel Prize in Literature 1993." *The Nobel Prize in Literature 1993*. Nobel Media, 2014. Web. 12 Oct. 2015.

"The Norton Lectures." *Norton Lectures/Mahindra Humanities Center*. Harvard University, n.d. Web. 12 Oct. 2015.

"Toni Morrison Papers to Reside at Princeton." *News at Princeton*. 17 Oct. 2014. Web. 12 Oct. 2015.

CRITICAL
CONTEXTS

Margaret Garner, Rememory, and the Infinite Past: History in *Beloved*

Kristine Yohe

While Toni Morrison's *Beloved* demonstrates a deep concern with the legacy of slavery in the United States, it also makes comprehensible for contemporary readers the dehumanizing personal experiences of enslaved individuals. As Morrison has said in multiple interviews, her intention in this novel was to create a "narrow and deep" internalized view of slavery instead of the wide, epic sweep that she had found to be more often depicted elsewhere. *Beloved* both draws on the historical record and creates an individualized past for her formerly enslaved characters, especially Sethe, Paul D, Baby Suggs, and Stamp Paid. These characters, in addition to Denver, who is born while Sethe is escaping, are simultaneously obsessed with and repelled by the horrors of their histories, haunted with pain while struggling to understand and make peace with their vivid "rememories." In order to develop the depth of authenticity in *Beloved*, Morrison blends historical fact with imagination, thus resulting in a greater effect than either one could achieve separately. She simultaneously works to excavate hidden elements of American history for the culture at large, as well as for her specific characters, thus resulting in the potential of healing for all.

Throughout her novels, Toni Morrison regularly focuses on history and its influence on the present. Whether this tendency manifests as characters stuck in the guilt of past mistakes, as we see in works ranging from *The Bluest Eye* (1970) to *Home* (2012) to *God Help the Child* (2015), or where family and communal history dominates, as in *Song of Solomon* (1976) and *Paradise* (1998), Morrison's created world frequently looks back in time. Morrison explains her point of view and her novels' historical preoccupation: "There is infinitely more past than there is future.... The past is infinite" (qtd. in Fowler & Abadie 27). This concept of the infinite past is one that recurs throughout Morrison's work and which she comments upon repeatedly elsewhere. In creating her fiction, she sees history as a bottomless well from which to draw inspiration and content. Her own family history contributes to this focus because she has strong influences from her close relationships with her siblings, parents, and grandparents. For example, she heard first-hand accounts of Alabama slavery from her maternal grandfather and great-grandmother, both of whom lived with her family, resulting in her intimate awareness of this most horrific part of American history. In addition, as she has explained in interviews, these familial ties have influenced Morrison's geographical awareness, as her parents' and grandparents' stories of their lives in Alabama and Georgia gave her a sensibility of the US South not always available in such communities as Lorain, Ohio, where she was born and raised (Denard 178). All told, this sense of personal history fits within Morrison's broader cultural consciousness, resulting in distinctive foundational undercurrents throughout her fiction.

Margaret Garner and Cultural History

Although Morrison has explained that she intended to create a novel, not a documentary, key elements of the plotline of *Beloved* were inspired by the historical record, especially concerning Margaret Garner. As Angelita Reyes explains, here, "Morrison is not as concerned with recording historical facts as she is with constructing meaning and emotional *truth* out of them" (77). The fraught history of United States slavery permeates *Beloved*, with powerful examples both narrow and broad. With its setting focused on Sweet Home, a farm in northern Kentucky, and 124 Bluestone Road, a house in Cincinnati, Ohio, the novel draws upon geography and fact to undergird its imaginative explorations. As Morrison has explained, she initially was inspired to create the novel after learning about a significant historical figure, Margaret Garner, whom she first discovered through her work as a book editor on the seminal collection *The Black Book*, edited by Middleton A. Harris and published by Random House in 1974.

Margaret Garner is remembered today because of her daring reaction to her failed escape to freedom. On a snowy night in

January 1856, Margaret Garner, along with her husband, Robert, his parents, and their four children, escaped from Maplewood Farm in Richwood, Kentucky, where they were all enslaved, into what they hoped would be the beginning of freedom in Cincinnati, twenty miles away. Traveling by horse-drawn sleigh overnight to the riverfront town of Covington, Kentucky, the group then continued on foot over the frozen Ohio River into Cincinnati, specifically to the home of a free cousin, Elijah Kite. While the plan was for them next to proceed northward to freedom in Canada via the Underground Railroad, with the assistance of white Quaker abolitionist Levi Coffin, instead the house was surrounded, and they quickly were caught by the enslaver, Archibald Gaines, along with law enforcement officers. Faced with a certain return to the horrors of slavery, Robert and Margaret initially resisted capture: he shot and wounded two deputies, and she cut her toddler daughter Mary's throat with a butcher knife and struck the other children with a shovel. She later explained that her goal was to kill them and herself, preferring death for them all to re-enslavement. Mary died, and the surviving family members were captured and imprisoned.

The case drew national attention, with the dominant question being whether or not Margaret Garner would be charged with destruction of property or murder. Delores Walters explains the broader context: "Pro-slavery proponents considered Margaret's act of infanticide evidence of the savagery of Black women, thus justifying slavery, while anti-slavery activists vilified slavery itself, not its victims," who, they said, were forced to such violence by the evil system (4). Renowned abolitionist Lucy Stone spoke in the packed courtroom, shocking everyone with her blunt allegation that the pale skin of three out of four of Margaret's children—whom newspaper accounts describe as "almost white"—came about because they were conceived from rape by the enslaver, Archibald Gaines: "The faded faces of the negro children tell too plainly to what degradation the female slaves submit. Rather than give her little daughter to that life, she killed it. If in her deep maternal love she felt the impulse to send her child back to God, to save it from coming woe, who shall say she had no right to do it?" (qtd. in

Weisenburger 173). In his important book about Margaret Garner, *Modern Medea: A Family Story of Slavery and Child-Murder from the Old South* (1998), Steven Weisenburger supports Stone's allegation and corroborates this theory with documentation showing that Gaines was present at Maplewood before each of Margaret's three last pregnancies. Although newspaper accounts in *Cincinnati Gazette* state that Stone discussed possibly buying her freedom or beseeching Gaines to grant it, no mercy was offered to Margaret Garner, and the legal proceedings took their course. Because a murder charge would have meant that her deceased daughter was considered to be a human being, the overarching legal mandates instead prevailed. Margaret Garner, therefore, was convicted of the crime of destruction of property, returned to the custody of the enslavers, and literally sold down the river, dying two years later from typhoid fever in Mississippi.

Margaret explained the motivation for her courageous actions to P. S. Bassett when he visited the Garners in prison, stating that she preferred to "kill [her children all] at once, and thus end their suffering, than have them taken back to slavery and be murdered by piece-meal." In an article first published in *The American Baptist* in February 1856, Bassett, of Cincinnati's Fairmount Theological Seminary, sympathetically describes that meeting and remarks on Margaret's stoic reaction to the outcome: "She alludes to the child she killed as being free from all trouble and sorrow, with a degree of satisfaction that almost chills the blood in one's veins; yet she evidently possesses all the passionate tenderness of a mother's love" (10). It is telling that both Stone and Bassett, each of whom was white, recognize and comment upon the humanity and conviction of maternal love that Margaret Garner's bold actions demonstrate.

Margaret Garner's decisive act, to protect her child from slavery through death, was widely regarded by abolitionists as radical and brave because an enslaved woman deciding the fate of her child was unusual, and, while infanticide in such a circumstance was not unheard of, it was rare. In addition to Bassett's article, this case inspired other contemporary responses, including a dramatic 1867 painting by Thomas Satterwhite Noble, *The Modern Medea*, which now hangs in the National Underground Railroad Freedom Center in Cincinnati. In addition, shortly after learning about Margaret Garner, Frances Ellen Watkins Harper was prompted to create a powerful poem.

Harper's 1857 poem, "The Slave Mother: A Tale of the Ohio" (not to be confused with her 1854 poem simply entitled "The Slave Mother") brings to the fore the motivations and emotions of Margaret Garner and makes vivid her decision to save her daughter through death. In this sixty-four-line poem, Harper develops a domestic narrative where Margaret's devotion to her children, her "treasures," is beyond doubt. She tries to escape into Ohio and find sanctuary for her refugee family, but, when this proves impossible, her commitment to freedom does not waver, but shifts in its target from desire for a purported free state to the afterlife:

> I will save my precious children
> From their darkly threatened doom,
> I will hew their path to freedom
> Through the portals of the tomb. (Harper 45–48)

If safety cannot be achieved on earth, then this determined mother will transform her life-giving power into life-taking and send her children to heaven. Harper makes Margaret Garner's logic clear: if life is hell, then death is peace. Through exalting Margaret's "deed of fearful daring" by the poem's end, Harper exhorts her readers to join the fight against slavery's tyranny and seek abolition at all costs. In addition, by entitling this poem as she does, coupled with her earlier poem with a similar title, Harper draws attention to the impossible status of enslaved women; while routinely forced to give birth to offspring also destined to a hellish life of bondage, they often were prevented from truly mothering their children. Harper's 1854 poem, "The Slave Mother," depicts a helpless and desperate woman whose child is forcibly torn from her arms on an auction block, while in the latter poem, the mother chooses her child's fate.

Learning of Margaret Garner's singular actions inspired Toni Morrison in a similar way as Frances Ellen Watkins Harper, for both authors focused on this brave woman's maternal commitment and compassion. When reading a clipping in the early 1970s of Bassett's 1856 article on Garner, Morrison was struck by the audacity of this woman who dared to determine the ultimate fate of her child, although she and her child were enslaved. In a new foreword to the 2004 edition of *Beloved*, Morrison states that she was impressed with Margaret Garner, who "had the intellect, the ferocity, and the willingness to risk everything for what was to her the necessity of freedom" (xvii). As Walters describes it, "Margaret Garner's act of infanticide represents the most drastic and extreme form of woman-centered resistance to the brutality of slavery" (1). Pondering what it meant for Margaret Garner, an enslaved mother, to kill her child *out of love*, Morrison was prompted to create a fictional story that interrogates such difficult positions through the actions and anxieties of her novel's protagonist, Sethe. In a 1987 video interview with Alan Benson, Morrison explains her reaction to Garner's powerful sense of agency: "For me, it was the ultimate gesture of the loving mother. It was also the outrageous claim of a slave. The last thing a slave woman owns is her children" (qtd. in Benson).

Inspired by Margaret Garner, but departing significantly from the historical record, *Beloved* is unequivocally a work of fiction. Instead of writing a novel about Garner, in *Beloved*, Toni Morrison imagines the lives of her created characters, especially the enslaved mother, Sethe. In her foreword to *Beloved*, Morrison explains:

> The historical Margaret Garner is fascinating, but, to a novelist, confining. Too little imaginative space there for my purposes. So I would invent her thoughts, plumb them for a subtext that was historically true in essence, but not strictly factual in order to relate her history to contemporary issues about freedom, responsibility, and women's "place." The heroine would represent the unapologetic acceptance of shame and terror; assume the consequences of choosing infanticide; claim her own freedom. The terrain, slavery, was formidable and pathless. (*Beloved* xvii)

In seeking historical truth "in essence" rather than strictly through fact, Morrison keeps the Margaret Garner story at the center around which she deftly transforms history and layers on her created literary world. Significantly, her novel does borrow the Garner name, which is borne by both enslavers and enslaved, as well as the overall geographical setting where Margaret Garner lived, escaped, and committed infanticide.

Years after *Beloved* was published in 1987, Morrison returned to Margaret Garner's history in 2004, when she wrote the libretto (lyrics) for an opera of the same name, with music composed by Richard Danielpour. While here Morrison sticks closer to the available facts about Margaret Garner, she nevertheless continues to take liberties with the historical record on behalf of art. As in *Beloved*, an enslaved mother's protective infanticide again takes center stage in the *Margaret Garner* libretto, where Morrison's focus is consistent: "That black slave woman was a revolutionary who clung to freedom and said, 'I am in charge of my children'" (qtd. in Gelfand A6). Clearly, what gripped Morrison about Margaret Garner's story in 1974 seems not to have diminished two decades later.

The Underground Railroad and Memories of Slavery

Because of its failure, Margaret Garner's attempted escape reflects the experience of the majority of enslaved Africans who fled from bondage in the American South, vainly hoping to find sanctuary in the free North. While most enslaved people lacked the opportunity even to try to run away, scholars have determined that the vast majority of those who did were caught. In the fictional world of *Beloved*, Morrison incorporates both the foiled attempts of many refugees from slavery, as well as Sethe's own escape, which is fruitful in the short term, though it fails violently twenty-eight days later. Yet Sethe, like Margaret Garner, is also fully successful on one level, as each mother dispatches her daughter to the relative peace of heaven. As Sethe declares to Paul D when he questions her momentous decision, "I stopped him... I took and put my babies where they'd be safe" (*Beloved* 193). These innovative and determined mothers claimed another way.

With its escape theme, as well as in other respects, the novel incorporates numerous historical references to slavery, including elements of the Underground Railroad, the loosely organized system of places and people who assisted refugees seeking to flee bondage. Stamp Paid—who transports Sethe and her newborn, Denver, across the Ohio River—is a part-time conductor on the Underground Railroad with echoes of the renowned Harriet Tubman, as well as his Ohio Valley counterpart, John P. Parker, who was active in and around Ripley, Ohio, east of Cincinnati. *Beloved* also includes other Underground Railroad references, especially related to the plan on how the enslaved friends intend to escape from Sweet Home. Sethe hears the others talk about a hope to go north because "freedom is that way. A whole train is going" (Morrison, *Beloved* 233). As Paul D remembers, Sethe had told him she was fleeing alone after her young children "had already [been] packed into a wagonload of others in a caravan of Negroes crossing the river. They were to be left with Halle's mother near Cincinnati" (*Beloved* 10). The plan was for Sethe, Halle, their children, Paul D, Sixo, and the others all to travel with that caravan at a point in the summer when the corn is high, the moon is full, and they hear the sign: "They can hardly harvest, or chop, or clear, or pick, or haul for listening for a rattle that is not bird or snake. Then one midmorning they hear it. Or Halle does and begins to sing it to the others: 'Hush, hush. Somebody's calling my name. Hush, hush. Somebody's calling my name. O my Lord, O my Lord, what shall I do?'" (*Beloved* 264). In this example, Morrison uses a classic element of Underground Railroad history, the encoded alert songs that those about to flee would sometimes use to indicate that the time had come. But the enslavers learn of the plot, and the men are prevented—tied up, driven mad, hanged, shot—from getting to the meeting place. So Sethe, heavily pregnant, sends her three children onward with what she refers to as "the underground agent" in the wagon waiting in the corn and then tries and fails to find her husband, Halle (*Beloved* 82). Years later, she learns from Paul D that Halle had lost his mind, his suddenly blasted mental capacity the result of unspeakable trauma, evidently as a result of helplessly witnessing Sethe being brutalized when her breast milk is forcibly taken and she is whipped. Being unable to protect his wife from this horror apparently breaks him beyond all hope of recovery.

Yet Sethe, through sheer force of will to get her milk to her "crawling–already? baby" already in Cincinnati, manages to make it away from Sweet Home on foot and, eventually, all the way to the Ohio River. There, she encounters Amy Denver, a young white woman fleeing indentured servitude, who mercifully assists Sethe as she gives birth to her baby literally *in* the river, that mighty border between slave and free states. Then Sethe and her newborn, whom she names Denver, are helped further along the Underground Railroad by Stamp Paid, who takes them across the river in his boat. Ella joins the effort after she sees the Underground Railroad signal, which she explains to Sethe: "Stamp leaves the old sty open when there's a crossing. Knots a white rag on the post if it's a child too" (*Beloved* 108). Ella also informs Sethe that Stamp Paid earlier has helped to transport some of the group that includes her older children, who have successfully made it to the home of their grandmother; Ella then helps them all to reunite at Baby Suggs's house on Bluestone Road.

In addition to its Underground Railroad connections, *Beloved* includes references to other key elements of its historical context, particularly slavery. Set in the post-slavery period (1873–1874), with flashbacks to 1855 (when Sethe escapes and Denver is born), and even earlier at Sweet Home, the novel demonstrates the influence of the slave narrative tradition, especially the most famous examples, Frederick Douglass's 1845 *Narrative of the Life of Frederick Douglass* and Harriet Jacobs's 1861 *Incidents in the Life of a Slave Girl*. In each of these classic texts, the enslaved individual manages, under great duress, to escape the brutality of slavery, journey northward, make a new life, and struggle to evade being recaptured. All of these elements and more—such as Baby Suggs renaming herself once free, as Douglass does—ground Morrison's novel within the historical and literary tradition of the slave narrative. Furthermore, Morrison makes a direct connection to Frederick Douglass when Stamp Paid contemplates with horror the rampant violence of Reconstruction with a reference to Douglass's abolitionist newspaper, *The North Star*:

Eighteen seventy-four and whitefolks were still on the loose. Whole towns wiped clean of Negroes; eighty-seven lynchings in one year alone in Kentucky; four colored schools burned to the ground; grown men whipped like children; children whipped like adults; black women raped by the crew; property taken, necks broken. He smelled skin, skin and hot blood. The skin was one thing, but human blood cooked in a lynch fire was a whole other thing. The stench stank. Stank off the pages of the *North Star*, out of the mouths of witnesses, etched in crooked handwriting in letters delivered by hand. (Morrison, *Beloved* 212)

Not only would Stamp Paid know of the violent racist aftermath of slavery in his own community, but he follows these events nationally through Douglass's influential newspaper. All of these historical underpinnings and markers contribute to the atmosphere of reality and accuracy that Morrison achieves in this novel, even within its simultaneous emphasis on imagination, memory, and the supernatural.

Memory, Healing, and Fragments of the Infinite Past

While slave narratives inform *Beloved* in many ways, Morrison also reinterprets this form when she takes her exploration to deeper levels. In bringing concerns from the nineteenth-century genre of slave narratives into the twentieth and twenty-first centuries, Morrison makes her novel more relevant to her readers by emphasizing modern-day beliefs, such as personal growth and healing. As Marilyn Sanders Mobley explains, "Morrison uses the trope of memory to revise the genre of the slave narrative and to thereby make the slave experience it inscribes more accessible to contemporary readers. In other words, she uses memory as the metaphorical sign of the interior life to explore and represent dimensions of slave life that the classic slave narrative omitted" (Mobley 357–358). We see this emphasis on the depth of personal memory through the flashback techniques the novel employs, where the characters attempt to understand their pasts in order to be able to survive into the future.

While the novel's elliptical flashback structure of memory is jarring for some readers, a linear sequence does exist. In the 1987

Benson interview, Morrison explains that she wrote the story in the complex way that she did in order to capture "the way people remember" their own lives, which often is in fragments. Her novel's characters frequently are trying not to remember their traumatic pasts, which means that the fragments can be even smaller and more jagged. "To Sethe, the future was a matter of keeping the past at bay" (Morrison, *Beloved* 51). Some memories, however, can bring solace, even when they appear in the novel as discontinuous. For example, the second part of Sethe's story of her escape from Sweet Home picks up almost exactly where it leaves off—even though fifty pages of text transpire in between (from page 42 to page 92 in the 2004 edition). Morrison shows that Sethe's memory of this escape is one of the rare comforting stories from the past that Denver enjoys hearing, and both versions are filtered through Denver's consciousness. Denver even repeats this personal history—accessible to her via her mother's memory—to Beloved. Morrison's language draws attention to the function of this "rememory" for Denver: "Easily she stepped into the told story that lay before her" (*Beloved* 36). When Denver relates it to Beloved later, her own memories of the story blend with Sethe's, as the daughter tries to imagine her mother's ordeal of fleeing while pregnant with her: "Denver was seeing it now and feeling it—through Beloved. Feeling how it must have felt to her mother" (*Beloved* 91). This layering of memory with current experience deepens the effect of their shared family history, where Sethe's remembered experience merges into Denver's understanding of who she is.

Early in the novel, when Sethe and Paul D first are reunited, after eighteen years apart, being together stirs up many memories from their shared past at Sweet Home. While they experience some comfort in revisiting this personal history, their reminiscences also tear open old wounds and slice new ones. When they piece together what must have precipitated Halle's mental breakdown, for example, their ability to compare memories yields new realizations that are intensely disturbing. Sethe is horrified to comprehend that Halle must have witnessed her assault by schoolteacher's nephews in the barn, and so she asks Paul D what was said. But Paul D reveals that he had not been able to speak because of having a bit in his mouth, one of the many forms of torture employed by schoolteacher at Sweet Home (Morrison, *Beloved* 82). Overwhelmed with this new information, Sethe struggles over whether to reject or absorb it, while she also tries to offer a sympathetic ear to Paul D. In this way, they share their horrors and articulate, perhaps for the first time, the infinite depths of their pain. Morrison encapsulates this moment through the figure of a rooster named Mister that Paul D realizes is, compared to him, "free. Better than me." Because of the brutality he experiences, Paul D is forever altered: "Mister was allowed to be and stay what he was. But I wasn't allowed to be and stay what I was... Schoolteacher changed me." Although Sethe and Paul D open up to each other a great deal in this scene, they stop themselves from speaking further out of fear, instead resuming their long-term practice of "beating back the past" (*Beloved* 86). If the past is infinitely vast enough to bring new and sharp pain after eighteen years, keeping it stifled, it seems, may be the only way to survive.

One of the primary ways that Morrison demonstrates her novel's focus on the past is through the character of Beloved. Not only is she the reincarnation of the murdered baby girl—who is unnamed, only referred to as "crawling-already?" when a living toddler—but her active haunting of Sethe and the family has been another manifestation of the past dominating the present. In an interview in 1994, Morrison describes Beloved as "the embodiment of the past," and also "like a catalyst. She opens up everybody's vulnerability" (qtd. in Carabi). After years of haunting, her in-the-flesh arrival at 124 Bluestone seems to be an intentional act of vengeance; she wills herself into physical form to enable more specific retaliation against Sethe. After Paul D returns to Sethe's life, the ghostly haunting first accelerates and then is subdued. But this spirit needs Sethe's undistracted attention, so she appears in the flesh, as Beloved, with the decisive goal of first removing Paul D, and then Denver, and then sucking Sethe's life force dry.

What interrupts Beloved's quest for dominance is communal remembering, which leads to healing. When Denver realizes that she, too, has been cast aside by Beloved and Sethe—who become totally fixated on each other, no longer caring whether they eat or sleep—she must seek help from the outside community. In order to ask her neighbors for food assistance, Denver first summons Baby Suggs, who gives her the courage to venture outward. Then, she must remember her way back to her former teacher, Lady Jones, and she must humble herself before the community, opening herself up to the possibility of rejection, but instead actually finding compassion. By making herself vulnerable, Denver is able to begin to grow up, to venture outward, and to begin to heal herself and her family. After Denver reaches out first to Lady Jones, the community women begin to help with food and other expressions of kindness. Then, when she visits Janey Wagon looking for work, Janey will not help until Denver shares some of the details of how Beloved is harming Sethe. This opening up on Denver's part enables the community women to begin to sympathize with her, which leads them then to gather for a sort of exorcism. In this moment in the novel, the thirty women converge at 124 Bluestone and remember past happiness with Baby Suggs at that house. Their singing prompts Sethe also to recall earlier times, especially the spirituality of healing and self-love that Baby Suggs practiced: "it was as though the Clearing had come to her." She hears the women's joined voices as a mighty "wave of sound," which "broke over Sethe and she trembled like the baptized in its wash" (Morrison, *Beloved* 308). When Sethe, confused with emotion and memory by all that transpires, ends up trying to attack Edward Bodwin—there to pick up Denver for her new job, not to attack her, though Sethe mistakes him for schoolteacher—the spell with Beloved breaks, and she disappears.

Though this loss of Beloved leads Sethe to despair, as she retreats to bed, it also enables Paul D to return to 124 Bluestone to help. Again, their reunion stirs up the painful past, but this time real healing is possible. They begin to understand and honor each other's vulnerabilities with tentative hope for renewal. Sethe realizes that Paul D has something special, "the thing in him, the blessedness that has made him the kind of man who can walk in a house and make the women cry. Because with him, in his presence, they could." He sees in her "too many things to feel," but remembering their shared history of anguish, Paul D also recalls her "tenderness" and sensitivity: "Only this woman Sethe could have left him his manhood like that" (Morrison, *Beloved* 321). Seeking healing, he wants to lay their infinite past to rest and tells her so: "me and you, we got more yesterday than anybody. We need some kind of tomorrow." They must learn to heal themselves from the traumas of the past and move forward, something that seems much more possible if done together. Morrison closes this scene with Paul D invoking Baby Suggs's mighty preaching to heal oneself from slavery's onslaught through self-love, as he tells Sethe that she is indeed worthy: "You your best thing, Sethe. You are." Sethe's first steps towards healing come through in her final utterance, "Me? Me?" (*Beloved* 322).

Because of this potential for healing, which continues in another form in the last two pages of the novel, Sethe and Paul D begin to break through their previous log-jammed positions. As Morrison describes it in an interview in 1994, "if you just dwell on the past, you can't go forward. If you confront the past, there is a possibility to move on" (qtd. in Carabi). In this way, memory can be liberating rather than crippling. Beyond her novel, Morrison's message seems to be that this promise could also be true for the nation at large; if we all try to face the past with honesty and grace, cultural healing may be possible.

When readers struggle with the complexity of this novel, one helpful perspective is to consider the context, especially how figures from history experienced the reality of the world it represents. In describing her challenges in writing *Beloved*, Morrison says that really remembering slavery is so intensely painful that "Nobody wants to go back and try to remember all that stuff. You think that you might be devastated." But when she was struggling through writing the novel, if it got too overwhelming, she reminded herself how much easier she had it than those who were really enslaved: "If they could live it, I could write about it" (qtd. in Carabi). And if the ancestors could live through and survive slavery, and if Toni Morrison could summon this crucial history in her magnificent novel, then we indeed can read it.

Works Cited

Bassett, P. S. "A Visit to the Slave Mother Who Killed her Child." 12 Feb. 1856. *The Black Book*. Ed. Middleton A. Harris. New York: Random House, 1974. 10.

Benson, Alan. Interview with Toni Morrison. *Profile of a Writer: Toni Morrison*. Dir. Alan Benson. RM Arts, 1987. Videocassette.

Carabi, Angels. Interview with Toni Morrison. *Belles Lettres: A Review of Books by Women*. 9.3 (Spring 1994): 38. *Literature Resource Center*. Web. 22 Aug. 2015.

Denard, Carolyn C. "Blacks, Modernism, and the American South: An Interview with Toni Morrison." *Toni Morrison: Conversations*. Ed. Carolyn C. Denard. Jackson: UP of Mississippi, 2008. 178–195.

Douglass, Frederick. *Narrative of the Life of Frederick Douglass, An American Slave*. 1845. New York: Barnes & Noble, 2003.

Fowler, Doreen & Ann J. Abadie. Interview with Toni Morrison. *Toni Morrison: Conversations*. Ed. Carolyn C. Denard. Jackson: UP of Mississippi, 2008. 24–28.

Gelfand, Janelle. "Author brings focus to Boone slave's life: Nobel, Pulitzer Prize winner reflects on opera's premiere." *The Cincinnati Enquirer*. 11 July 2005: A1, A6.

Harper, Frances Ellen Watkins. "The Slave Mother." 1854. *The Norton Anthology of African American Literature*. Vol. 1. New York: Norton, 2004. 450–451.

_____. "The Slave Mother: A Tale of the Ohio." 1857. *Toni Morrison's 'Beloved': A Casebook*. Eds. William L Andrews & Nellie Y. McKay. New York: Oxford UP, 1999.

Jacobs, Harriet. *Incidents in the Life of a Slave Girl*. 1861. New York: Norton, 2000.

Mobley, Marilyn Sanders. "A Different Remembering: Memory, History, and Meaning in *Beloved*." *Toni Morrison: Critical Perspectives Past and Present*. Eds. Henry Louis Gates, Jr. & K. A. Appiah. New York: Amistad, 1993. 356–365.

Morrison, Toni. *Beloved*. New York: Vintage, 1987, 2004.

_____. Foreword. *Beloved*. 1987. By Toni Morrison. New York: Vintage, 2004. xv-xix.

_____. Libretto. *Margaret Garner*. Music by Richard Danielpour. New York: Schirmer, 2004.

Parker, John P. *His Promised Land: The Autobiography of John P. Parker, Former Slave and Conductor on the Underground Railroad*. Ed. Stuart Seely Sprague. New York: Norton, 1996.

Reyes, Angelita. "Using History as Artifact to Situate *Beloved*'s Unknown Woman: Margaret Garner." *Approaches to Teaching the Novels of Toni Morrison*. Eds. Nellie Y. McKay & Kathryn Earle. New York: MLA, 1997. 77–85.

Weisenburger, Steven. *Modern Medea: A Family Story of Slavery and Child-Murder from the Old South*. New York: Hill & Wang, 1998.

Walters, Delores M. "Introduction: Re(dis)covering and Recreating the Cultural Milieu of Margaret Garner." *Gendered Resistance: Woman, Slavery, and the Legacy of Margaret Garner*. Ed. Mary E. Frederickson & Delores M. Walters. Urbana: U of Illinois P, 2013. 1–22.

Toni Morrison's Paradoxical Novel: Thirty Years of Critical Reception_____

Touria Khannous

From its date of publication in 1987, *Beloved* has remained Toni Morrison's most-analyzed novel. Within the fields of literature and literary theory, the novel, as a subject, has been important. *Beloved* is taught in undergraduate classrooms and graduate seminars alike, and criticism of it is featured in studies of modernist literature, feminist writing/theory, Gothic literature, and Black literature. Over twenty years ago, when I first read Toni Morrison's novel, I thought it was a compelling narrative about female empowerment. A year after its publication, a group of Black writers and scholars published a signed statement, in which they reproached the book industry organizations for not giving a National Book Award to Morrison:

> Despite the international stature of Toni Morrison, she has yet to receive the national recognition that her five major works of fiction entirely deserve.... We, the undersigned ... here assert ourselves against such oversight and harmful whimsy.... We write this testament of ... our simple tribute to the seismic character and beauty of your writing. And, furthermore, in grateful wonder at the advent of "Beloved," your most recent gift to our community, our country, our conscience, our courage flourishing as it grows. (Allen 36)

Beloved, they add, is a novel about "a universe of complicated, sweetly desiring, fierce and deeply seductive human beings hitherto subsumed by, hitherto stifled by, that impenetrable nobody-noun: 'the slave'" (36). Two months after this signed petition was published in the *New York Times*, Morrison was awarded the Pulitzer Prize. In 1993, she won the Nobel Prize for Literature. Subsequently, the novel was adapted into a drama-horror movie directed by Jonathan Demme and starring Oprah Winfrey. In general, a large number of interviews, articles, reviews, as well as books have been published on *Beloved*. There have also been national and international conferences dedicated to Morrison. In fact, the sheer amount of scholarship on *Beloved* has fueled interest in Morrison's earlier novels and consolidated her status as one of the foremost figures of the African American literary tradition.

Critical literature on Morrison has often tried to assign her to one particular sociopolitical/cultural/historical side or another. Oftentimes, the critical reception of her work points to critical categories in which she does not seem to fit. Such critical categories have in fact been reconfigured through questions raised by Morrison's fiction. On the side of Western modernism, critics place her alongside such modernist writers as William Faulkner, Henry James, and Virginia Woolf. As the field of African American studies expands, Morrison's importance in that field has also gained prominence. Barbara Christian's landmark study *Black Women Novelists: the Development of a Tradition* explicitly seeks to place Morrison's writings within a longer genealogy of African American women's writing, while Valerie Smith devotes an entire chapter to *Beloved* in her book-length study on Toni Morrison and identifies its complex position in literary criticism as a text read from a variety of critical perspectives. This testifies to the fact that Morrison's work is rich in possibilities for scholars in different disciplines, including modernism, postmodernism, Black studies, feminism and gender studies, cultural studies as well as postcolonial studies. The fact that Morrison's identity as a writer is American, because all her novels are set in the American context, and African American, given the tropes of blackness that pervade her narratives, is responsible for the divergent criticism of her work. This variety of criticisms lends itself better to the fact that the novel is read through many different lenses. In claiming Toni Morrison as their own, African American critics call attention to the themes about Black people's experiences that punctuate her work, while other critics tend to place her work within the larger canonical Euro-American literary tradition.

Modernist Tendencies

Early interpretations of *Beloved* tried to reposition Morrison's writing among that of modernist writers. A number of critics have explored the intertextual connections between Morrison's and Faulkner's work, emphasizing the similarities between the two authors in terms of narrative techniques and the use of lyrical language to portray strong community ties in an anarchic world characterized by racism and sexism. Such chaos is all the more magnified through innovative modernist narrative techniques, such as the moving backward and forward in time. Morrison has admitted the great influence Faulkner's work has had on her (Denard 25). In an edited volume entitled *Unflinching Gaze: Morrison and Faulkner Re-Envisioned*, scholars cite Morrison's revision of Faulkner, the mythic consciousness they both share, the intersection of "history" and story in their narratives, as well as their disruption of linear chronology. Readers note in particular the striking similarities between Faulkner's novel *Absalom! Absalom!* and *Beloved*, since both "are concerned with constructing monuments to the past[,]… are ghost stories[,]… [and] use a family catastrophe as a synecdoche for a larger social drama; both narratives must work through a repressed memory of an interfamilial order" (Kolmerten xiv). Morrison is also alleged to be strongly influenced by the Faulknerian theme of women's oppression and rebellion. Sethe, the main protagonist in *Beloved*, is reminiscent of Faulkner's female characters, who challenge vigorously any potential victimization. According to Larry Schwartz, Faulkner's individualism in the era of liberating cold war nationalism resonates with the way Morrison represents the voices of Blacks and women in an era where racism and sexism are still prevalent: "For Morrison, racism and sexism are psychological disorders. And in each of her novels the central characters who do survive, find redemption, liberation, and justice in individual resistance, not as group or community even" (Schwartz).

Many critics have shed light on Morrison's novels through relationships with other modernist writers. In one of the earliest essays to be published on Morrison, Joan Bischoff compares Henry James' novel *What Maisie Knew* to Morrison's characterization of female protagonists in *The Bluest Eye* and *Sula*. Nancy J. Peterson dismisses such comparison as a calculated gesture in order to garner Morrison more attention from academics not acquainted with her work at the time. According to Peterson, "this comparison is also significant in terms of race. Morrison's work is made to resemble James's in order to suggest that books speak to more than 'just' a black audience. Indeed, Bischoff goes on to invoke the problematic language of universalism to promote Morrison" (3). This view reveals the fact that a Caucasian critic who judges an African American work by standards of universal literary value can be open to the charge of using Eurocentric criteria. But this is just "one" view of what some critics make of Peterson's statement.

Yet, creating an unbridgeable difference between the Euro-American canon and Toni Morrison would be a limiting way of viewing her work. Some critics have stressed instead that it is important to consider what is common across the two literary traditions. They conducted racial re-readings of canonical writers as a way of including Euro-American literature within the African American literary tradition. In her book *The Artist as Outsider in the Novels of Toni Morrison and Virginia Woolf*, Lisa Williams focuses on common racial tropes of domesticity and gender tropes of inequality in Morrison's and Woolf's works, despite the different contexts of their novels. Williams's comparison of the two authors "serves to redefine modernity in terms of the tremendous influence of the African American oral tradition" (170). Such references to the racialized discourse of canonical authors in comparison with Morrison's work have been noted before in other critical texts. Later critical readings of her novels make mention of Mark Twain, Nathaniel Hawthorne, Ernest Hemingway, among other canonical authors. Some critics view this as imposing Eurocentric values and downplaying the cultural specificity and uniqueness of Morrison's work within the African American tradition.

Multivocal Critiques

Other critics have tried to sketch out a map of different positions, ranging from African American perspectives to Eurocentric criteria of criticism. These shifting critical positions correspond to Morrison's own changing perspectives and to the nature of the novel itself as a genre, which is seen as multivalent and complex in the postmodern era. What we see in this kind of criticism is a body of complicated readings in which every term is contested—in other words, challenged. This is evident in critiques that engage with the history and psychoanalysis of the novel, using Eurocentric models of analysis that also allow for the privileged position of the author's African American perspective.

History

A large body of criticism has focused on *Beloved* as a work of historical interpretation. These studies show how the novel places emphasis on what happened in the past, offering closer analogies that can be made between Morrison's methods and those of Eurocentric historians. Because she uses the experiences of past lives, Morrison's reconstruction of history can be compared to a historian's analysis of historical documents. Sethe is governed by an obsession with the past, specifically with her daughter Beloved's death. As such, a historical reading suggests that Beloved's ghost forces Sethe to come to terms with her past and her subconscious. For example, Homi K. Bhabha argues that "Morrison describe[s] the historical world, forcibly entering the house of art and fiction in order to invade, alarm, divide and dispossess" (18). For him, Morrison also "demonstrate[s] the contemporary compulsion to move beyond; to turn the present into the 'post' or... to touch the future on its hither side" (Bhabha 18).

Poststructuralist critics have read the novel as an example of historiographic discourse and what literary theorist Linda Hutcheon calls "historiographic metafiction." Kimberly Davis, for instance, argues that, while Morrison's novel enacts many of the theories of postmodern fiction formulated by Linda Hutcheon and Frederic Jameson, such as the fictionality of history and the questioning of grand historical narratives, it is also deeply committed to African American cultural memory and to recreating the past in order to build a better future. Davis situates Morrison between postmodernism and the genre of African American social protest, allowing her "to draw the best from both and make us question the more extremist voices asserting that our postmodern world is bereft of history" (243).

For literary critic Caroline Rody, however, while the novel "can be read as a historiographic intervention, a strategic re-centering of American history in the lives of the historically dispossessed," it is still difficult to interpret *Beloved* as a historical text (21). According to her, in placing historiographic authority in the hands of its slave heroine, *Beloved* does not stand in relation to some "history" outside itself as in most Euro-American historical novels that profess to be a record of a particular period of time (Rody 21). It rather offers a rendering of "history" with the various characters relating what happened to them in dialectical form. She concludes that Morrison is more concerned with the recreation of history, as the author, her characters and the reader are all involved in probing a problematic past through dialog and stream of consciousness. Therefore, it is in this dramatic form that Morrison's sense of history emerges.

Adding to the conversation on Morrison's historical representation, Valerie Smith argues that Morrison turns to visual and sensory forms of historical representation in a variety of ways. For Smith, "history" is bound up with sensory embodiments in the novel: "Not only do Sethe's memories of slavery come to her sensorily, through her body, but perhaps more obviously, she wears on her body the signs of her greatest ordeal at the Sweet Home plantation" (*Toni Morrison* 68). Her traumatic experiences are encoded in the visual scars on her back. Through this mode of representation, Morrison transforms history into a spectacle, as visual forms allow her to picture a history where "real human beings did suffer the whipping and chaining, and torture, and rape and murder" (V. Smith, "Circling the Subject" 354), thus asserting "the subjectivity of the former slaves and the depth of their suffering" (354). Understanding how historical representation in *Beloved* is depicted and what it means offers the best example of the complexity of the novel. Rather than promoting either the Eurocentric or Afrocentric modes of criticism, critics such as Kimberly Davis and Caroline Rody see the positive way in which the novel can allow for readings using a Eurocentric model that privileges Morrison's perspective on African American history.

Psychoanalytical Models

Psychoanalytic readings of *Beloved* have also offered a model for combining Eurocentric criteria of analysis and the author's African American context. In her essay "Is Morrison Also Among the Prophets? Psychoanalytic Strategies in *Beloved*," scholar Iyunolu Osagie argues that the novel uses psychoanalysis to explore the psychic aspects of American slavery. Furthermore, Morrison's use of psychoanalysis in her novel highlights "the deliberate indeterminacy of the text's meaning" (Osagie 423). Osagie focuses on problems of "indeterminacy," "uncertainty," and "assumptions" about Morrison's use of the ghost of Beloved. She postulates that Morrison uses psychoanalysis as a literary device not only to negotiate the boundary between the "physical and the spiritual," "the invisible and the visible," and "the conscious and the unconscious," but also to involve the reader intimately in the novel (423). Rather than trying to determine objective meanings, critics who adopt a psychoanalytic approach to the novel focus on the subjective experience of the reader. While psychoanalytic models are Eurocentric paradigms that dominate cultural notions of language, authority, and subjectivity, Morrison uses those very same models to describe a specific historical formation in order to interrogate its psychic dimensions. Hortense Spillers has argued in an essay on psychoanalysis and race that Eurocentric theories of psychoanalysis are also connected to race and racism. She asks "how might psychoanalytic theories speak about 'race'... and how might 'race' expose the gaps that psychoanalytic theories awaken?" (Spillers 376). Similarly, Morrison questions the omission of race in the psychoanalytic model by probing a past that is a continuous enigma: "Is the young woman who enters Sethe's life her daughter come back from the grave? Is Beloved someone else whose identity must be discovered? Does Beloved really exist?" (Osagie 423). Osagie offers two contradictory, but complementary readings of the character of Beloved. The first reading alleges that the novel is based on the true 1855 story of a slave woman who, when followed by her owner to Cincinnati where she had escaped, tried to kill her four children. The second reading attests that Beloved is a different woman who came back bearing the same name engraved on the headstone of the daughter Sethe had killed (423). By offering such contradictory readings, Osagie convincingly advances the argument that the intimate relationship the reader has to a text makes one realize that no one interpretation is inherently true. She also insinuates that using European models to interpret African American texts will always produce incomplete interpretations.

The African American Paradigm

The temptation to interpret Morrison's work using modernist and postmodernist literary criticism has provoked controversy. Morrison's disappointment with the interpretations of her work is made clear during an interview with Nellie McKay, in which she calls for a kind of literary criticism that does justice to her work:

> My plea is for some pioneering work to be done in literary criticism...
> Our—black women's—job is a particularly complex one in that
> regard. But if we cannot do it, then nobody can do it. We have no
> systematic mode of criticism that has yet evolved from us, but it will.
> I am not like James Joyce; I am not like Thomas Hardy; I am not like
> Faulkner. (McKay 408)

What Morrison is thus looking for is a type of criticism "that will illuminate whatever story black people have to tell from its inside" (McKay 408). She believes that only a criticism that emanates from the Black literary tradition will tell her story accurately. What becomes clear here is that Morrison places the Eurocentric reader on the outside, as "Other," while the African American or Black reader is granted a privileged position, especially given the important social and historical questions she raises in her work by challenging the "Master Narrative" of white-American history.

Earlier debates about Morrison's status as a Black woman writer laid the foundation for considering the multiple identities and spaces that Morrison occupies. African American literary critic Henry Louis Gates, Jr. provides a thoughtful discussion of the first of these debates over Morrison's status as an African American writer. While he acknowledges her influence by canonical writers, to him, that does not make her work less representative of the Black experience. Gates places Morrison's work within the larger African American canon, in which her novels can be analyzed through African American literary theory and according to "indigenous black principles of criticism" (Gates xxi). He sees the positive way in which her work can cater to its different readerships and yet allow a privileged position to the African American critic as insider. While acknowledging outside influences on Morrison's work from the magical realism of authors such as Gabriel Garcia Marquez and William Faulkner, Gates situates Morrison in the philosophical, literary, linguistic, religious, and artistic contexts of the Black tradition. This is evident, he states, in the meaningful affiliations she draws between the Afro-American literary, cultural, and spiritual elements that underpin the Black tradition, such as:

> James Baldwin's densely...fictional prose...as well as jazz, blues, and the whole range of Black secular vernacular speech rituals and discourses. . . . Her work, in this sense, spans that great divide between the lyrical modernism of Zora Neale Hurston ...and the existential naturalist experimentation of Richard Wright on the other (Gates ix).

In the context of this debate, Barbara Christian describes Morrison's work as "fantastic earthy realism" that is "deeply rooted in history and mythology" (137). Morrison's writing has helped to reconfigure the critical terrain of the Black literary tradition as new critical perspectives help shed light on the complexity of her work. African American critics in particular have credited Morrison for creating space for Black women writers who had been for too long "the subjugated, the voiceless, the invisible, the unpresented and the unrepresentable" (Gates 197). For this reason, criticism of her work is infused by a vigorous black feminist discourse.

In her groundbreaking essay "Towards a Black Feminist Criticism," Barbara Smith points out that race and gender are both inseparable from Black women's identities and experiences and that it is African American women who are in the best position to create an effective criticism, which takes into consideration not only race, but also gender, class, and sexuality in Black women's literature.

Morrison was, in fact, rediscovered during the late 1980's by Black feminist critics, such as Barbara Christian, Hortense Spillers, Hazel Carby, Susan Willis, Deborah McDowell, and Alice Walker, who revalued her work and explored the concept of a female literary tradition. Studies on Toni Morrison and other African American women writers include Hazel Carby's *Reconstructing Womanhood* (1987); Marjorie Pryse and Hortense Spillers's edited volume *Conjuring: Black Women, Fiction, and Literary Tradition* (1985); Mari Evans's *Black Women Writers* (1984); Bessie W. Jones and Audrey L. Vinson's *The World of Toni Morrison*; and Barbara Christian's *Black Women Novelists: the Development of a Tradition*, which did much to generate interest in Toni Morrison.

Common Subjects of Black Feminist Criticism

Womanhood

A core theme in Black feminist criticism on *Beloved* is womanhood. Critics allege that Sethe's problems stem from the sexualized racism that excludes her from the ideology of true womanhood, a nineteenth-century notion that associated women with domesticity, virtue, and submissiveness. Historian Barbara Welter has defined this ideology as "piety, purity, submissiveness and domesticity. Put them all together, and they spelled mother, daughter, sister, wife—woman" (Welter 152). Black women, however, were not able to meet the ideals of true womanhood given how they were treated within the slavery system. Hazel Carby argues that the notion of true womanhood describes "the parameters within which [Black] women… were declared… not to be women" (23). The dichotomy, according to Carby, is between the black slave as a "breeder," and the "glorified" propriety associated with the lady of the plantation manor (30).

Sethe is a slave at Sweet Home plantation in Kentucky, where life has become unbearable, especially after the death of slave owner Mr. Garner and subsequent takeover of the plantation by schoolteacher. In addition to making the slaves' conditions worse, schoolteacher makes dehumanizing observations about Sethe in comparing her human attributes to those of an animal, thus putting her outside the ideological construction of true womanhood. Sethe and her husband Halle plan their escape to freedom, but before they can carry out their plan, schoolteacher's young nephews sexually assault Sethe. Mrs. Garner's empathy with Sethe, when the latter tells her about the rape, remains futile, since she is herself under the tyrannical authority of schoolteacher. Mrs. Garner's relative power, however, is reinforced by the idea of true womanhood, which ensures her superiority to the black female slaves at Sweet Home. Thus, the hierarchical relationship between Sethe and Mrs. Garner is therefore "determined through a racial, not gendered categorization" (Carby 55).

The Body

Themes within the framework of sexuality and the black woman's body have also been central to Black feminist critiques of Morrison's work. The novel invites a reading of Sethe's body as a site of resistance to universal masculine subjectivity, the condition of enslavement and the commodification of Black womanhood. At Sweet Home plantation, Sethe's body is marked as a "breeder" to increase the slave master's stock of slaves. Morrison represents the rhetoric, whereby the Black female body is objectified, through schoolteacher's "book of learning," which divides Sethe's body into human and animal characteristics. Carole Boyce Davies scrutinizes the theme of the Black woman's body, as she draws a distinction between "marking which is the product of abuse and is linked to social inscriptions on the body of the "other" [and] naming... [which] has to do with redefinition" (138). In this way, Sethe's body is also the site of different markings. As a black female slave, she is "a marked woman—marked physically by abuse, pregnancy, motherhood and other societal inscriptions by white female, by Black male and by the white male inflictor of the abuse that marks her initially" (Davies 138). Davies discusses the association of racial marking to the bodily marking of pregnancy as signifiers of both Sethe's captivity and enslavement: "Sethe is represented as multiply captive. And significantly, while she can flee slavery, she cannot flee motherhood or the body that has been captured by the needs of her children" (138).

Valerie Smith remarks that Sethe not only remembers her slavery through her body, but also "wears on her body the signs of her greatest ordeal at the Sweet Home Plantation" ("Circling the Subject" 68). Her traumatic experiences are encoded in the scars on her back. The power of those scars lies in the multiple ways other characters in the novel read them: Amy Denver names the scars a chokecherry tree; Baby Suggs compares them to roses of blood, suggesting that scars can leave an imprint on sheets the way blood can, while Paul D compares the scars to "the decorative work of an ironsmith" (Morrison, *Beloved* 17). According to Smith, the novel is about the suffering of bodies under slavery, and its project is "to reclaim those bodies, to find a way to tell the story of the slave body in pain" (V. Smith, "Circling the Subject" 348).

Motherhood

There is a plethora of feminist criticism that focuses on themes of the maternal in Morrison's novel *Beloved*. Critics contend that it is through its exposition of black motherhood that the narrative undermines the violent inscription of the black female under slavery. They conjecture that Sethe's escape is her only way of affirming her identity and renaming herself as a mother, for it is her motherhood and pregnancy after all that have provoked the desire to resist her enslavement. Critic Sally Keenan argues in her essay "Myth, History, and Motherhood in Toni Morrison's *Beloved*" that what makes the novel extraordinary is the way it combines Sethe's desire for freedom and her fierce devotion to her children, thus highlighting "something that historiography has largely been unable to represent" (64). Feminist critic Andrea O'Reilly admits that she feels more connected to Morrison's motherhood than Anglo-American feminist writings that are "daughter-centric and [approach] motherhood only as it had been defined by patriarchal culture" (x). To Anglo-American feminists who were influenced by the dominant ideology of "true womanhood" and its characteristics of "piety, purity and passivity," motherhood specifically refers to "work women did in the privacy of their home that had no political import or cultural value and was oppressive to women" (O'Reilly x).

For African American women who were on the margins of the ideology of "true womanhood," motherhood is rather a site of liberation. For O'Reilly, "Morrison portrays motherhood in all its dimensions as motherwork, motherlove, and the motherline—as a political enterprise with social consequences" (x). Drawing upon the work of African American feminist criticism such as Patricia Collins' *Black Feminist Thought* and Patricia Bell Scott's edited anthology *Double Stitch: Black Women Write about Mothers and Daughters*, O'Reilly constructs Morrison as a maternal theorist and analyzes how such maternal theory plays out in her novels, where motherhood is portrayed as a site of power for both mothers and their children. O'Reilly credits Morrison's maternal philosophy for reworking the strategies for African American women's emancipation in America: "In this Morrison emerges as one of the most important and instructive voices in contemporary debates on race and gender; indeed, a voice that does and should keep you awake at night" (xi).

As feminist studies on Morrison have become more numerous and contributed to the development of race and gender studies, African American feminist scholars are increasingly critical of their forbearers. They warn that the association of Black women with the body and motherhood tends to reinforce gender and racial hierarchies. They also question the essentialization of womanhood, pointing out that no identity—be it racial, sexual, or gendered— is innate, and that all identities are socially constructed. Some of these critics have crossed over into several other areas such as queer studies. Critics such as Barbara Smith and Anthony Warde, who have analyzed sexuality in Morrison's work, implicitly question the heterosexual bias of feminist studies, alleging homogenization in a way that replicates the same hegemonic normalcy that Morrison critiques in her narratives. Readings of the homosexual aspect of *Beloved* engage in particular with the scene of the chain gang, where Paul D is held prisoner and forced to perform fellatio on the male guards on demand. Critics contend that the homosexual content of this scene has been elided from most critical studies of the novel.

Juda Bennett goes so far as to identify the ghost in *Beloved* as a figure of homosexual desires and "disruption[s] to compulsory heterosexuality" (2).

As these critical approaches to *Beloved* demonstrate, the power and appeal of the novel extend beyond those with a personal interest in literature. The critical trajectories charted by the studies assembled in this chapter begin with defining Morrison's status as a canonical writer alongside other modernist writers and extend to exploring its reach to African American history and culture, tapping into deeper themes. Ultimately, the perspectives gathered here provide a powerful argument that *Beloved* and the diversity of readings it inspires represent the primal academic challenge of becoming readers of complex narratives.

Works Cited

Allen, Robert, et al. "Black Writers in Praise of Toni Morrison." New York Times Book Review 24 Jan. 1988: 36.

Bennett, Juda. *Toni Morrison and the Queer Pleasure of Ghosts.* Albany: State U of New York P, 2014.

Bhabha, Homi K. *The Location of Culture*. New York: Routledge, 1994.

Bischoff, Joan. "The Novels of Toni Morrison: Studies in Thwarted Sensitivity." *Studies in Black Literature* 6.3 (1975): 21–23.

Carby, Hazel. *Reconstructing Womanhood: The Emergence of the Afro-American Woman Novelist.* New York: Oxford UP, 1987.

Christian, Barbara. *Black Women Novelists: the Development of a Tradition, 1892–1996.* Westport, CT: Greenwood, 1980.

Davies, Carole Boyce. *Black Women, Writing and Identity: Migrations of the Subject.* New York: Routledge, 1994.

Davis, Kimberly. "Postmodern Blackness: Toni Morrison's *Beloved* and the End of History." *Twentieth Century Literature* 44.2 (1998): 242–60.

Denard, Carolyn. *Toni Morrison: Conversations.* Jackson: UP of Mississippi, 2008.

Gates, Henry Louis, Jr. & Anthony Appiah, eds. *Toni Morrison: Critical Perspectives Past and Present.* New York: Amistad, 1993.

Keenan, Sally. "'Four Hundred Years of Silence': Myth, History, and Motherhood in Toni Morrison's *Beloved*." *Recasting the World: Writing After Colonialism*. Ed. Jonathan White. Baltimore: Johns Hopkins UP, 1993. 45–81.

Kolmerton, Carol, et al. *Unflinching Gaze: Morrison and Faulkner Re-Envisioned*. Jackson: UP of Mississippi, 1997.

McKay, Nellie. "An Interview with Toni Morrison." *Toni Morrison: Critical Perspectives Past and Present*. Ed. Henry Louis Gates, Jr. & Anthony Appiah. New York: Amistad, 1993. 396–411.

Morrison, Toni. *Beloved*. New York: Knopf, 1987.

O'Reilly, Andrea. *Toni Morrison and Motherhood: A Politics of the Heart*. Albany: State U of New York P, 2004.

Osagie, Iyunolu. "Is Morrison also Among the Prophets? Psychoanalytic Strategies in *Beloved*." *African American Review* 28.3 (1994): 423–40.

Peterson, Nancy J., ed. *Toni Morrison: Critical and Theoretical Approaches*. Baltimore, MD: Johns Hopkins UP, 1997.

Rody, Caroline. *The Daughter's Return: African American and Caribbean Women's Fictions of History*. New York: Oxford UP, 2001.

Schwartz, Larry. "Toni Morrison and William Faulkner: The Necessity of a Great American Novelist." *Cultural Logic: An Electronic Journal of Marxist Theory and Practice*. Cultural Logic, 5 (2002): n. page. Web. 5 Jul. 2015. <http://clogic.eserver.org/2002/schwartz.html>.

Smith, Barbara. "Towards a Black Feminist Criticism." *But Some of Us Are Brave: Black Women's Studies*. Ed. Gloria T. Hull, et al. New York: Feminist Press, 1982. 157–75.

Smith, Valerie. "'Circling the Subject': History and Narrative in Beloved." *Toni Morrison: Critical Perspectives Past and Present*. Ed. Henry Louis Gates, Jr. & Anthony Appiah. New York: Amistad, 1993. 342–55.

_____. *Toni Morrison: Writing the Moral Imagination*. Malden: Blackwell, 2012.

Spillers, Hortense. "'All the Things You Could Be by Now if Sigmund Freud's Wife Was Your Mother:' Psychoanalysis and Race." *Black, White, and in Color: Essays on American Literature and Culture*. Ed. Hortense Spillers. Chicago: U of Chicago P, 2003. 376–427.

Warde, Anthony. "'One Was a Woman, the Other a Man': A Psychoanalytic Study of Sexual Identity in the Novels of Toni Morrison." *Anachronist* 11 (2005): 270–293.

Welter, Barbara. "The Cult of True Womanhood: 1820–1860." *American Quarterly* 18.2 (1966): 151–74.

Williams, Lisa. *The Artist as Outsider in the Novels of Toni Morrison and Virginia Woolf.* Westport, CT: Greenwood, 2000.

Black Feminist Literary Criticism and Feminist Archetypal Theory: Exploring Connections in *Beloved*

Anne Herbert

Myths and archetypes that inform Feminist Archetypal Theory are amenable to black feminist critical approaches based in West African belief systems. Thus, they sustain interpretive integrity in the critical analysis of contemporary literature by women of the African Diaspora. Toni Morrison's deployment of Africanist and African American cultural codes in *Beloved* effects a narrative site for exploration of interpretive connections between the two critical camps. The image of the Great Mother or the Universal Feminine, for example, has its Africanist articulation in the Earth/Mother goddess of West African cosmology. As Morrison's narrative strategy in *Beloved* demonstrates, this universal feminine archetype resonates as an arbiter of African American cultural memory.

Informed by Morrison's statements in her nonfiction writings and interviews, this essay offers a black feminist reading of *Beloved* through the critical lens of both black cultural semiotics and Feminist Archetypal Theory. Commensurate with her stated goals of celebrating and preserving African American cultural memory, Morrison encodes archetypal aspects of The Great Mother, The Mother/Daughter Dyad, Memory/Water, and Protection/Enclosure in a narrative strategy based in Africanist epistemology and aesthetics. Indeed, Morrison masterfully manipulates her authorial relationship with the reader as co-producer of the meaning of *Beloved* as a powerful, mythically mediated narrative of cultural affirmation that is deeply invested in Jungian and corresponding Africanist archetypes.

Seeking Cross-cultural Common Ground: Feminist Archetypal Theory

Carol S. Rupprecht explains that in the revisionist Archetypal Feminist movement:

Feminist archetypal theory, proceeding inductively, restored Jung's original emphasis on the fluid, dynamic nature of the archetype, drawing on earlier feminist theory as well as the work of Jungian Erich Neumann to reject absolutist, ahistorical, essentialist, and transcendentalist misinterpretations. Thus "archetype" is recognized as the "tendency to form and reform images in relation to certain kinds of repeated experience," which may vary in individual cultures, authors, readers. Considered according to this definition, the concept becomes a useful tool for literary analysis that explores the synthesis of the *universal and the particular*. (39, italics mine)

Rupprecht's entry on Archetypal Theory in the *Johns Hopkins Guide to Literary Theory and Criticism* (1994) codifies and validates what I will argue as a useful critical grid for contemporary literature by women of the African Diaspora, such as Toni Morrison, whose works engage cultural semiotic narrative strategies invested in Jungian and corresponding Africanist archetypes. Indeed, in her dedication of *Beloved* to "Sixty Million and more" African slaves (those who survived the Middle Passage and those who did not), Morrison asserts her commitment to invoke and preserve *the particular*—the "long memory" ("Rootedness" 344) of African American culture.

Important to the explication in this essay of how Morrison illuminates *the particular* is Rupprecht's assertion that feminist archetypal criticism valorizes the role of the reader as a co-producer of meaning. She notes that the revisionist Archetypal Feminism movement has been bolstered by "new theories [that] increasingly give credence to the requirement, historically asserted by Jungian readers, that each text elicit a personal, affective, and not 'merely intellectual' response" (Rupprecht 39). Indeed, Morrison has definite ideas about how the novel as a repository of cultural memory should "work"—how the text should make meaning in order to accomplish its ends. As in the oral literature from which Black art originates, she believes there must be a "participatory relationship between the artist... and the audience... to make the story appear oral... to have the reader work with the author in the construction of the book" (Morrison, "Rootedness" 341); and she has defined narrative as "one of the ways in which knowledge is organized" (Morrison,

"Memory, Creation and Writing" 388). Thus, Morrison's ideas about narratology and active communication between the writer and the reader toward the common goal of making meaning suggest that *Beloved* is amenable to a cultural semiotic analysis.

Morrison's Cultural Semiotics: A *Recit/Diegesis* Analysis

In *Semiotics and Interpretation,* Robert Scholes observes that meaning is "a function of human experience" and that the meaning (signification) of words used for life experience will be different for those readers who have no experience with the concept or event that the word refers to. Scholes posits that "much of literature is based on attempts to generate semiotic equivalents for experiences that seem to defy duplication in mere signs" (35). I would suggest that much of contemporary literature by black women is based, necessarily, in manipulation of language to "generate semiotic equivalents for experiences" that can only be signified best in a culture-specific manner. Within the context of strategic deployment of cultural codes and signs in a literary work, semiotic equivalence would entail life experience as a black female, or at least an empathy with and receptivity to a black female aesthetic.

In an interview with Claudia Tate, Morrison notes that she perceives an apparent experience-based, cultural differential in black and white female literary expression:

> It seems to me there's an *enormous difference* in the writing of black and white women. Aggression is not as new to black women as it is to white women. Black women seem able to combine the nest and the adventure. They are both safe harbour and ship; they are both inn and trail. We, black women, do both. We don't find these places, these roles, mutually exclusive. That's one of the differences... how one perceives work, how it fits into one's life. (123, italics mine)

Moreover, Morrison notes a cultural distinction grounded in a compulsion to preserve history. Speaking of the historical context of *Beloved*, Morrison admits, "It was an era [American slavery and its aftermath] I didn't want to get into—going back into and through grief" (McKay 45). However, as a black woman, writing to preserve in *Beloved* the African American cultural memory of a specific period in the history of that culture, and writing from the poignant perspective of a black female protagonist (escaped slave) who lived in and through (and survived) that specific segment of "long memory," Morrison, indeed, writes with an "enormous difference."

Thus, Morrison's culture-conscious aesthetic agenda, in which preservation of cultural memory is paramount, enables a semiotic reading of *Beloved* in the manner of Scholes récit/diegesis approach to narrative analysis.[1] Semiotic analysis of a literary text focuses on discovering how meaning is produced in the text, how meaning is constructed or built; and (in an epistemological sense) how we come to know. As a literary semiotician, in "Decoding Papa: 'A Very Short Story' as Work and Text," Scholes decodes Ernest Hemingway's narrative by analyzing the text (words/*recit*) as well as the *diegesis* (the reader's creation of meaning during the reading process). Scholes also analyzes what he calls the "dialogue" between the *recit* and the *diegesis* and shows how the creation of meaning by the reader is controlled by the words (manipulated by the writer). The diegetic order (chronological sequencing of events) is, according to Scholes, discrete and metatextual, "independent from the text," and therefore must be inferred by the reader. This diegetic order is nevertheless "constrained by rules [conditions/codes] of inference that set limits to the legitimacy of the reader's constructions" (Scholes 112). These "limits to legitimacy" can be set by the writer. Although the writer cannot change the reader's diegetic impulse to always arrange events in chronological sequence, the writer can, as Scholes describes, set up a "dialogue between text (*recit*) and *diegesis*." Scholes explains that the literary semiotician can then look at this dialogue for intentional interruptions in the diegetic order, deployed to manipulate the reader's reception and control the interpretation of the narrative.

For example, consider the following general questions that, according to Scholes (114), a literary semiotician should ask to isolate a writer's intentional disturbances of the diegetic process:

"Does the text return obsessively to one episode of the diegetic history?"
[Sethe's murder of Beloved]

"Does it disturb diegetic order to tell about something important to its own discursive ends?"
[Sequence of events surrounding Beloved's murder evolves in a nonlinear, reiterative, and recursive narrative]

"Does it change its viewpoint in diegetic events?"
[Multiple narrative voices and points of view: Sethe, Baby Suggs, Paul D, Stamp Paid, Denver, Beloved]

"Does it conceal things?"
[Beloved's identity discovered in non-sequential, fragmented narrative increments]. (Scholes 114)

As noted above, the dialogue between the text and the diegetic process in *Beloved* is interrupted and influenced toward the ends of creating culture-specific meaning. Semiotics, then, is an illuminative critical lens for analysis of the nonlinear, recursive, multi-voiced narrative of *Beloved*, which registers characters' individual experiences in response to the central event—Beloved's murder. According to Morrison's statements in essays and interviews regarding her narrative techniques and goals as a writer, her motivation for manipulation of the text is based in epistemological as well as aesthetic concerns. Indeed, as Africanist/African American mythmaker, Morrison's goal in *Beloved* is to "put [her] own stamp on the diegetic process" (Scholes 37).

At the outset of each of the three sections of the novel, for example, Morrison both instigates and constrains the "diegetic impulse" in a frank, three-word declarative sentence: "124 was spiteful (I); 124 was loud (II); 124 was quiet (III)." With these cues, the reader reflexively summons the requisite tone and texture of the yet-to-be-told story as Morrison wants it to be received—i.e., toward making the meaning that Morrison intends. Moreover, at the beginning of each section, a stylized, emblematic image concretizes the adverb in each declarative sentence ("spiteful," "loud," "quiet"), as it proclaims the theme of the section and prescribes the mood of the haunted house at 124 Bluestone Road.

In "Unspeakable Things Unspoken," Morrison explains her motivation for this manipulative narrative strategy as a determination to "take the risk of confronting the reader with what must be immediately incomprehensible in that simple, declarative authoritative sentence." She describes her desire to disorient and destabilize the reader with the first sentence in the "in medias res opening" that was "abrupt" and "excessively demanding" (Morrison, "Unspeakable" 32). Accordingly, she adds, "the reader is snatched, yanked, thrown into an environment completely foreign... just as the slaves were from one place to another... without preparation and without defense." Setting the diegetic impulse toward an acutely empathic relation to the condition of the characters in the narrative, Morrison thereby ensures that the reader experiences the "compelling confusion of being there as they (the characters) are; suddenly, without comfort or succor from the 'author,' with only imagination, intelligence, and necessity available for the journey" (33).

Morrison's Mythmaking Journey—Guided by *Nommo*

Jane Campbell defines *mythmaking* as "the process whereby writers throw into relief the values, perceptions, and behaviors they want the audience to acknowledge within a particular culture" (Campbell x). *Mythmaking* can be seen as: culture-specific imagery/codes/signs + semiotics (making or building meaning), and in that manner, Morrison uses mythmaking to manipulate the reader's *diegesis* in *Beloved*. Moreover, Morrison's culture-specific manipulation of the diegetic process pivots on language and alludes to the Africanist belief system of *nommo* as an energizing creative force.[2]

Morrison has stated that in writing *Beloved*, she did not want to know any more than the few facts gleaned from *The Black Book* about Margaret Garner (the slave woman upon whom Sethe's character is based). Rather, she "wanted to depend on her imagination and *shared cultural knowledge* to construct the interior life of the characters"

(Showalter 223, italics mine). Speaking to the creative impulse of mythmaking in Morrison's enlistment of the true story of a female escaped slave to share cultural knowledge, Black feminist critic, Karla Holloway, characterizes *Beloved* as a "mythic revisioning" of the Margaret Garner story (516). I would argue that Morrison's rendering of Garner's lived story as a neo-slave narrative invested in Africanist myths and belief systems pivots on both imagination (the subconscious) and shared (African American) cultural knowledge. Such an authorial construction would depend heavily on imagery, symbols, and signs guided by *nommo*, with which Morrison aligns her creativity.

Nommo figures prominently into Morrison's mythmaking and manipulation of the narrative. African in origin, *nommo* ("word magic"), is understood as the tradition of connection to a benevolent spirit world. Janheinz Jahn relates the religious orientation of *nommo* to the African concept of all "living forces being hierarchically arranged. The thinking forces are the most powerful... by virtue of their control over the magic of the word, the *nommo*." In his study, *Neo-African Literature: A History of Black Writing*, Jahn explains the working relationship between the living and thinking forces:

> The [superior] thinking forces include living people, dead people, deified people, the ghosts, and the gods... It is through [the living people] that all other thinking forces can go on affecting the world... he invokes them by virtue of his nommo, his word magic...he brings the gods into life, by realizing their latent capacities in himself. He does not accept their orders, but asks them to 'work '... through the 'sympathetic magic' of his nommo, he invokes their activity, as handed down in myths, depicted in legends or demonstrated by historical actions, to bring the gods into his living presence, indicating to them the present concrete task. He nominates the gods as instruments of his will. (158)

Other African American critics have discussed this African concept in relation to Morrison's work and point to *nommo* as a particularly positive creative force in the hands of black women. [2]

Morrison is aware of *nommo* and its power to evoke cultural memory. Indeed, she claims to "sometimes know when the work works, when *nommo* has effectively summoned by reading and listening to those who have entered the text" (Morrison, "Unspeakable" 33). In Morrison's mythmaking process, *nommo* invokes the ancestral presence or voice necessary to achieve a distinctly African American cultural aesthetic based in a distinctly Africanist epistemological source.

Toward a Critical Perspective Informed by Africanist Cosmology

In articulating her aesthetic, Morrison asserts that she writes "without gender focus," that it is the "culture of black people" that "provokes [her] imagination" (McKay 54). In this regard, Yuri Lotman and B. A. Uspensky's essay ("On the Semiotic Mechanism of Culture") is relevant to a semiotic analysis of Morrison's narratology in *Beloved*. Lotman and Uspensky explain the relationship of semiotics to historical experience and cultural memory. They write that "culture appears as a system of signs" and that whether these signs are considered to be "man made," "conventional," or the "primordial quality of nature," they each represent discrete elements of cultural semiotics. Lotman and Uspensky further define culture as the "long... memory" or the "record of the memory of what a community has experienced... and is [therefore] connected to past historical experience;" culture thereby becomes a "mechanism for organizing and preserving information in the consciousness of the community." In such a construct, the "longevity" of memory is therefore of prime cultural concern (Lotman & Uspensky 410–413).

Lotman and Uspensky's observation regarding the role of forgetting in the preservation (or, conversely, in the "destruction") of a shared cultural consciousness is significant: "One of the sharpest forms of social struggle in the sphere of culture is the obligatory demand to forget certain aspects of historical experience (413). Significantly, Morrison believes that we must not forget—rather, we are obligated to preserve the "long memory" of African American culture in order to achieve an orientation to the past that is based in reality, however terrible or painful that reality may be. She further believes that the novel, as a record of "long memory," can be a "healing art form for Black people" (Morrison, "Rootedness" 344).

"Long Memory" and the Feminine Archetype: A Semiotic Reading of *Beloved*

The remainder of this essay provides a semiotic analysis of *Beloved* and illustrates Morrison's masterful use of sentient, rhythmic prose to culturally encode crucial passages in the narrative. I will argue that the narrative of *Beloved* is informed by the Feminine or Great Mother Archetype and its Africanist articulation in the Earth or Great Mother Goddess, as imagery of this archetype proliferates the narrative. Indeed, it is the connection of the African American system of cultural semiotics (symbols/images, signs/codes) to a specific historical experience (slavery) and the desire to ensure the longevity of the collective cultural memory, which energize Morrison's semiotic strategies in *Beloved*.

This semiotic reading of *Beloved* focuses on three aspects of the Feminine or Great Mother Archetype, each a meaningful sub-code in African American cultural memory: the Mother/Daughter Dyad; Protection/Enclosure; and Memory/Water imagery. My interpretative assumptions regarding this imagery are supported by Erich Neumann's comprehensive study of multicultural representations of this archetype (*The Great Mother: An Analysis of the Archetype*); his explanations of the significance of these images and symbols are incorporated into the analysis.

Narrative Desire and the Diegetic Order

Although this semiotic reading does not analyze the archetypal images as they appear sequentially in the narrative, it does begin at the beginning. In his essay "Narrative Desire," Peter Brooks presents an intriguing assumption about the "the opening paragraph of most novels":

Desire is always there at the start of the narrative, often in a state of initial arousal, often having reached a state of intensity such that movement must be created, action undertaken, change begun. . . . One could no doubt analyze the opening paragraph of most novels and emerge in each case with the image of desire taking on shape, beginning to seek its own object, beginning to develop a textual energetics. (132)

Brooks' assumption implicates the writer's control of narrative diegetic order. Although testing this assumption at the beginning of *Beloved* requires going to the end of the second paragraph, one paragraph farther than Brooks, indeed, one perceives the narrative "desire taking on shape."

The first paragraph of *Beloved* begins with Morrison's already discussed intentionally loaded line, which sets up an aura—an attitude of evil, malice, malignant (dis)order, a house and a household decidedly gone awry—something/somebody is "shattered," sick, needs healing. At the end of the second paragraph, the narrator tells us that "Baby Suggs' past had been like her present—intolerable— and since she knew death was anything but forgetfulness, she used the little energy left her for pondering color" (Morrison, *Beloved* 4). Thus, the narrative desire of *Beloved* is to emphasize the preservation of long memory and the danger of forgetfulness. At the beginning of the narrative, the potential for even "intolerable" memories to effect personal as well as communal healing is clear. The last lines of the second paragraph signal narrative "desire taking shape" in words and phrases, such as: "her past," "her present," "forgetfulness," and the last word, the last thing upon which Baby Suggs resolves to direct her focus and expend the "little energy left to her"—"color" (4). Erich Neumann's observation on the mythic quality of universal elements (including colors) is relevant here:

> The early magical psychic image of the body and the outside world is correlated not only with certain powers but also with colors, regions, plants, elements... The resulting participation mystique of the world in certain zones and organs of the body, and conversely from the zones of man's body and the substances connect with them to the mythical universe. (41)

After life had "worn her out" and the "whitefolks had won" (Morrison, *Beloved* 170), Baby Suggs resolves to reconnect with the primordial, immutable powers of the universe and expend the remainder of her life force "pondering color." Her terminal reconnection with the universe, mediated by the "magical psychic imagery" of color, is the only bond that makes sense to the former slave who, for most of her temporal life, was not allowed to form lasting, nurturing human bonds, or to "live" unbound and free.

Mother/Daughter Dyad

The Mother/Daughter Dyad, imaged in the Demeter and Persephone/ Kore archetype, is "central to feminine identity, spirituality and affirmation" and is also the "symbol for futurity, promise, and hope for humanity" (Dematrakopoulos & Holloway 32, 40). This archetypal image, therefore, can be seen as one aspect of the universal feminine that is of vital importance to the spiritual survival of a culture. In relation to Morrison's cultural semiotic narrative strategy, the Mother/Daughter Dyad can also allude to an image of ancestral or mother country connection, a connection important to maintain in order to ensure the survival of African American culture.

The narrative energy of *Beloved* centers on the Mother/Daughter Dyad, and several critics have entered the text on this interpretive impulse. In part, this semiotic reading and discussion of the dynamics of narrative *diegesis* relate to the reception (the processing) of this archetypal imagery by those critics who address it. I find that this imagery yields a (predictable) polarity of interpretation or *diegesis*: either *Beloved* is a ghost, or she is not.

A review of these critical works reveals that the differential is not whether the Mother/Daughter Dyad in the narrative is of positive mythical/archetypal significance, but whether one side of that dyad is supernatural or symbolic. Some may see Beloved as a ghost, Sethe's murdered, reincarnated daughter who has come back for vengeance, for love, or for both. Others may see Beloved as the embodied symbol of a generic "beloved" slave girl, who has survived the Middle Passage, which permits a plausible explanation for the enigmatic slave ship stream-of-consciousness narrative passages in Part II (Morrison, *Beloved* 259–263). At least one critic grounds Beloved firmly within an Africanist context, with the observation that "ghost stories told within the African tradition often insist that the natural and the supernatural intertwine… Beloved's immense power to draw Sethe back into the past, and indeed her presence as a reincarnation of the dead, blurs the neat divisions of time, again echoing African traditions" (Sanders 143). Others see Beloved as somebody else's daughter, not Sethe's. They subscribe to the encoded Mother/Daughter Dyad and all the positive cultural and personal implications of that relationship; they reject the supernatural, explain it away. The latter end of this polarity of perception [Beloved as some other slave girl] would, of course, require the reader/interpreter to exclude—refuse to process—important narrative supernatural occurrences as cultural codes.[3]

For psychoanalytic critics, it can be argued that *Beloved* permits a psychoanalytic interpretive option to explain the supernatural events. I suggest that a rejection of the supernatural or providing a psychoanalytic explanation can be seen as a diegetic impulse toward a diegetic order that is different and, therefore, not as amenable to interruption by the author's codes and signs—i.e., the codes and signs are experientially, perhaps even culturally, unfamiliar. These codes are so far to the left of the reader's epistemological grounding that the tendency is to not see or to exclude rather than incorporate these codes into the diegetic process.

The polarity of plausible interpretations of the character Beloved reflects the dynamics of the diegetic process. According to Scholes: "Where authors and texts delight in equivocation [Beloved as ghost?], the reader needs certainty and closure to complete the diegetic processing of textual materials" (114). Significantly, Scholes posits that *"neither the author nor the reader is free to make meaning"* [italics mine]. Cultural codes as well as "literary tradition," though perhaps "enabling communicative adventures," at the same time, constrain "the messages they can exchange" (110, 112). In other words, from a cultural semiotic perspective, *who* or *what* Beloved is, is equivocal. *How* Beloved functions in Morrison's narrative is not. Whether she is a slave girl symbol or Sethe's supernatural murdered daughter, by virtue of her being a black female, within the historical context of *Beloved*, she is Morrison's sign: one of millions of thwarted black lives that need to be remembered.

Protection/Enclosure Imagery

Archetypal images and metaphors of protection imbricate the Mother/Daughter Dyad imagery. For example, all the characters have enclosures (literal and metaphoric) that protect them physically or emotionally. Baby Suggs, "worn out" by a black woman's life and "whitepeople," peacefully closes off the outer world to contemplate color as she lay dying. Sethe, after the "click" (Morrison, *Beloved* 167) of recognition that Beloved was her murdered, re-born/returned baby girl, begins to "sleep like the drowned" in rememory, closing off, emotionally enclosing, protecting herself and her daughters from the pain of an outer world where she seems to have no control.

Denver's protective enclosure is the secret "green bush house," her "emerald closet" in the woods: "five boxwood bushes, planted in a ring… form a round, empty room seven feet high, its walls fifty inches of murmuring leaves" (Morrison, *Beloved* 27). In this "emerald closet," Denver is protected, "closed off from the hurt of the world." (27) In addition, encoded within the description of Denver's enclosure are feminine archetypal images of protection: "ring" and "round" symbolize the *uroboros*—"The 'Great Round,' the positive/negative, both male and female elements of consciousness" (Neumann 18).

Another physical enclosure for Denver is constrictive and malignant rather than protective and nurturing and represents the dark side of the Great Mother Archetype, "a dark dangerously dual figure, both benevolent and terrifying" (Paglia). Denver describes the jail cell where she was locked up with Sethe after the murder of Beloved and the rats that terrify her in the darkness: "a dark place, with scratching noises… where something little watched us from the corners. And touched. Sometimes they touched" (Morrison, *Beloved* 196). The boy Nelson Lord's question, "Wasn't you in there with her when she went [to jail]?" (97), reminds her of that traumatic experience and instigates a metaphoric enclosure for Denver: the descent into two years of deafness to protect her psyche from further trauma. Denver regresses into the willed, womb-like protection of silence, fortified by compulsive withdrawals into the boxwood *uroboros.*

Enclosure enables Sethe to sustain her sanity and protect her daughters. After recognizing that Beloved is her daughter, she isolates and encloses herself and her daughters from the rest of the world, in "their" space, the house at 124 Bluestone Road: "Whatever is going on outside my door ain't for me. The world is this room. This here's all there is and all there needs to be" (Morrison, *Beloved* 174). And, upon returning from work one evening, to "a body returned to her—just like it never went away, never needed a headstone," Sethe "opened the door and walked in and locked it behind her" (188), sealing herself and her children inside the protective enclosure of 124 Bluestone. Later, this enclosure begins to consume them, as Sethe/ Beloved/Denver become "locked in a love that wore everybody out" (230).

Archetypal imagery of protection/enclosure also pertains to Paul D, who is outside, yet on the periphery of influence of the Mother/Daughter Dyad. When Paul D learns of Sethe's crime, he accuses her of a stifling, unwise, and unsafe "thick love," i.e., a metaphoric enclosure. Contrarily, Sethe's answer connotes an image of "thick love" as protective: "Too thick?" Love is or it isn't. Thin love ain't no love at all" (Morrison, *Beloved* 156). For Sethe, love is protection; a mother can't protect with superficial, "thin love." When Paul D replies that Sethe's kind of love did not protect ("didn't work"), Sethe firmly insists that it did protect, "It worked." In Sethe's assessment, love enabled her to protect her children, was thick enough to provide a shield when they needed it most: "to keep them away from what I know is terrible. I did that" (156).

For Beloved, "the other side" (death? a slave ship in the Middle Passage?) was an oppressive enclosure before her "return," her resurrection/reincarnation. The stream-of-consciousness narrative passages (Morrison, *Beloved* 200–207) are heavy with the repetition of oppressive metaphors ("hot thing"), constrictive imagery ("crouching" occurs thirteen times in this stream-of-consciousness

---

Critical Insights

soliloquy), and confusing, fragmented sentences delineated by gaps rather than punctuation marks. These passages enclose and constrict the reader within the narrative, as if packed into the ship's hold with Beloved, the dead man on her face on the reader's as well.

Paul D, too, has a protective enclosure—the "tobacco tin lodged in his chest," where he keeps his memories of Sweet Home—i.e., all the memories that he needs to lock up and forget. Before he came to 124 Bluestone Road, "nothing in this world could pry it open" (Morrison, *Beloved* 106). When the protective tobacco tin finally opens, all the enclosed painful memories spill out in a scornful, syncopated litany: "bad whiskey, nights in the cellar, pig fever, iron bits, smiling roosters, fired feet, laughing dead men, hissing grass, rain, apple blossoms, neck jewelry, Judy in the slaughterhouse, Halle in the butter, ghost-white stairs, chokeberry trees, cameo pins, aspens, Paul A's face, sausage, or the loss of a red, red" heart (224). The rhythm of the prose helps the reader "hear" the tin box bursting, Paul D's protective enclosure giving way. Having come this far with Paul D in the story, having experienced Sweet Home and the iron bit and the prison box with him, all we need are the two- and three-word hints (codes): the reader can feel Paul D surrender and can understand his poignant need to know—"How much is a nigger supposed to take? Tell me. How much?" (224).

In a metaphoric gesture of ultimate protective enclosure, Baby Suggs, the purportedly invincible matriarch and community healer/ preacher—"worn out" by "whitepeople" and life lived as a black woman—decidedly closes off the tyranny of the outer world to peacefully ponder color as she lay dying.

Water/Memory Archetypal Imagery

Water is an aspect of the central symbolism of the Feminine or Great Mother Archetype, "the primordial womb of life, from which in innumerable myths, life is born" (Neumann 47). Water symbolizes memory in *Beloved*. Sethe tells Beloved that before she came back, her [Sethe's] "mind was homeless," but now reunited with Beloved, Sethe says she can "sleep like the drowned, have mercy" (Morrison, *Beloved* 194); she could now immerse herself in the peace of rememory, having done the deed she had to do—keep her children safe from slavery. When recalling for Beloved the story that Nan had told her about Sethe and her mother at sea, Sethe is overcome by a surge of remembrance and yearning: "A mighty wish for Baby Suggs broke over her like surf," and it became "quiet following its splash" (59). Beloved is reborn from water (memory); and Sethe's water breaks (memory returns) when Beloved returns from the other side on a slave ship that crosses the Middle Passage, bridging the gap of "long memory" between ancestral and African American culture

The ice skating episode in Book Two is a powerfully descriptive passage which imbricates all three archetypal images of the Feminine/Great Mother to build the central myth (meaning) of the narrative. Sethe, Beloved, and Denver skate together on the ice (frozen memory —the pain numbed now that Beloved is back). Having only three skates, Sethe (now spiritually strong) chooses to skate without—she can "shoe slide" (Morrison, *Beloved* 166); Denver (growing stronger spiritually) skates on one; the spiritually ambivalent, re-born baby Beloved skates on two.

With prose of sentient power, in this passage, Morrison builds from a reference to spiritual strength to a sense of Sethe/Beloved/ Denver (mother/daughters) "falling" into an isolated closeness/ protection, which "nobody saw." Each needs only the burgeoning spiritual strength of the others to help her "step glide over the treacherous ice" (Morrison, *Beloved* 166) of painful memories. Sethe/ Beloved/Denver, at last, are safely enclosed within a regenerative mother-daughter physical and spiritual unity: "Each seemed to be helping the other two stay upright, yet every tumble doubled their delight. The live oak and soughing pine on the banks enclosed them and absorbed their laughter while they fought gravity for each other's hands… Nobody saw them falling" (166). This passage is the climax of the episode: we the readers can "feel an understanding" of Morrison's codes. We not only read, but can "feel" an acute sense of words such as "soughing," "enclosed," "absorbed," "laughter," "fought," "gravity," "falling."

Then, having let us fall with Sethe/Beloved/Denver into their protective enclosure, Morrison jerks us, too, back into the real world with Sethe when she abruptly falls "on all fours," with "laughter shaking her chest, making her eyes wet" with tears, melting that part of her frozen memory that being on all fours reminds her of. Indeed, Paul D—just before he left her—had accused her, judged her before he "junkheaped her" (Morrison, *Beloved* 165), told her that she should not have killed her own child, that she was not an animal: "You got two feet, Sethe, not four" (156). When Sethe's "laughter died" and the "tears did not, Beloved and Denver knew the difference… [and] touched her lightly on the shoulders." Now, spiritually fortified and resolutely reconciled to whatever lay ahead, they walked together "over hard snow," holding on "tight,"—back to 124 Bluestone (166).

To "Talk About How as Well as What"

Commenting on her aesthetics in "The Site of Memory," Morrison articulates what I perceive to be her cultural semiotic strategy in *Beloved*:

> Writing is thinking and discovery and selection and order and meaning, it is also awe and reverence and mystery and magic… a kind of literary archeology; on the basis of some information and a little bit of guesswork you journey to a site to see what remains were left behind and to reconstruct the world that these remains imply. What makes it fiction is the nature of the imaginative act: my reliance on the image on the remains—in addition to recollection, to yield up a kind of truth. (92)

Thus, moving from the "remains" of the African Earth/Mother goddess and the archetypal Great Mother/Universal Feminine to the text of *Beloved*, Morrison encodes the narrative to "yield up a kind of truth" that invokes the universal as well as the particular. Accordingly, with a cultural semiotic analysis of *Beloved*, attuned to feminine archetypes, Africanist cultural codes, and Morrison's black aesthetic, as Morrison suggests, one can "talk about how as well as what… identify the workings as well as the work" ("Unspeakable" 33).

Notes

1. Robert Scholes writes about the diegesis semiotic in "Decoding Papa: 'A Very Short Story' as Work and Text," (*Semiotics and Interpretation* 110–126).

2. Karla F. C. Holloway (*New Dimensions in Spirituality*), defines *nommo* as "life force… Its power can be destructive or sustaining, but its power seems to be best held by women who have remembered its creative potential" (41). In another section of her book, she identifies *nommo* as "a procreative act assuring civilizations a connection to generations past and future" (22).

3. Martha Bayles, for example, in "Special Effects, Special Pleading," *The New Criterion*, (January 1988), states that in her "heretical opinion, *Beloved* is a dreadful novel, final proof of Morrison's decline from high promise into fashionable mediocrity." Accusing her of "embrace of magic realism," Bayles sees *Beloved* as "reverse racism... so intent is she on showing the inhumanity of the master, she dehumanizes the slave" (34–40).

Works Cited

Campbell, Jane. *Mythic Black Fiction: The Transformation of History.* Knoxville: U of Tennessee P, 1989.

Dematrakopoulos, Stephanis & Karla C. Holloway. *New Dimensions of Spirituality: A Biracial and Bicultural Reading of the Novels of Toni Morrison.* Westport, CT: Greenwood Press, 1987.

Holloway, Karla F. C. "Beloved: A Spiritual." *Callaloo* 13 (1993): 516–525.

Jahn, Janheinz. *Neo-African Literature: A History of Black Writing.* New York: Grove Press, 1968.

Lotman, Urij & B. A. Uspensky. "On the Semiotic Mechanism of Culture." *Critical Theory Since 1965.* Ed. Hazard Adams & LeRoy Searle. Tallahassee: Florida State UP, 1986. 410–422.

McKay, Nellie Y. *Critical Essays on Toni Morrison.* Boston: G. K. Hall & Co., 1988.

Morrison, Toni. *Beloved.* New York: Penguin Books, 2000.

_____. "Rootedness: The Ancestor as Foundation." *Black Women Writers (1950–1980),* Ed. Mari Evans. Garden City, NY: Anchor/ Doubleday, 1984. 339–345.

_____. "Memory, Creation and Writing." *Thought* 59 (1984): 385–390

_____. "Site of Memory." *Inventing the Truth: The Art and Craft* of *Memoir*. 2nd ed. Ed. William Zinsser. Boston & New York: Houghton Mifflin, 1995. 83–102.

_____. "Unspeakable Things Unspoken: The African-American Presence in American Literature." *The Michigan Quarterly Review* 28 (1989): 1–34.

Neumann, Erich. *The Great Mother An Analysis of the Archetype*. Vol. 47. Princeton, NJ: Princeton UP, 1974. Bollingen Ser.

Paglia, Camille. "Erich Neumann: Theorist of the Great Mother." *Arion* 13.3 (Winter 2006): 1–14. Web. 1 Jun. 2015. <http://www.bu.edu/arion/files/2010/03/Paglia-Great-Mother1.pdf>.

Rupprecht, Carol. "Archetypal Literary Theory." *The Johns Hopkins Guide to Literary Theory and Criticism*. Eds. Michael Groden & Martin Kreiswirth. Baltimore, MD: Johns Hopkins UP, 1994.

Sanders, Joe Sutliff. *The Tony Morrison Encyclopedia*. Ed. Elizabeth Ann Beaulieu. Westport, CT: Greenwood Press, 2003. 142-143.

Scholes, Robert. *Semiotics and Interpretation*. New Haven, CT: Yale UP, 1982.

Showalter, Elaine, Baechler, Lea & Litz, A. Walton. *Modern American Women* Writers. New York: Simon & Schuster, 1993.

Tate, Claudia, Ed. *Black Women Writers at Work*. New York: Continuum Publishing, 1983.

"Not If You Are Scared They Ain't": Escaping the White Masculine in *Beloved*_____

Herman Beavers

> For excellent reasons of state...the process of organizing American coherence through a distancing Africanism became the operative mode of a new cultural hegemony.
>
> (Toni Morrison, *Playing in the Dark*)

Readers of *Beloved* will recall Toni Morrison's description of life on Sweet Home, the Kentucky farm from which Sethe and Paul D escape and where Baby Suggs lived prior to being relocated to 124 Bluestone Road on the outskirts of Cincinnati, Ohio. Morrison's decision to set the novel just across the river in Ohio resonates when we put *Beloved* (1987) into conversation with Harriet Beecher Stowe's *Uncle Tom's Cabin* (1852).[1] According to Askeland, "both novelists use and remodel traces of slave history to create narratives that will also remodel the ideologies that dominate the country's power structure" (787–88). Askeland's contention that "*Beloved* sets itself up as a remodeling of *Uncle Tom's Cabin*" is provocative, especially in light of how she characterizes the former as an effort to complicate our understanding of the ideological underpinnings of domesticity. She notes further that *Beloved* insists that reifying patriarchal power structures is ill-advised as a strategy for overcoming the lingering effects of bondage (Askeland 787).

Though commentators on Morrison's novel are aware that its main source text is the story of Margaret Garner's infanticide, close examination of *Uncle Tom's Cabin* reveals *Beloved* to be a product of both invention and revision. I will attend to the cultural ramifications that follow Morrison's decision to revise Stowe in the pages below, but for now, consider that the clearest evidence that *Beloved* is a revisionary text can be found in Chapter Eleven of Stowe's novel. There, the scene shifts from Tom's departure from the Shelby plantation to a Kentucky tavern, where men gather to drink and discuss matters of the day. When one man holds up a handbill advertising George Harris' escape, the exchange takes on a peculiar—and perhaps unexpected—tenor. Though one might expect a white man to blame a bondsperson's escape from a life of bondage and toil on the slave's disloyalty and waywardness, the men conclude differently. Instead, they claim that George's flight was caused by acts of unkindness, if not outright incompetence, on the part of his owner. Indeed, one man states without a hint of irony, "Any man that owns a boy like that, and can't find any better way of treating him, deserves to lose him" (Stowe 91). Another man states that his "gang of boys" are "free to run any time," concluding that "it jest breaks up their wanting to." Moreover, the man declares that he has "free papers" for each of his slaves, "all recorded." But the most striking claim this character makes comes when he insists, "… I tell ye, stranger, there ain't a fellow in our parts gets more out of his niggers than I do" (179). And he continues:

> Why my boys have been to Cincinnati, with five hundred dollars' worth of colts, and brought me back the money, all straight, time and agin. It stands to reason they should. Treat 'em like dogs, and you'll have dogs' works and dogs' actions. *Treat 'em like men* and you'll have men's works. (Stowe 179, italics mine)

The passage above might be familiar to readers of Stowe's novel who will note how it demonstrates the manner in which the ideology of the slaveholder is as much a matter of semantics as it is a matter of racial superiority. Indeed, the scene depicts slave holders who disable their slaves' desire to be free by creating documents that will bestow freedom upon them, allowing travel back and forth across the Ohio River, thus, providing opportunities for slaves to move from slave state to free state and back. The scene is resonant of a scene in Chapter One of Stowe's novel, where Mr. Shelby asserts his trust in Tom's integrity and honesty, "Why, last fall, I let him go to Cincinnati alone, to do business for me, and bring home five hundred dollars" (Stowe 43). Despite the fact that upon his return, Tom's fellow slaves accost him by stating, "Tom, why don't you make tracks for Canada?" (43) Tom's reply: "Ah, master trusted me, and I couldn't..." (43) confirms Shelby's insistence that selling a slave of Tom's honesty and integrity make him valuable enough to cover his entire debt. Though she does not state it directly, Stowe's narration in Chapter Eleven insists that white men's power is best quantified when they do not have to display it. To be a slave, Stowe suggests, is to be stripped of self-possession. Tom's reduction from heroic character in the nineteenth century to the dismissive epithet ("uncle tom"), as it has come to be used in the present, has much to do with the ways that his actions fortify and sustain white masculine power. A slave who travels into free territory and willingly returns to bondage is little more than a human being living under an evil spell.[2]

These scenes in Stowe's novel help us understand the attitude of Morrison's Mr. Garner, who feels his slaves should be "believed and trusted." As Morrison describes it, Sweet Home is a farm worked by men who happen to be slaves. The phrase "happen to be slaves" denotes how Sweet Home is a departure from convention, a place where a slave knows he will be "listened to" (Morrison 147). The five male slaves Garner owns label themselves the Sweet Home men. Paul D Garner, Paul A Garner, Paul F Garner, Halle, and Sixo, experience a form of bondage ironically shaped by their belief that they are, in fact, men and not brutes, beasts of burden, or tools. Indeed, Paul D has grown up "thinking that, of all the Blacks in Kentucky, only the five of them were men" (147). We find out that the Sweet Home men were:

> [a]llowed, encouraged to correct Garner, even defy him. To invent ways of doing things; to see what was needed and attack it without permission. To buy a mother, choose a horse or a wife, handle guns, even learn reading if they wanted to—but they didn't want to since nothing important to them could be put down on paper. (Morrison 147)

In such a circumstance, it is difficult not to feel that Sweet Home is a veritable paradise for slaves, but the philosophical foundations of antebellum slavery make such a conclusion difficult to reach.[3] Nonetheless, Mr. Garner is a slave owner who departs from the conventional wisdom on how to manage his slaves. In a scene that reprises the one described above, Mr. Garner makes a series of aggressive claims about his five male slaves in his conversations with fellow slaveholders: "Y'all got boys, he told them. "Young boys, old boys, picky boys, stroppin boys. Now at Sweet Home, my niggers is men every one of em. Bought em thataway, raised em thataway. Men every one" (Morrison 12). This is an extraordinary claim for a slaveholder to make, which is signaled when his white companion replies, "Beg to differ, Garner. Ain't no nigger men" (12). As we will discover, cultural mechanisms working at the intersection of race and gender help to clarify Garner's larger objective. In a clear instance of throwing down the proverbial gauntlet, Garner declares, "Not if you scared they ain't... But if you a man yourself, you'll want your niggers to be men too" (12). For reasons difficult to discern at first, Garner's claim has little to do with the Sweet Home men. The complexity of Garner's insistence that "[his] niggers is men," functions on several levels. First, it challenges the conventional wisdom that a slave's inferiority locates him outside the realm of humanity. Second, by insisting that the decision to confer manhood on his slaves is contingent on having an unwavering belief in his own manhood, Garner problematizes what it means for a white man to own slaves.

But this attitude points to a third level of complexity, namely, that the challenge Garner issues to the manhood of the white men in his midst happens only within the space of language. When Garner hears, "I wouldn't have no nigger men round my wife," the narrator relates, "It was the reaction Garner loved and waited for" (Morrison 12). This becomes clear only after we realize that Garner has maneuvered his companion to use the word "have" as a double entendre denoting sexual congress. The narrative states, "there was always a pause before the neighbor, or stranger, or peddler, or brother-in-law or whoever it was got the meaning" (12). The silence Garner's comment elicits suggests that language is an inadequate vehicle of masculine self-assertion, and it is necessary to ponder the question as to why. The reader needs to remember that the narrator is not describing a singular event; the sentence makes it clear that Garner has had conversations with other white men that originate with his claims about the Sweet Home men on multiple occasions. Further, at no point in any of the exchanges is he involved in a debate about the morality of owning slaves, nor is he voicing uncertainty about his ability to exert control over them. The complexity of the exchanges becomes clear if we conclude that Garner's purpose is to demonstrate his superiority over other white men.[4]

In a novel that focuses on the travails of black characters seeking what Sethe terms taking "ownership of [a] freed self," it is easy to assume that men of the same race stage homosocial encounters free of adversarial intent. But such a conclusion is only possible if we fail to locate Garner's ideological investment in manhood at the intersection of race, gender, and affect. In other words, it does not matter that white men constitute a community because they share the belief that racial superiority legitimizes their right to own human flesh because the requirements of manhood are such that men who hold power over black bodies are only partially realized as men.

This brings us to the fourth level of complexity in Mr. Garner's assertion about the Sweet Home men, namely, that masculine subjectivity is perhaps best understood within the context that "the image of violent adventure as a test of manhood has influenced American literature since at least the nineteenth century" (Armengol 81). The error that white men make when they encounter Garner is failing to understand that conversation with him is an adversarial event. As he would have it, racial superiority is not a pretense for claiming masculine superiority over other white men. Returning to the moment of silence that follows what appears to be a harmless rejoinder to the reasonable assertion by a slaveholder that he would not put his slaves in close proximity to his wife, "neither would I" seems an incongruous response. But as Morrison frames it, the exchange turns on Garner's adroit understanding that in addition to being a vehicle for self-assertion, language is also a means of self-concealment. Navigating the silence that follows Garner's remark, the adversary comes to understand that language can function to declarative ends, but it can also function connotatively. Matters escalate into violence because Garner sets the stage for his companion to "out" himself as homosexual, and he is, by turns, discrete about practicing it within a domestic space while masquerading as patriarch. In the time it takes to glean the significance of Garner's retort, the distinction between closet and public stage is blurred. When Garner states, "Neither would I," the comment seems to suggest that he, too, engages in illicit sexual encounters with his slaves. But here we need to recall that the conversation began with his declaration that his "niggers [are] men." By insisting that his fellow slave owners (or the man sympathetic to slaveholders) "got boys," and listing the variety of boys a slaveholder can own, Garner insinuates that control over their slaves is enforced through acts of pedophilia rather than masculine force. When Garner insists, "But if you a man yourself, you'll want your niggers to be men too," he asserts that the power he holds over his slaves also signals the masculine superiority he exerts over men of his own race.

Once Garner's adversary realizes that he has been manipulated into revealing himself as both a complicit and duplicitous practitioner of dishonesty, pedophilia, and sodomy, violence becomes the only way they can regain their position inside the category of manhood. Consider, then, the way the encounter reaches a state of closure via "a fierce argument, sometimes a fight" (Morrison 12). And Garner's assertion of masculine authority is verified by the fact that he comes "home bruised and pleased, *having demonstrated one more time* what a *real Kentuckian* was: one tough enough and smart enough to make and call his own niggers men" (13, emphasis mine). Morrison's use of the adjectives "bruised and pleased" indicates how the uncertainty of manhood can only be managed through violence. Hence, Garner's willingness to be contradicted and defied by the Sweet Home men is mediated through his violent encounters with other white men.

Though the Garner scene occupies less than a page, Morrison reveals white masculinity to be a performance that requires the constant policing of boundaries separating the races as well as those separating licit and illicit forms of sexuality. Brevity notwithstanding, this scene is integral to any arguments we might wish to make about *Beloved* as a rumination on the transition from bondage to freedom. The novel demonstrates that because white men like Mr. Garner believe manhood can only be achieved by subjecting themselves to the rigors of physical trial, racial allegiances do not countermand the imperative for men to seek ways to dominate and exercise authority over other men. Garner demonstrates how verbal dexterity is hierarchically situated beneath physical violence, thus suggesting that masculine embodiment trumps language.

Morrison plays on Stowe's own assessment of what makes a Kentuckian unique among men and thus interrogates the politics inherent to the pursuit of authentic forms of masculinity because they are associated as much with the frontiersman as the plantation owner. Hence, as a "real Kentuckian," Mr. Garner's declaration that his "niggers is men," revises the slaveholder's declaration, "Treat em like men, and you'll have men's works." Note how Garner equates "nigger" with manhood, while Stowe couches slaveholding within the space of simile, where all that is required is that slaves be treated "like men." Though the difference would seem on its face to be a matter of degree, on closer inspection the nature of masculine anxiety is entangled here with the paradox of slavery, and it suggests that the real reason slaves were "men," even as they were property is because that configuration works in the service of white men's struggle to become "authentic" men. Though it is counterintuitive to refer to a slave as a man, doing so is part of the overall test a white man might undertake to confirm his own manhood.

Morrison's revision of Stowe is meant, then, to decipher the issues she deems to be most important to her as an author writing in the twentieth century, namely that violence in the black community is a product of an intricate social design. This is the only way we might fully ascertain Morrison's decision to use "Sixty Million and more" as the epigraph to *Beloved*. Though it can easily be read as a gesture of commemorating the Africans who died during the Middle Passage, it can more aptly be read as a way to comment on the practice of blacks inflicting violence on other blacks. Where *Beloved* departs from *Uncle Tom's Cabin* is in its depiction of the traumatic impact of slavery as a modality that proves to be inexhaustible because it reprises slavery's parasitic relation to black subjectivity. Sethe's decision to murder her baby is suggestive of how freed persons (and their descendants in the twentieth century) failed to discern the pattern created by social erasure and mistreatment at the hands of whites, where rather than resisting white supremacy via direct confrontation, they turned the rage in upon themselves. In a manner that reflects the inclination to equate acts of self-destruction with noble sacrifice, Sethe assumes a form of radical individualism whose most salient feature is self-mutilation. But this is because the communal mechanisms that might have warned Sethe and Baby Suggs of schoolteacher's imminent arrival have failed, leaving Sethe to her own resources.

That self-mutilation has been rehearsed at the feast Baby Suggs holds at 124 Bluestone Road to celebrate Sethe's successful escape from Sweet Home. As they consume the turkey, strawberry shrug, corn pudding, and meal-fried perch that has grown out of Baby Suggs effort "to do something with the fruit [picked by Stamp Paid] worthy of the man's labor and his love," the freed persons in the community get angry and turn that anger upon Baby Suggs:

> Too much, they thought. Where does she get it all, Baby Suggs, holy? Why is she and hers always the center of things? How she always knows exactly what to do and when? Giving advice; passing messages; healing the sick, hiding fugitives, loving, cooking, cooking, loving, preaching, singing, dancing, and loving everybody like it was her job and hers alone. (Morrison 161)

What is mutilated, of course, is the community's integrity, its ability to use adversity as a binding principle and catalyst for community resistance. But Baby Suggs realizes that she is culpable, her act of honoring Stamp Paid's labor the product of her hubris, discerning that her "friends and neighbors were angry at her because she had overstepped, given too much, offended them by excess" (Morrison 163).

If *Beloved* and *Uncle Tom's Cabin* exist in a state of complementarity, it could be because both novels are concerned with what happens when one individual falls under the control of another, which compromises their self-possession. Here, I do not mean to privilege the relationship between white slave-owners and their slaves. Rather, it is clear that both Stowe and Morrison are concerned with what happens when self-possession is jeopardized via acts of excessive forms of self-indulgence. Because self-indulgence, as Morrison and Stowe portray it, is often a matter of the false consciousness that accompanies the misuse or misidentification of personal or financial capital, both novels provide us with instances in which miscalculation places the characters at odds with the very thing that sustains and fortifies them.

In the case of Baby Suggs' neighbors, their anger in the face of abundance grows out of the act of equating the feast with Christ's feeding of the multitudes. Recalling the travails of slavery, they conclude that Baby Suggs' experience in slavery does not rival their own. They conclude she has never had to carry "one hundred pounds to the scale," or pick okra "with a baby on her back" nor was she "lashed by a ten-year-old whiteboy" or even had to escape slavery, "had, in fact, been *bought* out of it by a doting son and *driven* to the Ohio River in a wagon" (Morrison 161–62). In an effort to sustain their enmity, Baby Suggs' neighbors reprise the humiliation and abuse that marked their lives as slaves. Rather than serving as a means for repudiating their dispossession, the community makes injury a source of self-authentication. In spite of the fact that slavery has crippled her hip, Baby Suggs' status as a binding force in the community, as the one who "calls" the community to the Clearing where they can experience healing and self-recovery through the reintegration of flesh and spirit, is the target of collective disapproval.

Self-indulgence is also evident in the Sweet Home men's masculinity and the relative amount of freedom they enjoy. Looking once more at the names of Paul A Garner, Paul D Garner, and Paul F Garner, we find that none of them has a period after their middle initial, which would signify that the letters, "A," "D," and "F" are abbreviations for middle names—Andrew, perhaps, or David, or Frederick. But the absence of the period also means that they are individuals who share the same first and last name, who are distinguished by a single letter between them. What appears on its face to be a circumstance in which the Sweet Home men are a collection of individuals whose opinion matters to the man who owns them, can be described as being trapped in a liminal state between symbol and personhood. If we presume that Mr. Garner's first name is "Paul," then we can surmise that the three black men on his farm he raised to be men are named after him. This is the prerogative of the patriarch, but in failing to give them middle names that might allow them space to figure out how each exists apart from the others, Mr. Garner's claim that his "niggers is men," fails to identify them as individuals imbued with free will and self-possession. Rather, they are variations on a singular theme whose main purpose is to buttress his manhood.

After his death, Mr. Garner's self-indulgence is mediated by the arrival of schoolteacher, who interprets Sweet Home as a model of disorder in need of reconfiguring. Subsequently, we find that schoolteacher, "a little man [who]… [a]lways wore a collar, even in the fields" is Mr. Garner's brother-in-law, called by Mrs. Garner because she "didn't want to be the only white person on the farm, and a woman too" (Morrison 44). After Mrs. Garner sells Paul F to help pay off the farm's debts, the remaining Sweet Home men are confirmed in their sense that they could run the farm without supervision. Schoolteacher's arrival disrupts this belief in their autonomy. But, his arrival also should be understood within the context of our introduction to Mr. Garner. Recall that Garner's adversaries included neighbors, strangers, peddlers, and brother-in-laws. Though it might seem pure conjecture, it is likely that Mr. Garner and schoolteacher argued (if they did not engage in physical combat as well) at his intimation that the latter was a pedophile. Such an accusation would have even greater resonance for a man who "had book learning" and who made his living working with children.

As a man whose bearing is the antithesis of Stowe's description of a Kentuckian as a man who wear hats "with true republican independence," and is "altogether the frankest, easiest, most jovial creature living," (Morrison 176–77). Schoolteacher's quiet ways, his soft voice, his use of eugenics to confirm black inferiority, suggest that the use of force need not be accompanied by excessive forms of affect. The disciplinary measures he takes rest on his belief that "definitions belong to the definers—not the defined" and thus "everything [the Sweet Home men] touched was looked on as stealing" (225). Thus, when, "schoolteacher took away the guns from the Sweet Home men and, deprived of game to round out their diet of bread, beans, hominy, and vegetables, and a little extra at slaughter time, they began to pilfer in earnest, and it became not only their right but their obligation" (225). Just as St Clare's sale of Tom to Simon Legree (Stowe 479) constitutes a descent into hell, where he will give his life rather than abandon his Christian principles, schoolteacher's arrival at Sweet Home radically alters the symbolic landscape. For one thing, it reveals that the manhood the Sweet Home men enjoyed under Garner was largely provisional. Years later, Paul D thinks back on his time at Sweet Home, where Garner believed that "what [the Sweet Home men] said had merit and what they felt was serious" (Morrison 147). But it is "schoolteacher who [teaches] them different," by using force to reinforce what Paul D comes to understand as an essential truth:

> A truth that waved like a scarecrow in rye: they were only Sweet Home men at Sweet Home. One step off that ground and they were trespassers among the human race. Watchdogs without teeth; steer bulls without horns; gelded workhorses whose neigh and whinny could not be translated into a language humans spoke. (Morrison 147–48)

But this begs the question: How did the most prominent male characters in *Beloved*, Paul D and Stamp Paid, set about inventing a form of manhood that is not contingent on white men's whim?

For Stamp Paid, it is simply a matter of recognizing that to be black is to be in a constant state of deficit. His act of renaming himself, abandoning the name Joshua in favor of Stamp Paid, is meant to suggest how freedom is an occasion for the total erasure of debt. Morrison writes:

> Born Joshua, he renamed himself when he handed over his wife to his master's son. Handed her over in the sense that he did not kill anybody, thereby himself, because his wife demanded he stay alive.

Otherwise, she reasoned, where and to whom could she return when the boy was through? With that gift, he decided that he didn't owe anybody anything. Whatever his obligations were, that act paid them off. (228)

In this, he is a revision of Haley, the slave trader, who revels in accruing power by holding benign slaveholders like Shelby in financial thrall. Rather than engaging in ostentatious forms of self-display (which Stowe equates with Haley through her description of his gaudy and outlandish clothes), Morrison's Stamp Paid embodies his debtlessness by extending it to others, "by helping them pay out and off whatever they owed in misery. Beaten runaways? He ferried them and rendered them paid for; gave them their own bill of sale, so to speak. "You paid it; now life owes you. And the receipt, as it were, was a welcome door that he never had to knock on" (Morrison 218). However, Stamp Paid makes two tactical errors: one is showing Paul D the newspaper clipping describing Sethe's act of infanticide, and the other comes when Baby Suggs retires to her bed to fix on color. Believing it is his duty to remind her of her responsibility to issue the Call in the Clearing, Stamp Paid underestimates that she has suffered a mortal wound. Because he does not share her sense of total defeat, Stamp Paid has little empathy for her refusal "to go to the Clearing because she believe[s] *they* had won" (227). But Stamp Paid's function in the narrative is similar to Tom's in *Uncle Tom's Cabin* because he gives voice to the Christian values of charity and sacrifice. What makes him a variation on Tom, however, is that he quickly learns that in the wake of Sethe's act, the community surrounding 124 Bluestone has fallen into a state of self-interestedness that he is powerless to break.

For Paul D, however, the transition from bondsman to convict to ex-slave to citizen proves to be very onerous. The challenge for him comes from the fact that his behavior is guided by conflicting models of manhood. The memory of Sweet Home is perhaps the closest he comes to a sense of personal autonomy, but the discipline schoolteacher enforces on the Sweet Home men proves how his manhood is a product of white men's whim. Remembering Alfred,

Georgia, leads to Paul D's realization that black men can resist white supremacy by relying on symbolic forms of resistance. Once he is free of the chain gang and headed north, Paul D must find a way to fashion a life. Morrison writes, "It was some time before he could put Alfred, Georgia, Sixo, schoolteacher, Halle, his brothers, Sethe, Mister, the taste of iron, the sight of butter, the smell of hickory, notebook paper, one by one into the tobacco tin lodged in his chest. By the time he got to 124 nothing in this world could pry it open" (Morrison 233). But Morrison opts not to leave Paul D in this state of emotional deferment. The final model of manhood he adopts arises when he accepts his own powerlessness and remembers Sixo's description of how he feels about the Thirty Mile Woman, "She is a friend of my mind. She gather me, man. The pieces I am, she gather them and give them back to me in all the right order. It's good, you know, when you got a woman who is a friend of your mind" (321). What Paul D realizes is that he does not need to be solely responsible for creating a viable form of selfhood. Sixo's words help him realize that manhood can be a product of collaboration, provided men are willing to abandon their patriarchal desire to reside at the top of the gender hierarchy. He thinks about the empathy and tenderness Sethe extends to him when she first sees his "neck jewelry," the last visible remnant of his life as a slave. "How she never mentioned or looked at it, so he did not have to feel the shame of being collared like a beast. Only this woman Sethe could have left him his manhood like that" (322). Thinking about this, Paul D concludes that he "wants to put his story next to hers" and thus recognize the need "for some kind of tomorrow" (322). Unlike Stowe's depiction of Tom and George Harris respectively as the most moral upstanding character and the most ambitious in *Uncle Tom's Cabin*, Morrison does not seek to use Stamp Paid and Paul D in this manner. The question of whether they are better men than the white men from their past is rendered moot by Morrison's sense that black communities are often undermined by the hubris that drives such thinking. And by declaring that everything that has transpired prior is "not a story to pass on," Morrison insists, finally, that healing is a product of forward-thinking acts of conscious design.

Notes

1. Though the novels' respective themes radically diverge once we consider that *Beloved* is concerned with slavery's traumatic aftereffects, Lori Askeland observes that the parallels in the texts are numerous. Beloved is set in part in the same place and during the same period as *Uncle Tom's Cabin*: Sweet Home's northern Kentucky must be near the location of the Shelby plantation, and both novels' initial action represents a response to the Fugitive Slave Act. Moreover, *Beloved*'s main action takes place near Cincinnati in 1873, which was the location of the Beecher family home from 1832–1849—a significant factor in her writing of *Uncle Tom's Cabin*, since it was there that she gained first-hand experience of recently "freed" slaves (Askeland 787).

2. Though Uncle Tom's Cabin is not to be mistaken with a fairy tale, it is hard not to think about the distance between Stowe's Tom and the derisive epithet, "uncle tom" and the fact that it may have to do with the manner in which Tom's selflessness and Christian piety are interpreted as vehicles of self-nullification, as if they are meant to serve as indicators of his goodness, but not his agency, as if he is under a spell that can only be broken in the Hereafter.

3. One thinks here of Frederick Douglass's observation in his autobiography that his master, fortuitously named Mr. Freeland, was "the best master I ever had, till I became my own master" (Douglass 83, italics in original). Douglass's point is that while the words "best master" might intimate a slave owner who lives by a set of principles that lead him to treat his slaves humanely (he states that he went a year with Freeland "without receiving a single blow"), he is nonetheless part of a system in which black bodies are held in captivity. Situated in *The Narrative of the Life of Frederick Douglass* (1845) at a point in the text right before Douglass makes his escape from slavery and lands in New Bedford, Massachusetts, escaping from Mr. Freeland is no different from escaping from his prior master, who treated him harshly.

4. We come to understand Mr. Garner's motivation through Jeff Hearn's observation that men are not situated in a single public domain (2). Rather, they move across multiple public domains and thus the power they exert can fluctuate despite men's wholesale investment in masculinism, which Arthur Brittain describes as "the ideology that justifies and naturalizes male domination" (4). In a representation of

masculinism, such as the one found in *Beloved*, men in the public sphere seek not only to dominate women, "but also different types of men dominate other men—able-bodied over men with disabilities, heterosexual over gay, and so on" (Brittain 4). Mr. Garner's motivations are clarified when Brittain further observes, "what is paramount in representations of masculinity in a capitalist society is competition and achievement" (16). It is important to recognize the intersectionality of white men's presence in the public sphere.

Works Cited

Armengol, Josep M. "Gendering Men: Re-Visions of Violence as a Test of Manhood in American Literature." *Atlantis*. 29.2 (2007): 75–92.

Askeland, Lori. "Remodeling the Model Home in *Uncle Tom's Cabin* and *Beloved*." *American Literature*. 64.4 (1992): 785–805.

Brittain, Arthur. *Masculinity and Power*. Oxford: Basil Blackwell, 1989.

Douglass, Frederick. *Narrative of the Life of Frederick Douglass*. 1845. New York: Anchor Books, 1973.

Hearn, Jeff. *Men in the Public Eye*. London, New York: Routledge, 1992.

Jehlen, Myra. "The Family Militant: Domesticity Versus Slavery in *Uncle Tom's Cabin*." *Criticism*. 31.4 (1989): 383–400.

Morrison, Toni. *Beloved*. 1987. New York: Vintage Books, 2004.

Stowe, Harriet Beecher. *Uncle Tom's Cabin; or, Life Among the Lowly*. 1852. New York: Penguin Books, 1984.

CRITICAL
READINGS

Slavery in Toni Morrison's *Beloved*_____

Joseph McLaren

Toni Morrison's *Beloved* (1987) can be classified as a neo-slave narrative that retells a particular history of the "peculiar institution," the term used by Kenneth Stampp to describe slavery in the United States. The historical archive of nineteenth-century slavery is extensive, and Morrison's choice of the Margaret Garner story suggests its emblematic possibilities and supports what Wilfred Samuels and Clenora Hudson-Weems refer to as showing the "workings of the plantocracy that denied...basic human and political rights (96). Margaret Garner's 1856 escape from slavery in Kentucky to assumed freedom in Cincinnati, Ohio, demonstrates the fragility of "free" status and the social problems generated by the Fugitive Slave Act of 1850, which was followed by the Dred Scott Decision of 1857, further restricting the legal rights of those who escaped to "free" territories. Both rulings are mentioned in the novel as part of "the discussions, stormy or quiet," which took place in the "Clearing," where Baby Suggs presides (Morrison 173). In the novel, Morrison offers what Adrienne Lanier Seward and Justine Tally have called "stories that open our consciousness to realities that many have willfully refused entry" (xv).

Although *Beloved* can stand as a story of personal relationships and a black family's torn legacy, it also can serve as a corollary to the various histories of slavery. In creating the character Beloved, Morrison, as Ashraf Rushdy observes, "resurrect[s] one of its anonymous victims" (578). The Sweet Home plantation in Kentucky, from which Sethe escapes, symbolizes the physical and psychological abuses of slavery, shown in situations that define the so-called "master-slave" relationship. Morrison's portrayal of Mr. and Mrs. Garner, who "own" Sweet Home, shows a "benign" form of slavery and the existence of humanizing emotions and actions. Although Sethe, the fictionalized Margaret Garner, has not arrived directly from Africa, her characterization reflects historian Michael

Gomez's explanation of an acculturation process in which "there was obviously interaction with the host society—the white world-both slaveholding and nonslaveholding" (8). However, the novel does not diminish the cruelties or severe aspects of the institution as seen in the characterization of schoolteacher, who is the successor to Mr. Garner in running the plantation. For Sethe, under schoolteacher's control, "there is no aspect of her self that is in fact secure against the violations of that society" (Moglen 29). Morrison's portrayals of the physically demeaning acts committed against Sethe by schoolteacher and his nephews add to historical understandings of abuses experienced by enslaved women. Furthermore, the black male characters at Sweet Home, Paul D, Halle, and Sixo, for example, demonstrate the predicaments of enslaved men.

While the novel exemplifies the conditions of enslavement in Kentucky, it also presents modes of escape and liberation through the Underground Railroad, where such characters as Amy Denver and Stamp Paid are fictionalized representations of those who defied the restrictions of slavery. Overall, Morrison, as noted by Tessa Roynon, "depict[s] the black experience of slavery and its aftermath in tragic terms" (83). Morrison represents slavery in its many facets, but especially through its effects on human relationships, both "romantic" and familial. The origins of *Beloved* are directly linked to Margaret Garner as explained by Nellie McKay: "The Garner incident was well known when it occurred and was taken up as a cause célèbre by abolitionists such as Frederick Douglass and by abolitionist newspapers" (7–8). The incident was described in detail by Samuel May in *The Fugitive Slave Law and Its Victims*, published by the American Anti-Slavery Society in 1856. May used materials from Cincinnati newspapers, which identified Margaret Garner as the wife of Simon Jr. and mother of four children (25). The Garner incident "disturbed the North more than a hundred arguments of antislavery philosophers" (Yanuck 47).

The horrific incident itself was detailed by May: "In one corner of the room was a nearly white child, bleeding to death. Her throat was cut from ear to ear, and the blood was spouting out profusely, showing that deed was but recently committed" (25). Garner was the so-called property of Archibald K. Gaines and John Marshall "of Richwood Station, Boone, County, Kentucky" (May 27). However, "Morrison blots the undisputed historical fact that Garner was taken back into slavery, after which recapture she vanished" (Serpell 121).

Forms of Slavery: Memories of Dehumanization

In the novel's three parts, the slave experience is revealed through allusions and flashbacks. Morrison shapes the novel around two central locations, the present, located in Cincinnati at 124 Bluestone Road, and the past at the Sweet Home plantation in Kentucky, under the Garners and later schoolteacher. There is also a transitional space, the crossing of the Ohio River through the agency of Amy Denver and Stamp Paid. This crossing is a literal movement from slave territory to free, but also an emotional and psychological break with the dehumanizing experiences of servitude that linger into the future.

The opening of the novel suggests the past experiences of enslavement. One of the first representations of Sweet Home is through Sethe's conversation with Paul D, "the last of the Sweet Home men," who arrived at 124 Bluestone Road (Morrison 9). Paul D was one of the "six of them who belonged to the farm, Sethe the only female" (9). Here the term "belonged" suggests that people are property in the language of slavery. Furthermore, the selling of Paul D's brother had psychological effects on Sethe, whose eyes were like "two open wells that did not reflect firelight" (9). Most important, the death of Mr. Garner and the beginning of schoolteacher's control is marker of time, earlier suggested as 1855. Later in Part One, there is a flashback to the crossing of the river and the meeting with Amy, who observes Sethe's scarred back, evidence of the whippings that Sethe has experienced. The scars are described as a "'chokecherry tree" where the "trunk—it's red and split wide open, full of sap, and this here's the parting for the branches'" (Morrison 79). The scar can also be understood "As an element of the grotesque…a sign of degradation" (Corey 35).

The flashback retelling the birth of Denver also shows the fear that runaways experienced: "A pateroller passing would have sniggered to see two throw-away people, two lawless outlaws—a slave and a barefoot whitewoman with unpinned hair—wrapping a ten-minute-old baby in the rags they wore" (Morrison 84–85). The so-called "pateroller" or slave catcher was the agent of the system sanctioned by the Fugitive Slave Act. The novel also describes the arrival at 124 Bluestone Road, where "Sethe climbed off a wagon, her newborn tied to her chest, and felt for the first time the wide arms of her mother-in-law, who had made it to Cincinnati" (Morrison 87). Baby Suggs as mother-in-law creates a place of refuge in the "Clearing," where she preaches, heals, and, according to La Vinia Jennings, "calls worshippers from the trees encircling the Clearing to perform the ring shout" (21). In the "Clearing" Sethe "claimed herself" despite the reality that "Freeing yourself was one thing; claiming ownership of that freed self was another" (Morrison 95). Sethe's memory is important because through an understanding of the past, one "can begin to imagine a future" (Zauditu-Selassie 145). The character Stamp Paid is also connected to slavery, but as an agent of the transition to freedom. Described as "the sly, steely old black man: agent, fisherman, boatman, tracker, savior, spy," he contributes to the nurturing of Denver as an infant. When he brings the blackberries to the infant "Twenty days after Sethe got to 124," he becomes symbolic of the community of free blacks in Cincinnati (Morrison 136–137).

The novel also explores slavery through Paul D, who experiences the rigors of enslavement and the chain gang when he is marched "in a coffle with ten others, through Kentucky into Virginia." Having attempted to kill Brandywine, who is sold, too, after the attempted escape from Sweet Home, Paul D survives the next phase of his servitude. In this part of the novel, the treatment of the enslaved men is described: "The wrists he held out for the bracelets that evening were steady as were the legs he stood on when chains were attached to the leg irons" (Morrison 106–107). Morrison's use of descriptive language is impressive, as when the narrator describes the manacles as "one thousand feet of the best hand-forged chain" (107). The chain gang experience in Georgia reveals further modes of control as prisoners are confined at night to trenches. However, the will to escape is shown as well, and freedom is described as "Free North. Magical North. Welcoming, benevolent North" (112). Most important, schoolteacher is used to show the controlling element of slavery and the curious relationship between the "Sweet Home men" and Garner. For Garner, "Deferring to his slaves' opinions did not deprive him of authority or power" (Morrison 125). In contrast, schoolteacher, who "taught them otherwise," is unyielding (Morrison 125).

The effects of enslavement are also developed through the memories of Baby Suggs and her relationship to her children. As a mother, although she does, as Ato Quayson suggests, "carry impairments" (88), she is able to maintain a link to her children through memories. Prior to Sweet Home, she had been enslaved in "Carolina" and had lost her many children. The strength of her maternal memory is shown through her connection to their physical presence: "Seven times she had done that: held a little foot; examined the fat fingertips with her own—fingers" (Morrison 139). This aspect of slavery, the separation of mothers from their offspring, is part of the cycle of inhumanity inherent in the system. The novel also suggests mobility and movement as a result of such separations. Baby Suggs is emblematic of this forced mobility, where at Sweet Home, unlike in "Carolina," "there wasn't a rice field or tobacco patch in sight, and nobody, but nobody, knocked her down" (139). These depictions suggest that Sweet Home, where she is called Jenny, was a respite from the drudgery of field work experienced in "Carolina." Even in the kitchen duties, Baby Suggs would "stand beside the humming Lillian Garner while the two of them cooked" (139). Although under Mr. Garner "Sweet Home was a marked improvement," it was also where Baby Suggs experiences personal conflicts of the enslaved woman who "never had the map to discover" her own self-identity (Morrison 140).

Nevertheless, slavery under Mr. Garner allowed for certain leniencies related to labor.

> The Garners, it seemed to her, ran a special kind of slavery, treating
> them like paid labor, listening to what they said, teaching what they

wanted known. And he didn't stud his boys. Never brought them to her cabin with directions to "lay down with her," like they did in Carolina, or rented their sex out on other farms. (Morrison 140)

Here, Morrison alludes to certain practices of slavery, "hiring out" and slave breeding, what is later referred to as "the danger of men-bred slaves on the loose" (Morrison 141). In the US, the practice of "hiring" oneself out, discussed, for example, in Frederick Douglass's autobiography, was a means for acquiring one's own money or being further exploited by a slave owner.

Most important, Baby Suggs's liberation is achieved through the agency of her son Halle. The negotiation or the "agreement" made between Mr. Garner and Halle, who was allowed to purchase his mother's freedom, shows how "it meant more to him [Halle] that she go free than anything in the world" (Morrison 141). The transition to freedom, described as allowing oneself to be "taken 'cross the river,'" is the ultimate goal of the enslaved person. However, for Baby Suggs, it is conflicted with realizations of her own years of servitude and what freedom will actually constitute. As noted by Evelyn Schreiber, "Later, freed slaves carry the generational memory of abuse, and their post- slavery reality reactivates the prior bodily experience and threat of real bodily harm" (36). When Baby Suggs thinks, "What does a sixty-odd-year-old slavewoman who walks like a three-legged dog need freedom for?" (Morrison 141), the psychological effects of liberation are implied, not solely in relation to longevity or the age at which one achieves freedom, but through a comparative process involving the mother-son relationship. Baby Suggs considers that for Halle, "who had never drawn one free breath…there was nothing like it in this world" (141). Here the consciousness of liberation is transferred from Halle to Baby Suggs, who is "scared" of the new status (141). Furthermore, liberation is defined through its effects on Baby Suggs's body: "These hands belong to me. These *my* hands." The repossession of the body and the ownership of the tools of labor is a moment of "discovery" that involves the life force, "her own heartbeat" (141). Mr. Garner understands the fragile nature of Baby Suggs's consciousness, her fear of free status, counseling her when he says, "'Nothing to be scared of, Jenny. Just keep your same ways, you'll be all right'" (141).

The conversation between Baby Suggs and Garner uncovers additional layers of Baby Suggs's past through the fundamental idea of naming. Baby Suggs's question to Garner, "'why you all call me Jenny?'" not only shows the act of her purchase in "Carolina," where she was named Jenny Whitlow, but her desire to claim her marriage (Morrison 142). Moreover, the importance of freedom is revealed in Baby Suggs's relationship with her "husband," who "taught her how to make shoes," and with whom a "pact" was made for running away; "whichever one got a chance to run would take it; together if possible, alone if not, and no looking back" (142). Although the "pact" might appear destructive to the marriage, it suggests that freedom was the paramount objective. In addition, Baby Suggs's goal to retain her husband's name, despite Garner's suggestion that "'Mrs. Baby Suggs ain't no name for a freed Negro,'" is strategic. By using "some bill-of-sale name,'" such as Jenny Whitlow, the possibilities of reunion would be less (142).

Transition to Freedom: Escape, Family Connections, and the Economics of Slavery

One of the key transitional moments to freedom involves the handing off by Garner of Baby Suggs to the Bodwins, white abolitionists in Cincinnati, where Baby Suggs realizes the possibility of reuniting her family and announces, "'I'm free, you know'" (Morrison 143). The Bodwins "'don't hold with slavery, even Garner's kind'" (Morrison 145). When Baby Suggs, who spent ten years at Sweet Home and was a skilled cobbler, considers that someone might "write old Whitlow," she proves that the scattered branches of family might be brought together but with the caveat that "if she searched too hard and they were hiding, finding them would do them more harm than good" (143). In the conversation with the Bodwins, Baby Suggs's ultimate retort reveals the economics of manumission, the benefits that will accrue to Garner: "'But you got my boy [Halle] and I'm all broke down. You be renting him out to pay for me way after I'm gone to Glory'" (146). "Hiring out" becomes the mode of payment.

Furthermore, manumitting a senior enslaved person, a practice in US slavery, was not necessarily done for humanitarian reasons. Baby Suggs's free status is not without labor, where, in exchange for housing at 124 Bluestone, she is expected to wash clothes for "[t]wo cents a pound" (145) and work as a cobbler. Freedom also meant continuing the search for her family and dealing with "the heart that started beating the minute she crossed the Ohio River" (147).

Sethe, Baby Suggs's daughter-in-law and Halle's wife, also experiences "freedom" in Cincinnati, but she is vulnerable to recapture. Her pursuit by schoolteacher is one of the central parts of the novel. Schoolteacher arrives at 124 Bluestone Road with "one nephew, one slave catcher and a sheriff" (Morrison 148). Experienced at this process, they are aware that "likely as not the fugitive would make a dash for it." Morrison shows the ingenuity of runaways who might be found "folded up tight somewhere: beneath floorboards, in a pantry—once in a chimney" (148). The places of seclusion also include a "press" or a "hayloft." The narrator suggests the mindset of schoolteacher and his group toward runaways: "Caught red-handed, so to speak, they would seem to recognize the futility of outsmarting a whiteman and the hopelessness of outrunning a rifle" (148).

The attitude of the slave catcher is presented as cruelly economic, when the capture of a human is compared to that of "a snake or a bear," and if deadly force were used "you ended up killing what you were paid to bring back alive" (Morrison 148). One of the free black persons is referred to as "[a] crazy old nigger" and Sethe's children as "pickaninnies" (149), the derogatory word used to identify enslaved children. The repetition of the word "crazy" suggests the perspective of the slave owner, who perceives the defense by the group as a sign of madness. Morrison's use of irony accents this moment, for although presented from the perspective of the slaveholder, this event shows an act of salvation by "the old nigger boy, still mewing, [who] ran through the door behind them and snatched the baby from the arch of its mother's swing" (149). Although explained in the novel, Sethe's killing of her baby "runs counter to the slave community's response of resistance, namely, their determined effort to keep family ties alive despite the master's attempt to sunder them" (Grewal 97).

This section of the novel, the shed description of the killing of Sethe's child, reinforces the economics of slavery where the goal is to reclaim children whom they could "take back and raise properly to do the work Sweet Home desperately needed" (Morrison 149). Sethe's killing of her child "can be tied directly to the existence of the harsh new Fugitive Slave Law that took effect in 1850" (King 167). However, Sethe, in many ways, reflects what Karla Holloway and Stephanie Demetrakopoulos describe as "the sexual stripping that Black women experienced through the systems of slavery and racism" (22). Schoolteacher's thoughts at the horrific scene, "that there was nothing there to claim," show the crass economic viewpoint (Morrison 149). Sethe, viewed as "having at least ten breeding years left," has been ruined by "the nephew who'd overbeat her" (149). This language is consistent with the concept of chattel slavery, where humans are considered as animals. The shed scene is also used to show the corrupting psychological effects of such cruelty on schoolteacher's nephew, whose "shaking" is a sign of his trauma and confusion. While at Sweet Home, Sethe had been held down by one of schoolteacher's nephews, while this nephew took her milk, "nursed her" (Morrison 150). Schoolteacher's nephew recognizes that although he is white, he, too, had "been beat a million times" (150). The killing of the child is, for him, an unexplainable act, and he wonders, "What she go do that for?" For the reader, the explanation can be found in Theresa Washington's analysis, that the act was done "[r]ather than subject their progeny to the financially motivated, sexually depraved, and morally bankrupt whims of their oppressors" (174–175). Also, "from a traditional view, death is not an ending but rather a transference to another but not distinctly separate sphere" (Jennings 62).

Also, the tenuousness of runaway status is developed through flashbacks and the emotional and psychological effects on Paul D, who recollects Alfred, Georgia. Slavery can be understood as a corrupting element in interpersonal and familial love, which are sought but never fully realized. When Baby Suggs reminds Paul D later in Part One, "what it was like for [her] to get away from there [Sweet Home]" (Morrison 161), he remembers the obstacles "to get to a place where you could love anything you chose—not to need permission for desire—well now, *that* was freedom" (162). In many respects, Paul D is a blues figure who experiences the chain gang and "restless wandering" (Eckstein 275).

Part Two of the novel continues with allusions to slavery and freedom. Stamp Paid uses the term "the Misery" to describe Sethe's killing of her child, also called her "rough response to the Fugitive Bill" (Morrison 171). In Cincinnati, Sethe gradually becomes part of "a community of other free Negroes—to love and be loved by them" (Morrison 177). The novel takes us some years past the slavery era to 1874, when "whitefolks were still on the loose. Whole towns wiped clean of Negroes; eighty-seven lynchings in one year alone in Kentucky," reported in the pages of the *North Star* (Morrison 180). Other aspects of slavery at Sweet Home under schoolteacher involve an incident in which Sixo cleverly articulates the nature of property, describing his act of butchering, cooking, and eating a "shoat" as "Improving your property," implying that if he were better fed, he would be more productive (190). After the death of Mr. Garner, the enslaved men find other means to provide for themselves:

> Schoolteacher took away the guns from the Sweet Home men and, deprived of game to round out their diet of bread, beans, hominy, vegetables and a little extra at slaughter time, they began to pilfer in earnest, and it became not only their right but their obligation. (Morrison 190–191)

Expressed as an "obligation," the act of pilfering becomes a mode of survival and is not perceived as morally or ethically incorrect.

Dehumanization under schoolteacher is also presented through flashbacks, where Sethe recalls hearing schoolteacher teaching "his pupils." He instructs "one of them," who is writing about Sethe, "'I told you to put her human characteristics on the left; her animal ones on the right'" (Morrison 193). Although Sethe tried to understand the word "characteristics," it is through a conversation with the ailing Mrs. Garner that she learns what it means, "'a characteristic is a feature. A thing that's natural to a thing'" (Morrison 195). Morrison allows this ironic answer to remain unresolved, letting the reader perceive the various possibilities of the words "thing" and "natural." Also, in this part of the novel, Sethe remembers a conversation with Halle, revealing more about schoolteacher, the Garners, and slaveholders. Sethe admits that the Garners "'ain't like the whites I seen before. The ones in the big place I was before I came here'" (195). The dialogue uncovers the motives of Mr. Garner in allowing Halle to purchase his mother's freedom. When Halle remarks, "'If he hadn't of, she would of dropped in his cooking stove,'" he implies that her age was the primary reason (195). The economic necessity of purchasing one's freedom is also indicated through Sethe's viewpoint: "getting away was a money thing to us. Buy out. Running away was nowhere on our minds" (197). The options of purchasing one's freedom, or that of a family member, are contrasted with the risks of running away. Significantly, Mrs. Garner survives for two years by selling Paul F, and the transfer to her brother-in-law, schoolteacher, is considered a necessity because "people said she shouldn't be alone out there with nothing but Negroes" (197).

By returning to characterizations of schoolteacher, the novel fills in the fragments of the past as in a description of his initial entry into Sweet Home: "So he came with a big hat and spectacles and a coach box full of paper. Talking soft and watching hard. He beat Paul A" (Morrison 197). Implicitly, the decision to escape to freedom is the result of schoolteacher's harsh treatment. The idea of a "train" to freedom is part of Sixo's understanding of the Underground Railroad: "Sixo say freedom is that way. A whole train is going and if we can get there, don't need to be no buy-out" (197). These flashback recollections in Part Two clarify the choices faced by Sethe, her family, and others after the arrival of schoolteacher.

The novel also imagines the trans-Atlantic slave trade, prior to plantation slavery in Kentucky. Through the character Beloved's perspective, the Middle Passage, the journey from the West African coast, is presented in a stream of consciousness section where the imagery describes a memory of the slave ship:

...the men without skin bring us their morning water to drink we have none at night I cannot see the dead man on my face (210)

...in the beginning the women are away from the men and the men are away from the women storms rock us and mix the men into the women and the women into the men (211)

Although Beloved does not experience the cruelties of Sweet Home, she is, nevertheless, connected to its effects. She is a "ghost" who is a "bridge of personal and historical memory" (Anderson 65). Following Beloved's version of the Middle Passage, another evocation involves the sea: "the men without skin came and took us up into the sunlight with the dead and shoved them into the sea" (Morrison 214).

Also in Part Two, Morrison continues the cyclical retelling of the Sweet Home experience through the memories of Paul D, who remembers his twenty years at Sweet Home and the importance of family linkages, which, in some cases, were not broken during slavery, exemplified by a Maryland family he encountered:

Once, in Maryland, he met four families of slaves who had all been together for a hundred years: great-grands, grands, mothers, fathers, aunts, uncles, cousins, children. Half white, part white, all black, mixed with Indian. (Morrison 219)

The reference to "mixed with Indian" reminds readers of the relationship between African-descended populations and Native Americans during the slavery era. Also, Paul D and the others who escaped Alfred, Georgia, were assisted by the Cherokee, who called them "Buffalo men" (Morrison 112). Through Paul D's perspective, the deleterious effects of schoolteacher's actions are reified: "For years Paul D believed schoolteacher broke into children what Garner had raised into men" (Morrison 220). Also, Paul D's recollections clarify the escape plans at Sweet Home, the connection to the Thirty-Mile Woman, Sixo's friend, and the plan she reveals "That seven Negroes on her place were joining two others going North" (Morrison 222). The whole process of escape is suggested through memory and the "plan" that is fraught with uncertainties: "Is it better to leave in the dark to get a better start, or go at daybreak to be able to see the way better?" (222). The ultimate confrontation, when they are caught by schoolteacher in the act of escape, is also presented in dramatic detail as is the burning of Sixo, although schoolteacher and his men "came to capture, not kill" (Morrison 226). Most important, this moment in the novel reveals Paul D's understanding of slavery and his status as property once he is captured, shackled, and placed in a "three-spoke collar" (226–227).

> Paul D hears the men talking and for the first time learns his worth. He has always known, or believed he did, his value—as a hand, a laborer who could make profit on a farm—but now he discovers his worth, which is to say he learns his price. The dollar value of his weight, his strength, his heart, his brain, his penis, and his future. (226)

Schoolteacher, who values Paul D at $900, is the antithesis of Garner, who supposedly broke laws in "letting niggers hire out their own time to buy themselves. He even let em have guns! And you think he mated them niggers to get him some more? Hell no! He planned for them to marry!" (Morrison 226–227). Here again, the economic purpose of Sweet Home is linked to slave breeding and the ultimate goal that schoolteacher and his nephews "would have seven niggers and Sweet Home would be worth the trouble it was causing" (227). In relation to breeding, Sethe represents "property that reproduced itself without cost" (Morrison 228).

In Part Three, the journey of Paul D reflects the Civil War when he encounters "the battlefields of Alabama" and a black soldier who "had been with the Massachusetts 54th," the famous first all-black regiment under Colonel Robert Gould Shaw that was heroic in the 1863 battle at Fort Wagner, South Carolina (Morrison 268–269). Indeed the past of slavery through the experiences of Sethe and Paul D is encapsulated in the closing of the novel, when he says to Sethe, "me and you, we got more yesterday than anybody. We need some kind of tomorrow" (273).

For Morrison, the importance of the future is connected to the past experience of enslavement. Through the use of flashbacks and retold memories, the novel depicts the gradations of slavery, its dehumanizing effects, and economics realities. However, the novel also shows various modes of liberation, resistance, and agency, including the purchasing of freedom and the will to escape. The desire to maintain family connections, despite inevitable separations, is also a central element of the novel and a communal response to enslavement.

Works Cited

Anderson, Melanie R. *Spectrality in the Novels of Toni Morrison.* Knoxville: U of Tennessee P, 2013. *EBSCO* eBooks. Web. 6 Sept. 2015.

Corey, Susan. "Toward the Limits of Mystery: The Grotesque in Toni Morrison's *Beloved.*" *The Aesthetics of Toni Morrison: Speaking the Unspeakable.* Ed. Marc C. Conner. Jackson: UP of Mississippi, 2000. 31–48. *EBSCO* eBooks. Web. 27 Aug. 2015.

Eckstein, Lars. "A Love Supreme: Jazzthetic Strategies in Toni Morrison's *Beloved.*" *African American Review.* 40.2 (Summer 2006): 271–283.

Gomez, Michael A. *Exchanging Our Country Marks: The Transformation of African Identities in the Colonial and Antebellum South.* Chapel Hill: U of North Carolina P, 1998.

Grewal, Gurleen. *Circles of Sorrow, Lines of Struggle: The Novels of Toni Morrison.* Baton Rouge: Louisiana State UP, 1998. *EBSCO* eBooks. Web. 6 Sept. 2015.

Jennings, La Vinia Delois. *Toni Morrison and the Idea of Africa.* New York: Cambridge UP, 2008.

Holloway, Karla F. C. and Stephanie A. Demetrakopoulos. *New Dimensions of Spirituality: A Biracial and Bicultural Reading of the Novels of Toni Morrison.* Westport, CT: Greenwood Press, 1987.

King, Lovalerie. "Property and American Identity in Toni Morrison's *Beloved.*" *Toni Morrison: Memory and Meaning.* Ed. Adrienne Lanier Seward and Justine Tally. Jackson: UP of Mississippi, 2014. 159–171. *EBSCO* eBooks. Web. 1 Aug. 2015.

McKay, Nellie Y. Introduction. *Toni Morrison's Beloved: A Casebook*. Ed. William L. Andrews and Nellie Y. McKay. New York: Oxford UP, 1999. 3–19.

May, Samuel J. "Margaret Garner and seven others." *The Fugitive Slave Law and Its Victims*. New York: American Anti-Slavery Society, 1856. Rpt in *Toni Morrison's Beloved: A Casebook*. Ed. William L. Andrews and Nellie Y. McKay. New York: Oxford UP, 1999. 25–36.

Moglen, Helene. "Redeeming History: Toni Morrison's *Beloved*." *Cultural Critique* 24 (1993): 17–40. *JSTOR*. Web. 6 Sept. 2015.

Morrison, Toni. *Beloved*. New York: Plume/New American Library, 1987.

Quayson, Ato. *Aesthetic Nervousness: Disability and the Crisis of Representation*. New York: Columbia UP, 2007. *EBSCO* eBooks. Web. 31 Aug. 2015.

Roynon, Tessa. *Toni Morrison and the Classical Tradition: Transforming American Culture*. Oxford, England: Oxford UP, 2013. *EBSCO* eBooks. Web. 3 Sept. 2015.

Rushdy, Ashraf H. A. "Daughters Signifyin(g) History: The Example of Toni Morrison's *Beloved*. *American Literature* 64.3 (Sept. 1992): 567–597. *JSTOR*. Web. 27 Aug. 2015.

Samuels, Wilfred D. and Clenora Hudson-Weems. *Toni Morrison*. Boston: Twayne, 1990.

Schreiber, Evelyn Jaffe. *Race, Trauma, and Home in the Novels of Toni Morrison*. Baton Rouge: Louisiana State UP, 2010. *EBSCO* eBooks. Web. 31 Aug. 2015.

Serpell, C. Namwali. "ADJACENCY: Toni Morrison, *Beloved* (1987)." *Seven Modes of Uncertainty*. Boston: Harvard UP, 2015. 119–152. *JSTOR*. Web. 27 Aug. 2015.

Seward, Adrienne Lanier and Justine Tally. Introduction. *Toni Morrison: Memory and Meaning*. Ed. Justine Tally and Adrienne Lanier Seward. Jackson: UP of Mississippi, 2014. xv–xxv. *EBSCO* eBooks. Web. 30 Aug. 2015.

Stampp, Kenneth. *The Peculiar Institution: Slavery in the Ante-Bellum South*. New York: Random House, 1956.

Washington, Teresa N. "The Mother-Daughter Àjé Relationship in Toni Morrison's *Beloved*." *African American Review* 39.1/2 (Spring–Summer 2005): 171–188. *JSTOR*. Web. 27 Aug. 2015.

Yanuck, Julius. "The Garner Fugitive Slave Case." *The Mississippi Valley Historical Review* 40.1 (June 1953):47–66. *JSTOR.* Web. 27 Aug. 2015.

Zauditu-Selassie, K. *African Spiritual Traditions in the Novels of Toni Morrison.* Gainesville: UP of Florida, 2009. *EBSCO* eBooks. Web. 25 Aug. 2015.

A Gathering of Trees: An Examination of Memory, Trauma, and Embodiment in Toni Morrison's *Beloved*

Kokahvah Zauditu-Selassie

Once when I was tree, Flesh came and worshipped at my roots. My ancestors slept in my outstretched limbs and listened to flesh Praying and entreating on his knees.
(Henry Dumas)

The axe forgets, the tree remembers.
(African American Proverb)

That we the black people are one people we know. Destroyers will travel long distances in their minds and out to deny you this truth.
(Ayi Kwei Armah, *Two Thousand Seasons*)

Topography

In *Song of Solomon*, Guitar Bains iterates the existential relationship between geography and memory saying, "Milk, I do believe that my whole life's geography" (Morrison, *Song* 114). Like Pilate Dead whose few possessions included a geography book to mark her journeys, Morrison interrogates geography and maps Black experience through her novelistic figurations. She was a child of the Midwest, born to parents who immigrated to Ohio from the South— Alabama for her mother and Georgia for her father. And the South, its tensions, and its attendant values accompany Morrison's inquiry, especially the ways in which Black people denied "the comfort of social belonging" navigate "the unheimlich terror of the space or race of the other" (Bhaba 3). For the novels set in the West or North, or "up south," her landscapes change, but inhumanity and brutality meted out to Black people doesn't vary appreciably. All cardinal points are triangulated for terror and Black bodies are sites on which to enact a brutal humanity. Addressing the impact of the trauma in a public letter to his son, Ta-Nehisi Coates narrates the various ways in which Black people are vulnerable in a system "that makes your black body breakable" (18).

Those who have read the episodic novels of Morrison, to date, have learned how to navigate through the historical narrative or "Long Song" of Black people's sojourn in North America. In these novels, Morrison depicts the hostile environments of America, the South where the venom of race is intensified and the North where more subtle practices interrupt the quality of life. Replete in her literary corpus are characters who must battle white supremacy and the inhospitable lands as marginalized, exiled people and, at the same time, assist one another and the larger community in deflecting the harmful assaults directed towards them.

In this essay, I extend this conversation of memory by examining rituals of healing and notions of spiritual embodiment as means to restore wholeness in a place where "boys hung from the most beautiful sycamore trees" (Morrison, *Beloved* 6) where black alterity and difference renders the body at once as a sign that embodies reduction and diminishment as property in the system of white supremacy and as a site of resistance, a deliberate response to Black ontology. This resistance is achieved through ritual. The importance of ritual cannot be understated. Grimes, writes, "Ritualization is not just a symbolic way of pursuing survival, but is a quest for a specific style of being in our bodies and world" (39).

In these literary spaces, Morrison helps readers to reclaim, reconcile, renew, and recover cultural identity through incorporation with the physical landscapes as they recover from alienation. My exploration includes an examination of trees as spiritual locations to heal characters. I argue that Sethe's embodiment of the tree is a necessary "rememory" reconnecting her to a Black cosmology. Among the compendia of things not to forget, *Beloved* references African cultural rituals such as dancing the antelope, the ring shout, singing, and dancing which allows Black people to control their bodies countering the intent of involuntary separations, violations, and traumatic personal losses embodying the American racial experience.

Morrison invokes the ancestor as a metaphor for the specific and requisite memory for African people. All human beings identify themselves as a matter of cultural memory. However, given the assaults to their personhood, the taking away of names, and other deprivations, their conceptual frame had to be as sturdy as the baobab tree whose roots spread above and below the earth. The fundamental basis for their remembering is their survival. Somé argues, "If some people forget their past as a way to survive, other people remember it for the same reason" (*Of Water and Spirit* 14). These memories may change based on various disruptions. Morrison ensures memory to counter this mass forgetting by restoring the ancestors. In this way, characters are able to repair their individual breaches.

In *Beloved,* Morrison invokes the ancestor. Constructing the story in non-sequential order, using Baby Suggs as the central focus for relating major story elements from the characters and omniscient narrator, she establishes the circle of Black beliefs and Black lives. This circularity, akin to the African tradition of call and response, allows for the affirmation of the ancestral ontological experience. Holloway adds texture to this idea of circularity. She says, "because she [ancestor] serves as recursive touchstone for the simultaneous existence of and revision in the idea of mediation, the ancestral presence constitutes the posture of (re)membrance" (Holloway 115).

Morrison establishes the frame for remembrance by recording those insufferable events that define both the communities highlighted in the novel and those in the realm of the ancestors. These ancestors and their historical experiences of captivity and enslavement recalled in the narrative posit African continuities and make historical commentary. Baby Suggs, who is an ancestor when the story begins, is invoked as an ancestor, and her story is told in a series of flashbacks. Although Baby Suggs has been dead for nine years at the novel's opening, she is a major character throughout the novel.

Morrison's works are flashbacks of history not taught in American schools. Remixed anachronistically, her novels contextualize historical memory, beginning with *A Mercy*, which related the penultimate terror of enslavement where Jacob Vaark prospers in a place of "lawless laws" that encouraged cruelty "in exchange for common cause, if not common virtue" (11) then on to *Beloved*, where Baby Suggs laments, "Those white things have taken all I had or dreamed... There is no bad luck in the world but whitefolks" (89). From there, Morrison records the brutalities of the Reconstruction period along with the rise of organized domestic terrorist groups and internalized oppression in *Paradise*, the terror of pre and post-World War I riots in *Jazz* and trauma in *Sula*, segregation and genocide in *Song of Solomon*, eugenics and "scientific" experimentation on black bodies in *Home*, ideas of globalization and world dominance (colonization) in *Tar Baby*, aesthetic and spiritual negation in *The Bluest Eye* and *God Help the Child*, and the destructiveness of integration on Black economics and police brutality in *Love*.

In an interview, shortly after winning the Pulitzer Prize for *Beloved*, Morrison remarked that the enslavement of African people is something that no one wants to remember. She states:

> I thought this is [*sic*] got to be the least read of all the books I'd written because it is about something that the characters don't want to remember, black people don't want to remember, white people don't want to remember. I mean it's national amnesia. (Angelo 120)

But if others forget to maintain the power to oppress, remembering is exactly what Sethe and other characters in *Beloved* do as they simultaneously endure the harshness of present realities. Readers are included in this literary memorial. According to Amos Wilson, black people insist on amnesia. He writes,

> They want to deny European's terroristic rule on Earth, deny his evil, deny his domination over them and deny his destruction of the Earth and life itself. So they choose not to see color, so they can't see White for what it is. They use it to justify not knowing their history and not knowing themselves because they don't see "color" hereby maintaining the amnesia. (Wilson 38)

Sethe's dismay with her "rememory" confirms this preference for the analgesic nature of amnesia. One does not have to do the hard work ahead to heal from these brutalities. Exiled from the community, Sethe treads the water of daily living taking care of Denver and supporting the two of them by working at the restaurant. Morrison writes, "Working dough. Working, working, dough. Nothing better than to start the day's serious work of beating back the past" (*Beloved* 73). This struggle that keeps her "not interested in the future" (70) is illustrated in the following passage, in which Sethe chides her memory for its insistence on recalling disturbing things:

> Why was there nothing it refused? No misery, no regret, no hateful picture too rotten to accept? Like a greedy child it snatched up everything. Just once, could it say, No thank you? I just ate and can't hold another bite? I am full God Damn it of two boys with mossy teeth, one sucking on my breast the other holding me down, their book-reading teacher watching and writing it up. (Morrison, *Beloved* 70)

As Sethe struggles to forget, memory wins out. Indeed, Sethe's persistence in remembering is key to beginning the healing process. This healing commences when Sethe reclaims the memory of Baby Suggs as an ancestor and begins to explore some of the stories that Paul D lays next to her own about life at Sweet Home.

Morrison's *Beloved* counters America's "Hunger Games," the insatiable demand for the bodies of Black people, the people "whose names had been erased, whose tongues had been cut from their mouths, whose traditions had been deemed punishable by death" (Rebecca Walker xiii–xiv). White supremacy disguised as political correctness requires that Black people exist in a state of historical amnesia. Morrison speaks for the group, liberating its tongues from the margins of silence demanded by white supremacist domination, thus, giving it access to a history denied it.

Forgetting creates vulnerability and exacerbates trauma. In *The Falsification of Afrikan Consciousness*, Amos Wilson discusses the harmful effects of forgetting, stating:

> Simply because we choose to forget a traumatic event, simply because we choose not to learn a traumatic history that may make us feel ashamed, does not mean that that history is not controlling our behavior. Simply because we don't know our history, and may not have heard of it, does not mean that the history does not control our behavior. (34)

Sethe learned this lesson in *Beloved*, as she is forced to confront the pain that her memory repressed. Shared history fosters a shared identity and a sense of collective purpose. But, the architecture of *Beloved* is constructed on a landscape that is tragic and at the same time, triumphant. Morrison illustrates this dialectic, resolving paradoxes in *Beloved*, where "rememory" and storying mediate the trauma where beauty and brutality can coexist in places where boys hung "from the most beautiful sycamore trees" (*Beloved* 6). She also constructs the body's geography as—frontiers defined by scarred backs resembling chokecherry trees and branded skin whose marks identify and represent the body as chattel and at the same time signify cicatrizations—ontic patterns expressing unbroken affiliations with African nations.

Using African value systems, Morrison's characters overcome the contours of unwelcoming and unwilling whiteness to withstand the trauma described in her 1993 Nobel Prize acceptance speech: the distress of not having had a home in this place, as well as the historical occurrence of being "set adrift from the one(s) you knew" and the social situation of being placed "at the edge of towns that cannot bear your company" (28–29). This dispossession can be altered by repossession—a psychic return to self through memory.

Through storying Morrison invokes the sacred imperative of memory and brings cosmogonic time to the present moment." In *Beloved*, Morrison writes, "All of it is now… it is always now" (210). Using traditional oral forms that reiterate identity and engender the cultural integrity of the community, Morrison transmits inter-generational culture, historical experiences, and collective memories that come and go not only in the "stream in back of 124," but also in the continuous stream of ancestral consciousness and within the concentric circle of community.

Middle Passage

In an essay titled, "Home," Morrison notes that the "forced transfer" of African people is the "defining event of the modern world" (5) and links death and the Middle Passage. In the dedication of her fifth novel, *Beloved* (1987), Morrison connects the trauma of those who lived to be bartered, sold, and bred to the circle of ancestors, those casualties of the Middle Passage who did not succeed in leaving "their bodies behind," (*Beloved* 210), those in the "ocean-deep place" (*Beloved* 264). In this way, she retrieves the lost contents of culture and mitigates the trespass caused by un-naming, thus, connecting the character Beloved to the unnamed "Sixty Million or more" (*Beloved* xii). Using conservative estimates, sixty million ancestors not only lost their names, but also their lives during the Middle Passage from the West Coast of Africa to the Americas. Recent figures, which take into account both the Arab and European trade, calculate the total as being close to 200 million. In *Unclaimed Experience: Trauma, Narrative, and History*, Cathy Caruth explains that the act of leaving illuminates the central core of trauma according to Freud's theoretical explanation of trauma. She asserts:

> It is departure that, in the full force of its historicity, remains at the same time in some scene absolutely opaque, both to the one who leaves and the theoretician linked to sufferer in his attempt to bring the experience to light. (22)

Unremembered, their presence remains as a strangling trauma that continues to choke the living as they call out for acknowledgement. Akasha Gloria Hull describes the ancestor's insistent presence as "Long black bones waving like angry spears under an ocean of years and water... in the cold and tropical seas" ("These Bones, These Bones").

In *Two Thousand Seasons*, Ayi Kwei Armah refers to the Middle Passage as a different part of African destruction—the first was the arrival of the Arabs and subsequently the Europeans. He writes, "Their hearing was of fantastic journeys over land, one long traversing of a place neither land nor water, and after, worse: the forced crossing of oceans with no life at the other end, only lifelong slavery... an endless cycle of ever sharper cruelties" (Armah 12–13). This place described as being neither land nor water suggests a transitional "other space" a space to access the spiritual power needed for the crossing.

In *Beloved*, the Middle Passage resembles Armah's idea of a spiritual portal where a fully dressed woman could walk out of the water and interact with the community of the living. Morrison recovers history in those spaces or breaches. Horvitz claims, "She is Sethe's mother, She is Sethe herself; she is her daughter" (163) Explaining these "blurred boundaries," she says, "Beloved exists in both the realm of the particular and the universal. She is a member of Sethe's family and a representative spirit "of all the woman dragged onto slave ships in African woman in America trying to trace their ancestry back to the mother on the ship attached to them" (Horvitz 157). Beloved's multiple identity is consistent with African cosmologies, which allow for intergenerational renewal and notions of time as being fluid using the Bantu concept of *Hantu*, which represents time and space as unities. According to Mintz and Price, after death:

> The sprit travels west in the direction of the setting sun. There lies the River of Death, which it must cross before reaching its final destination. Once in the Land of the Dead, the newly arrived soul is subjected to a number of ordeals whose duration is determined by the gravity of his past misdeeds. First, the person must sit on the top of a tree under the burning sun. (145)

Morrison's description of Beloved's arrival to 124 Bluestone is similar. Sethe first sees Beloved sitting down on a "stump not far from the steps of 124" (*Beloved* 50). "The rays of the sun struck her full in the face" (51). Upon seeing Beloved, Sethe has an urge to relieve herself, "for some reason she could not immediately account for, the moment she got close enough to see the face, Sethe's bladder filled to capacity... the water she voided was *endless*" (Morrison, *Beloved* 51, emphasis mine). This endless water represents both the rupturing and mending of birth waters and is also metaphorical for the river (memory) of life and death. The return of Beloved is necessary to heal the community and the inhabitants of 124 Bluestone Road.

The Ba Kongo have generally thought of the universe as divided into two worlds of the living and the dead, separated by water. Morrison recovers these ancestors of those spaces or breaches on land. As Diedrich, Gates, and Pedersen remind us, "The Middle Passage emerges not as a clean break between past and present, but as a spatial continuum between Africa and the Americas, the ship's deck and the hold, the Great house and the slave quarters, the town and the outlying region" (*Black Imagination* 8). That is to say, when we remember, we keep the circle unbroken, thereby, engendering the necessary healing. In *Beloved*, Morrison contributes to the sense of historical consciousness, emphasizing the individual's responsibility to the living named community through the active process of creating memory.

Roots and Routes

Trees are gateways or portals where characters harness the vital essences of life that bind them to the coils of perpetuity. Using African spiritual sensibility Morrison's depiction of the tree as a leitmotif invokes memory, alleviates trauma and reconnects the individual with the natural world of spirits, ancestors, and the African Gods. Since ritual is action, not thought, it must be performed. Morrison encodes performance of what Yoruba call *asé*, the Yoruba concept of vital essence and power, to enable Sethe and other characters in *Beloved* communicate directly with the Divine and ancestors, embody them as they petition them to effect solutions for the concentric circles of community.

The Yoruba and Fon similar to other West and West-Central African groups claim connections between themselves and natural sites such as trees, rivers, hills, and swamps, seen as places to petition God, primordial divinities and the deified ancestors. The word tree is etymologically related to the word tar, the black primordial earth. Symbolically, the concept of tree speaks of the capacity for endless regeneration: the Tree of Life. These symbolic roots once acknowledged and reconnected have the potential to knit the person to the cycle of perpetuity. Accordingly, the tree is a central feature of this spiritual landscape in Diasporic literature. Despite being forcefully uprooted and transported to the Western Hemisphere, and experiencing traumatic dispossessions, African people in America incorporate the tree as a sacred entity. In *A Mercy*, Morrison writes about a man from Lina's village whose name "meant "trees fall behind him,' suggesting his influence on the surroundings" (55). In that same novel, Morrison juxtaposes the Europeans' atrocities and disconnection from nature. "They would forever fence land, ship whole trees to faraway countries. . .chew up the world and spit out a horribleness that would destroy all primary peoples" (*A Mercy* 54). In *Home*, Morrison creates a character named Crawford, who refused to abandon his tree, "the oldest magnolia tree in the county," when he was told along with others that he had twenty-four hours to leave, or else—'else' meaning 'die' (*Home* 10). Morrison writes, "Maybe loving that Tree which, he used to brag, his great-grandmother had planted made him so stubborn" (*Home* 10). He was tied to the tree and beaten to death. In *Jazz*, Morrison warns readers again about the importance of memory in her indictment of Joe Trace's forgetfulness having journeyed from Virginia to Harlem. A man who used to sleep in trees, Joe has forgotten his connection. Morrison writes, "In no time at all he forgets little pebbly creeks and apple trees so old they lay their little branches along the ground and you have to reach down or stoop to pick up the fruit" (*Jazz* 35).

In *Beloved*, Sethe's scar is multivalent. For instance, Paul D disputes Sethe's story that the keloidal skin on her back is a tree. He has a tree named Brother. He tells Sethe, "Trees were inviting things you could trust and be near, talk to if you wanted to" (Morrison, *Beloved* 21). Sethe's tree mirrors the Adinkra symbol, *Nyame Dua*, the altar of God, which affirms the presence of God in the form of a sacred altar represented by two pieces of wood intersecting, such as the branches of trees. Morrison writes:

It's a tree, Lu. A chokecherry tree. See, here's the trunk—it's full of sap, and this here's the parting for the branches. You got a mighty lot of branches. Leaves too, look like, and dern of these ain't blossoms.

Tiny little cherry blossoms, Just as white. You got a whole tree on it. In bloom. (*Beloved* 79)

Sethe's body altar enshrines the memory of the brutality; its woven structure of keloidal tissue, a healing over of the skin, prefigures the layers and depth of mental healing that Sethe needs in order to be whole. Caruth notes that "a wound of the mind—the breach in the mind experience of time self, and the world—is not, like the wound of the body a simple and healable event" (4).

Sethe's back is a site for potential empowerment. It embodies her memory and stands as a living testimony to her experiences giving her the necessary resolve for resistance. She says, "I got a tree on my back and a haint in my house, and nothing in between but the daughter I am holding in my arms. No more runnin—from nothing. I will never run from another thing on this earth" (Morrison, *Beloved* 15).

The Yoruba of West Africa speak of complementary opposition being the structure of the universe dividing reality into two parts, forces that build up and forces that tear down. The Yoruba argue that anything that does not contain an element of opposition is incomplete, for God, Olodumare is a combination of opposites (Mason & Edwards 3). These dualities as philosophical ideas can be traced to ancient Kemetic ideas of the *ba* and *ka*. In the Kongo tradition, *kala* and *zima* are similar concepts of duality loosely translated as giving/ receiving. These are not really opposites but reflective and reciprocal forces that balance life. Morrison's narrative coheres to this structural unity by describing the forces that build up, the traditional spiritual and ritual models transported with as blueprints and primary sources of information for living. These affirming values exist alongside those inimical to them. The brutality and singular cruelty of chattel enslavement and systemic white supremacy are forces that tear down. So, fearing the return of her children into bondage, Sethe kills her unnamed infant daughter.

Resentment and jealousy over the excesses of the feast cause the community to fail to warn the inhabitants of 124 Bluestone that schoolteacher and his men were headed in their direction. The community registered its disapproval and demanded a sacrifice. Therefore, Baby Suggs' feast is the necessary event that provides one of the primary conflicts to be resolved in the novel leading to Sethe's vulnerability, which ultimately precipitates the sacrifice of the innominate baby. The narrator divulges the rancor of the community's malevolence juxtaposed to Baby Suggs' benevolent actions. Morrison writes:

> Where does she get it all, Baby Suggs, holy? Why is she and hers always the center of things; how come she always know exactly what to do and when? Giving advice; passing messages; healing the sick, hiding fugitives, loving, cooking, cooking, loving, preaching, singing, dancing, and loving everybody like it was her job and hers alone...Loaves and fishes were her powers...? (*Beloved* 137)

The Dance
> It sleeps after the night of howling, speaking-in-tongues, dancing to drums; watching strange lights streak across the sky.
> (Ishmael Reed, *Mumbo Jumbo*)

Notwithstanding the novel's cataloging of brutalities: the burning of Sixo, the iron collar that once yoked Paul D's neck, the broken hearts and bodies, and sagging spirits, the emergence of scientific racism in schoolteacher's collecting and recording of body data of the enslaved at Sweet Home, I argue that the breach between the residents of 124 Bluestone Road and the community is the central problem in the novel. In *Beloved*, Morrison asks how Black people can survive without the unity that protects them. The subsequent question is, if they could be disloyal to the community healer, aren't they all vulnerable? Who would defend them? Baby Suggs helped the community to recover identity and revitalize their diminished *asé* or vital life forces. Standing in the center of the ring, she reminded them of the assault to each part of their body to those outside the circle.

In *The Healing Wisdom of Africa*, Malidoma Somé notes that energy from the spiritual plane must be brought to the physical plane. This is achieved through the use of gateways—where the physical realm meets the spiritual. In Africa, as elsewhere, ritual behavior is a way of communicating with the divine, for the purpose of changing the human situation. In *Beloved*, that space is the Clearing, where Baby Suggs had performed the ring dance in the sunlight.

This "unchurched preacher" led "every black men, woman and child" to the "Clearing—a wide-open place cut deep in the woods" (Morrison, *Beloved* 87). Similar to experiences in Africa where sacred groves were dwelling places of individual deities and the loci of other supernatural beings, the Clearing represents the space for African to repair the ruptures of the past using rhythm to free their bodies from the trauma imposed by enslavement's limited opportunity for mobility. Baby Suggs commanded the men to dance, the women to cry, and the children to laugh. Morrison writes, "In the heat of every Saturday afternoon she sat in the clearing while the people waited among the trees" (*Beloved* 87). Cloke and Jones argue that trees are landscapes of memory that are significant from a cultural perspective as "deep currents of meaning swirl around our culture(s) and brush the branches of any tree place which is being encountered, experienced, narrated, or imagined at any given time" (19). Baby Suggs begins the ritual calling to the most vulnerable members of the community: "Then she shouted, 'Let the children come!'" "[a]nd they ran from the *trees* toward her," "the *woods*," (Morrison, *Beloved* 87, emphasis mine). The ritual dance is an emotional explosion and an embodiment of the power still residing in them, their bodies becoming sacred sites to resist the trauma of oppression and to push back against the absolute control of them by others.

This excursion into the remembrance of ritual dance is important because it links ritual to the ancestor, the central motivation for the narrative. Stuckey emphasizes the importance of these circles, "The ring in which Africans danced and sang is the key to understanding the means by which they achieved oneness in America" (*Slave Culture* 12). In the circle the community is reconnected, unified, and rendered whole, ready to thwart attacks from outside forces. As they become one force of moving energy in the dance, the lines blur signifying their embodiment and possession. Morrison writes:

It started out that way: laughing children, dancing men, crying women and then it got mixed up. Women stopped crying and danced; men sat down and cried; children danced, women laughed, children cried until, exhausted and riven, all and each lay about the Clearing damp and gasping for breath. (*Beloved* 88)

In *History and Memory in African American Culture*, Genevieve Fabre argues that the "celebrative spirit accompanied Africans to America and that Africans used creative ways to reinvent both ritual and forms to alter the time space framework prescribed or suggested by the whites" (72). The will to remember and construct an African memory is evidenced in this ritual activity. According to Fabre, through ritual the "dialectic of forgetting and remembering is worked out" (75). Spent from their ecstatic embodiment, the community is temporarily restored and healed from the indignities narrated by Baby Suggs. Her ritual dispossesses or disembodies the community removing the assaults to their flesh and hearts. She asks them to allow love to replace the embodied grief and disappointment. "Love it. Love it hard. Yonder they do not love your flesh. They despise it" (Morrison, *Beloved* 89).

Another memory of dance helps Sethe in her "rememory," specifically, her reflection on the birth of Denver, whom she thought of *in vitro* as an antelope. This memory of the antelope leads to another recollection, a girlhood memory of her own mother and her other mothers or Ma'ams—the corporate body of other enslaved women who watched over the children on the plantation. In this reminiscence, the women are dancing the antelope. The image of the antelope and the accompanying song and dance jumpstarts Sethe's stalled memory and connects her to a remembrance of a mother signified by a "cloth hat" in distinction to her "other mothers" all of whom "were also called Ma'am" (Morrison, *Beloved* 30). Similar to the indeterminate memories of vital statistics and parental separation documented in the enslavement narratives, Sethe's memories are fragmented. The power of the song and dance memories dominates her mind and after a brief digression to another resurrected thought, Sethe and the narrator jointly recall the liberating effect of the song and dance:

Oh but when they sang. And oh but when they danced and sometimes they danced the antelope. The men as well as the ma'ams, one of whom was certainly her own. They shifted shapes and became something other. Some unchained, demanding other whose feet knew her pulse better than she did. Just like this one in her stomach. (Morrison, *Beloved* 31)

What is significant in this passage is the idea that the narrator sees Sethe as one of the dancers, further reinforcing the continuity between the multi-tiered past and present symbolized by the image of the antelope and the ability of the enslaved to shape shift to embody the antelope. Among the Bambara people of Mali, this antelope, called *Tji-wara*, or *Chi-wara*, is said to have introduced agriculture to them. The dancers wearing the masks and aided by song and drum become the spirit symbolized by the antelope as they dance. The prime purpose for the masks is to serve as a temporary dwelling place for God the spirit represented zoomorphically. The dancers become possessed, embodying the energy of the mask.

Sethe's exercise of memory forces her to listen to her own voice and to remember her own mother, her ma'am, with the special mark on her body. Morrison writes,

Back there she opened up her dress front and lifted her breast and pointed under it. Right on her rib was a circle and a cross burnt right in the skin. She said, "This is your ma'am. This, and she pointed.' I am the only one got this mark now. The rest dead. If something happens to me and you can't tell me by my face, you can know me by this mark. (*Beloved* 61)

Here, Morrison asks the reader to consider Sethe's recognition of the *Dikenga dia Kongo* or *Iowa* symbol, the circle in a cross as a remembered spiritual memorate connecting her to her mother and Africa. Yoruba call this symbol, *orita meta*, the crossroads. Additionally, her mother's words, indicating that most of the people who had this are now dead, can be read as a reference to those bodies culturally inscribed from African ceremonial activities and not merely the identifying marks of bondage.

Sethe's remembrance of her mother's native language, songs, and dances is significant, since dance makes a smooth transition in Black worship and represents a primary vehicle to store sacred information. As a major cultural dynamic, singing is an essential ritual element. Morrison also highlights the power of song as a primary way to heal the fragmented African personality. Singing a major trope in the African American literary heritage, the importance of singing as a symbolic continuity with West and Central African cultural forms enriched by Black people's social and political encounters with oppressive forces here in the Americas. As primary ways to negotiate and give meaning to the world around them, singing helped Black people to cope, understand, and "re-make" their world by symbolically reconfiguring core beliefs and deeply spiritual ideas and cultural concepts. Helping them to create difference with the tonal languages of West and Central Africa.

In the essay "In Search of Our Mother's Garden," Alice Walker ask the reader to consider what life would have been if, like reading and writing, singing had been forbidden (234). It is unfathomable for Black people to live in a world where singing does not exist. Black arts movement writer and literary critic Larry Neal notes "a clear spiritual impulse revealed in African culture. This impulse helped to sustain the African in the Western Hemisphere" (122). Neal argues that African people shaped reality in "forms that were compatible with his [*sic*] own sensibilities" (122). Dance is a major part of that cultural sensibility. Thus, Morrison emphasizes the indispensability of dance. "Sixo went among the trees at night. For dancing, he said to keep his bloodlines open, he said" (*Beloved* 25).

Embodiment through dance opens up the spaces for remembrance and a chance to imagine a life on the other side of trauma. In *Beloved*, Sethe's recollection of her mother is limited to the mark. She did not know her mother's name, and she has forgotten almost everything except singing and dancing. As Sethe reflects upon the void that accompanied her after Baby Suggs' death, it was her message of love, of dance and song that Sethe yearned for, even just to "listen for the spaces that the long ago singing had left behind" (Morrison, *Beloved* 89).

At the end of the novel the women return to the house to heal the breach with Baby Suggs. The group of women assembles in the manner of an African council around the village tree. Ella, inspired by her own haunting memories, "set her jaws working" and "hollered" (Morrison, *Beloved* 259). The women followed in suit. "Instantly the kneelers and the standers joined her. They stopped praying and took a step back to the beginning. In the beginning was the sound, and they all knew what the sound sounded like (259).

The collective ritual frees Sethe and the inhabitants of 124 Bluestone, including the spirit of the other baby, Baby Suggs. The introduction of the women's names attached to the bottom of the plates of food begins the healing by reintroducing the women in advance of their physical arrival. The ritual gathering in front of the house seals the healing and reconnects the broken circle. In *Beloved*, Morrison asserts that by remembering, sculpting sounds, controlling language, and reclaiming dance, and protecting and defending one another, African people can evolve from the designation of vassal to become vessels of memory. By tapping into their sonic codes, dancing their dances, and remembering their trauma, Black people have the necessary keys for healing. This is a story to *pass* on.

Works Cited

Armah, Ayi Kwei. *Two Thousand Seasons*. London: Heinemann, 1979.

Baraka, Amiri. *Blues People*. New York: Perennial, 1998.

Bhabha, Homi K. *Nation and Narration*. New York: Routledge, 1990.

Bockie, Simon. *Death and the Invisible Powers: The World of Kongo Belief*. Bloomington: Indiana UP, 1994.

Caruth, Cathy. *Unclaimed Experience: Trauma, Narrative, and History*. Baltimore, MD: Johns Hopkins UP, 1996.

Coates, Ta-Nehisi. *Between the World and Me*. New York: Spiegel& Grau, 2015.

Dumas, Henry. "Root Song." *In Search of Color Everywhere: A Collection of African-American Poetry*." Ed. E. Ethelbert Miller. New York: Stewart, Tabori & Chang, 1994. 15.

Douglass, Frederick. *The Narrative of the Life of Frederick Douglass*. New York: Dover, 1990.

Cloke, Paul & Owain Jones. *Uprootings/Regroundings: Questions of Home and Migration*. New York: Berger, 2003.

Eliade, Mircea. *The Sacred and the Profane: The Nature of Religion*. 1959. Trans. Willard R. Trask. New York: Harcourt, 1987.

Fabre, Genevieve & Robert O'Meally. Ed. *History and Memory in African American Culture*. New York: Oxford UP, 1994.

Fu-Kiau, Bunseki K. *African Cosmology of the Bantu-Kongo: Principles of Life and Living*. Brooklyn: Athelia Henrietta Press, 2001.

Grimes, Ronald L. *Beginnings in Ritual Studies*. London: UP of America, 1982.

Henderson, Carol E. *Scarring the Black Body: Race and Representation in African American Literature*. Columbia: U of Missouri, 2002.

Hull, Akasha. G. *Soul Talk: the New Spirituality of African American Women*. Rochester, VT: Inner Traditions, 2001.

Gaines, Ernest J. *The Autobiography of Miss Jane Pittman*. New York: Bantam, 1971.

Horvitz, Deborah. "Nameless Ghosts: Possession and Dispossession in *Beloved*." *Studies in American Fiction* 17.2 (1989): 157–168.

Jahn, Janheinz. *Muntu: African Culture and the Western World*. New York: Grove Weidenfeld, 1961.

Mason, John & Gary Edwards. *Black Gods: Orisa Studies in the New World*. Brooklyn: Yoruba Theological Archministry, 1985.

Mintz, Sidney W. & Richard Price. *The Birth of African American Culture: An Anthropological Perspective*. Boston: Beacon Press, 1976.

Morrison, Toni. Afterword. *The Bluest Eye*. 1970. New York: Plume, 1993.

_____. *Beloved*. New York: Knopf, 1987.

_____. *The Bluest Eye*. 1970. New York: Plume, 1993.

_____. *God Help the Child*. New York: Knopf, 2015.

_____. "Home." *The House That Race Built*. Ed. Lubiano Wahneema. New York: Vintage 1998.

_____. *Home*. New York: Knopf, 2012.

_____. "Interview." *Black Writers at Work*. Ed. Claudia Tate. New York: Continuum, 1988. 117–31.

_____. *Jazz*. New York: Knopf, 1992.

_____. "Lecture and Speech of Acceptance upon the Award of the Nobel Prize for Literature." Stockholm. 19 Dec. 1993. New York: Knopf, 2000.

_____. *Love*. New York: Knopf, 2003.

_____. *A Mercy*. New York: Knopf, 2008.

_____. "The Pain of Being Black." *Time* (May 1989): 120.

_____. *Paradise*. New York: Knopf 1998.

_____. *Song of Solomon*. New York: American Library, 1977.

_____. *Sula*. 1974. Knopf. New York: Plume, 1987.

_____. *Tar Baby*. New York: Penguin, 1987.

Neal, Larry. "My Lord He Calls Me by the Thunder." *Visions of a Liberated Future; Black Arts Movement Writings*. Ed. Michael Schwartz. New York: Thunder's Mouth Press, 1989.

Ray, Benjamin C. *African Religion,* Symbol, Ritual, and Community. Englewood Cliffs, NJ: Prentice Hall, 1976.

Reed, Ishmael. *Mumbo Jumbo*. New York: Scribner, 1996.

Somé, Patrice Malidoma. *The Healing Wisdom of Africa: Finding Life Purpose Through Nature, Ritual, and Community*. New York: Tarcher, 1998.

_____. *Of Water and the Spirit: Ritual, Magic, and Initiation in the Life of an African Shaman*. New York: Putnam, 1994.

Stuckey, Sterling. *Slave Culture. Nationalist Theory and the Foundations of Black America*. New York: Oxford UP, 1981.

Walker, Alice. *In Search of Our Mother's Gardens*. New York: Harcourt Brace Jovanovich, 1983.

Walker, Rebecca. *Black Cool: One Thousand Streams of Blackness*. Berkeley, CA: Soft Skull Press, 2012.

Wilson, Amos. *The Falsification of Afrikan Consciousness: Eurocentric History, Psychiatry, and the Politics of White Supremacy*. New York: Afrikan World Info Systems, 1993.

"You May as Well Just Come On": African American Healing Ways in Toni Morrison's *Beloved*

Sarah L. Berry

Beloved captures a worldview that enslaved Africans brought with them to the New World, a worldview that places humans in relation to spirits, ancestors, and nature and that explains illness as an imbalance in this universal system. Enslaved Africans adapted the African worldview under the dehumanizing constraints of slavery. In *Beloved*, Morrison illustrates an Afrocentric view of suffering, death, and healing that concerns not a single patient, but an entire community. This view and the healing ways promoted by it are contrasted with the destructive effects of slaveholders' racist science, carried out by schoolteacher. This essay uses a health humanities perspective (viewing illness and health through artistic, literary, and social lenses) to examine African American knowledge about illness and practices of healing in *Beloved*. From this perspective, the novel is structured around an initial attempt at healing the ills of slavery by Baby Suggs, holy; next, the central trauma of schoolteacher's racist science prompts the murder of Beloved, causing not only Sethe's decline, but also decreasing the well-being of her whole community. The resolution of this collective affliction is a blend of African and American healing ways, a strategy that illustrates Toni Morrison's participation in third-wave feminism taking place in the late 1970s and 1980s.

"You may as well come on," a phrase that many characters utter at key turning points of the novel, invokes multiple layers of African American knowledge about human relationships, suffering, and healing. Sethe and Denver call the spirit that shakes up the house in order to reason with it, chanting, "Come on. Come on. You may as well just come on" (Morrison 4). Sethe encourages the newly returned Paul D to "Come on in... Come on. Just step through," when he senses past trauma pulsating at the threshold of 124 (10).

Amy keeps Sethe moving toward freedom by telling her to "come on" (41; 97). Beloved, a ghost, tells Denver "You may as well just come on" when she tries to get her to dance, bringing Denver out of her post-traumatic distress to live a full life (87). Near the end of the novel, Janey Wagon tells Denver to "come on in," inviting her into the community that will ultimately save her mother (298). Inviting kin, whether alive or in spirit form, illustrates African views of the universe carried on by enslaved people: humans, spirits, and nature are interdependent and humans are not separate or superior beings in this cosmology.

The invitation to "come on" also evokes community dynamics in enslaved conditions. "Come on" echoes the concept of "getting over" or "coming through," an experience of spiritual conversion, empowerment, and group belonging among some enslaved communities, such as the Gullah people of coastal South Carolina (Chandler xvii), of finding salvation in a mixture of Christian and African American beliefs shared by the community. In this worldview, Sethe and other enslaved characters experience illness and suffering within overlapping social, natural, and supernatural realms that are equally powerful. The experiences of illness and healing necessarily involve not a single patient, but the entire community. All of these concepts are central to the enduring wounds of slavery for Sethe, her family, and her community.

Illness as Cosmological and Social Disharmony

In many African cultures, humans, the spirits of ancestors, deities, and nature coexist in a universal balance. Elements of this African worldview include:

> the unity of the spiritual and physical realms of life, which enables harmony among all relationships while implying that negative experiences result from the disharmony between those two dimensions of life... [and] the integral relation between the family and the wider community that implies corresponding duties and responsibilities. (Paris 433)

This worldview survived when Africans were enslaved in the New World. Morrison implies that Sethe's mother spoke her original language (74) and practiced African religious rituals such as the antelope dance (37), all prohibited by slaveholders, who enforced this rule with a bit in her mouth (240) and ultimately by murdering her for participating in traditional song and dance (73).

Health, illness, and dying are situated in this fluid understanding of the universe. The natural world, imbued with a life force (for example, *ashé* in Yoruban culture), holds the power to both heal and harm. Plants and trees in particular contain vital force that influences human well-being, whether by visiting the forest or making herbal medicines. For instance, Paul D and Denver both commune with trees to soothe their aching bodies or troubled minds—Paul D with Brother, the oak tree at Sweet Home, and Denver with her "emerald closet" of boxwood (Morrison 25; 45). Yet in the duality of healing and harming inherent in African views of nature, trees also house the horrific trauma of Paul A's hanging and Sixo's burning at the stake.

Historian Sharla Fett describes one adaptation of the African worldview in the context of slavery as a relational vision of health (6). Unlike European American views of human disease after the Industrial Revolution as a mechanical problem of the body unrelated to spiritual feeling or social relationships, the relational view did not separate these aspects of human existence (mental, spiritual, physical, and social). Rather, the relational vision:

> connected individual health to broader community relationships; it insisted on a collective context for both affliction and healing; it honored kinship relations by bridging the worlds of ancestors and living generations; [and] it located a healer's authority in the wisdom of elders and divine revelation. (Fett 6)

From the perspective of Afrocentric healing ways, *Beloved* is structured around an initial attempt at healing the collective suffering from the physical and spiritual effects of slavery by Baby Suggs, holy; the trauma of schoolteacher's racist science leading to infanticide; the return of Beloved from the spirit world that injures Sethe, Denver, Paul D, and the whole community; and a final, collective ritual healing that restores balance among the living community, Sethe's reconstituted family, and the dead.

Healing the Wounds of Enslavement

Enslaved descendants of Africans combined African relational views of well-being with Christian beliefs so that the spiritual permeated everyday life, including the effects of slavery and its aftermath on mental, spiritual, and physical health. Morrison draws a historical lineage from Sethe's African mother to Baby Suggs, holy, an elder who "calls," not preaches, "her dance in the Clearing" to the community (208). Baby Suggs's healing is communal rather than individual. The spiritual power to heal the effects of slavery's degradation takes place outside a church, drawing instead on the vital force of forest plants and trees. Forests and fields were rich sources of plants for enslaved peoples' deep knowledge of herbal medicine and a place equally rich in the restorative vital force of the universe. The Clearing carries over for the free people from practices under slavery of meeting and communing outside the monitoring of whites; it was a safer space than the white church or gathering within sight of white overseers.

Baby Suggs's healing power also participates in the tradition of divine revelation, a practice that served healers, caretakers, and midwives in the treatment of everything from mundane physical ailments to emotional distress and relationship conflicts. Baby Suggs's denomination "holy" suggests the incorporation of Christian faith healing with the African view of spiritual sources of illness and healing. In the nineteenth century, enslaved people who attended white churches often received a separate sermon that exhorted them to obey slaveholders. By contrast, Baby Suggs in the forest attempts to heal her congregation of the physical and mental effects of slavery and Northern racism by teaching them to own their bodies and love themselves, reuniting each member with an alienated self. What is more, Baby Suggs is particularly qualified as a healer because of her age—elders were respected for their experience and wisdom among enslaved communities (Fett 55). She is marked as a healer because of her injured hip, as well. Her spiritual authority stems from her own physical suffering and survival along with her care of the young on the plantation, which would include feeding, minding, and doctoring infants and children. Enslaved healers were often marked by a physical difference, such as a withered limb or unusual size (Fett 97). In all of these respects, Morrison illustrates a world of power and spiritual healing in the character of Baby Suggs, holy, that directly contradicts the slaveholder's devaluation of old, injured, female slaves (because their ability to labor for commodity production is limited) as well as slaveholders' tendency to use Christian preaching to slaves as a means of mental and bodily control.

Baby Suggs, holy, temporarily heals the collective body of the resettled people of Cincinnati. The feast, in which the savory food magically multiplies, recalls the parable of Jesus feeding the multitude with only a few loaves of bread and fishes (e.g., John 6:5–15). Families and neighbors come together, functioning as a community—a great sign of well-being and harmony with the universe in African cosmology. Yet the sense of well-being is short-lived, and in fact, Baby's borrowing of healing power from the universe turns to harm; the people become resentful and fail to warn Baby and Sethe of schoolteacher's arrival, directly contributing to Beloved's death. This reversal of Baby's healing power gives us insight into the many layers of internalized oppression experienced by survivors of slavery and racism. In telling this story from a late twentieth-century perspective, Morrison asks readers to witness the interrelations among oppression, self-alienation, community fracture, and violent death. At the same time, the reversal of Baby's healing power leading to community fracture and infanticide aligns with nineteenth-century African American views of spirit and power as double-sided, containing both the ability to heal and to harm simultaneously. Baby's immense power is turned back on the people, causing equally immense harm to the community as a whole (people revert to distrusting one another and not helping one another in the hard task of surviving in a racist Northern city). Consequently, Baby's failure to heal the community ultimately causes her loss of hope and her slow death, setting the stage for Morrison to propose another healing way at the end of the novel that is more effective because it brings the community together.

Schoolteacher and the Human Cost of Racist Science

The worldview of many enslaved communities contrasted greatly with slaveholders' views of health and illness. In *Beloved*, schoolteacher is a scientist who studies the physical traits of slaves. He belongs to a larger group of scientists who sought to justify slavery by "proving" the biological inferiority of people of African descent. Proslavery scientists and physicians studied race and slavery in specialized branches of science that are now obsolete, but that held considerable sway in the nineteenth century. These branches of science asserted that Africans were happiest and healthiest in slavery, since they supposedly lacked both the physical and mental capacity to govern themselves or survive without the white man's resources. Particularly influential was Dr. Samuel Cartwright's medical assessment of African slaves, first published in 1851 in the *New Orleans Medical and Surgical Journal* and reprinted widely in Southern journals. The physician coined two diseases "peculiar to the Negro race," which gained currency among planters because it had "a direct and practical bearing upon... $2 billion worth of property," revealing how closely enslaved people were associated with livestock and other farm supplies (DeBow 64). "Drapetomania" was "the disease causing slaves to run away" and "Dysacsthesia Aethiopis" was the ailment of laziness (Cartwright 707; 709). Cartwright backed up his research with physiological findings, such as a perceived difference in the blood of African people (it could not carry as much oxygen). Cartwright also claimed that all Africans had a kneecap shape adapted to their "natural" posture of kneeling in subservience to superior people, like whites (708). The invention of these diseases speaks to the social power of medical researchers in a proslavery society rather than to real afflictions of enslaved people.

Racist medical study went hand in hand with another branch of science, anthropometry, founded upon measuring the size of skulls; the shape of facial features, such as jaws and noses; and the width of pelvises of people from different areas of the world. Scientists analyzed patterns and differences in these measurements in order to categorize all people into seven or eight races. Anthropometry was part of a debate among educated people in the nineteenth century about whether Africans and Europeans (including "Caucasian" Americans) were of different species. Those who believed that people of different races had separate origins were called polygenists, and this belief also justified slavery and racial segregation in their eyes because Africans were designated as closer to animals than Europeans. The most influential, comprehensive study of racial difference backed up by seemingly objective data was Josiah C. Nott and George Gliddon's eight-hundred-page book *Types of Mankind*, first published in 1854 and reprinted many times. In *Beloved*, schoolteacher is educating his nephews in the science of anthropometry. Rather than privileging schoolteacher's malicious but authoritative worldview, Morrison reveals the impact of this science on the "objects" of study, Sethe, Sixo, and the enslaved men of Sweet Home.

Morrison challenges the history of racist medicine and science not only by revealing its effects from the perspectives of Sethe and Sixo, but also by making racist science arguably the largest factor in the novel's central trauma of infanticide. Sethe's consciousness of the dehumanization of slavery begins when she overhears schoolteacher asking his students to list Sethe's human and animal characteristics, an activity that arouses Sethe's fear. Stunned by this attack on her humanity, she backs away from schoolteacher and his students with involuntary movements and feels a "prickly" sensation on her head, "like somebody was sticking fine needles in [her] scalp" (Morrison 228). Her terror of this inhuman view that another holds for her is confirmed when she gets the definition of the word "characteristics" from Mrs. Garner. Sethe's justified aversion to schoolteacher's view of her reveals the deep ignorance of scientists who claimed that Africans had a child-like or animal-like lack of intelligence.

The human cost of racist science is unforgettably illustrated by the events following Sethe's discovery. Racist science is the trigger for Beloved's murder, which also leads to the deep depression of Baby Suggs and Sethe's emotional and physical decline nearly to death. Sethe gets her children onto the Underground Railroad wagon insisting "No notebook for my babies and no measuring string either" (Morrison 233). After the initial trauma of seeing herself as a subhuman from schoolteacher's perspective, his racist science converges with the widespread practice of rape by white men of enslaved women. Morrison alters the rape scene described by many writers in the nineteenth century, such as Harriet Jacobs in *Incidents in the Life of a Slave Girl.* Instead of vaginal rape, schoolteacher's nephews suck milk from Sethe's breasts while schoolteacher takes notes (Morrison 83), a trauma that is central to the fate of her whole family: Halle goes into shock and never sees his family again; Sethe nearly loses her life escaping on foot; and Sethe reacts to reenslavement by killing one daughter and traumatizing the other three children. Morrison's alteration of the scene of rape to include breast milk underscores the human cost of scientific racism. Under its authority, the nephews literally consume the black female body, just as white infants were often nursed by enslaved women whose own newborns got less or no milk (babies did not legally belong to enslaved women but to the slaveholder). The ill effects of such denial of bodily autonomy are what Baby Suggs attempts to heal in the Clearing.

The scientific dehumanization of Sethe and the rape that it authorized is the primary trauma of *Beloved.* In this view, infanticide is the result of racist science—a cause and effect that is available to readers only by privileging Sethe's point of view. Her physical sensation of a prickly scalp, first felt when she overheard schoolteacher claim she was partly an animal, becomes amplified when schoolteacher arrives at 124 Bluestone to bring Sethe and her children back into slavery. This sensation is accompanied by ringing in her ears—the sensations of extreme panic that Morrison beautifully renders as the sound and feeling of hummingbirds buzzing and stinging her scalp. The swift killing of Beloved and attempted killing of Denver are the result of this trigger, determining the fates of Sethe and everyone in her family and community. Infanticide—reflexive and determined by a denial of autonomy in slavery so severe that it offers Sethe only one tragic way out—is thematically and logically linked by Morrison to schoolteacher's racist science.

African American Spirits and Sethe's Illness

The most obvious source of Sethe's decline almost to death is the return of Beloved from the dead. African American beliefs in ghosts are voiced by Stamp Paid, who can hear the "pack of haunts" at 124 Bluestone (Morrison 200). Also called "hants" and "haints," depending on regional dialect, the ghost in African American culture is a widespread collective belief. For example, in Gullah culture of the South Carolina Sea Islands, a group of formerly enslaved communities that retained African worldviews into the twentieth century, hants cause distress among the living. Attributed to people who died violent deaths, their presence causes sleeplessness, mental illness, and physical decline (Chandler 131; 356–7). Morrison draws heavily on these traditional, widespread beliefs in characterizing Beloved and illustrating her effects on Sethe's family.

Beloved starts out as a very traditional haunt or haint, first making disturbances in the kitchen (Chandler 356) and disarranging the house and even pitching the floorboards and furniture. But after Sethe and Denver invite her to "come on" or come through, Beloved joins a living community and takes on new flesh, grows, and becomes pregnant. True to an African American worldview, Beloved is an ambiguous agent of both healing and harming. At first, her presence rescues Sethe from her deep sorrow. Eventually, though, Beloved takes more and more from Sethe, diminishing her own vital force, making her thinner, distracted, and unable to care for herself or Denver.

Yet Morrison complicates the haint tradition in order to make a powerful statement about oppression, for as she grows, Beloved develops ancestral memories of the Middle Passage, which means that she too is haunted. Another form of ghost derived from West African culture, which Gullah people call hags, are especially dangerous. A hag is "a disembodied spirit of a living person roam[ing] the earth, skinless, perpetrating bad dreams on its victims, and 'riding' them" (Chandler 19). For Hagar Brown, a woman born enslaved in South Carolina, a hag is terrifying because it can "suck yuh en draw yuh blood" (Chandler 19). Brown links hags to white people, who command the hag to harass the victim while resting, showing an adaptation of African spirits to the context of mandatory labor (Chandler 19). In Morrison's novel, Beloved—already a "haunt" herself—gives readers perspective on the compounded suffering of Africans during the entire period of transatlantic slavery. The "men without skin" who haunt her are hags; they also illustrate African perceptions of white slave traders (African people who have never seen Europeans would assume that brown skin was the only kind of skin). These white men's unpredictable assaults aboard slave ships and on plantations make them hag-like. Morrison's incorporation of Afrocentric worldviews complements the spiritual healing ways influenced by Christianity and sets the stage for an African and American hybrid method of healing for Sethe and her surviving family.

The Final Healing

Healing Sethe ultimately fulfills the relational vision of health by bridging the deceased Baby Suggs, an ancestor, with the living members of the community. Recall that the relational vision of health "honored kinship relations by bridging the worlds of ancestors and living generations" (Fett 6). Beloved is banished when Stamp decides to help Baby Suggs's family expel the ghost. In this sense, Baby as an ancestor is central to the return of healthy community relationships and Sethe's recovery. The healing process begins slowly and requires the participation of multiple community members, while also situating the suffering of Beloved and Sethe among all Africans who were enslaved. Stamp Paid initiates the collective rescue as Sethe is reaching a peak of suffering; he visits Ella and reverses her prejudice against Paul D and Sethe, whom she believes are afflicted with haunts and whom she wants to exclude from the community (Morrison 221). Stamp's repair of relationships enables Ella to become a lead healer of the affliction at 124 Bluestone, as we will see.

The need for collective action to heal Sethe is counterbalanced with Beloved's progression from an individual who was hurt by another individual, her mother, to a growing collective body of all Africans, particularly girls and women, who endured injury, rape, and murder by white men (Morrison 284). The parasitic relationship between Beloved and Sethe illustrates how survivors of slavery suffer doubly: on one level, from personal experience of psychological and physical violence and on another level, from the grief of witnessing loved ones endure violence or die. Stamp experiences this double suffering as a feeling of "exhausted marrow," a physical sensation of illness in the innermost core of his body (213). Baby Suggs experiences this as a permanent loss of hope, taking to her bed like an ill person to slowly die as the only way to avoid re-injury by remembering the violence her family has suffered. After her death, however, her healing power manifests differently than did her work in the Clearing: Stamp changes his mind in a sudden empathic realization. Feeling remorse about rejecting Baby's right to die without reliving all the suffering of her family, he understands her reaction and decides to help her family. This reestablished bond, in turn, initiates the novel's second, more effective healing, performed by the community as a whole.

The process of healing continues with Denver entering the community that has been partly primed by Stamp's repair of broken relationships. Denver seeks work to provide for Sethe, who has become virtually paralyzed by Beloved's increasing demands for resources and attention. Denver first sees Janey Wagon, who asks questions about Denver's "sick" mother, deduces that the return of Beloved in the flesh is the cause, and tells other women in the community (Morrison 298–300). Ella, an herbalist and "practical woman who believed there was a root either to chew or avoid for every ailment," organizes the community to heal Sethe (301).

The women have a range of explanations for Sethe's ailment, but they share the relational vision of health because they all see Sethe's withdrawal from the community after her release from jail as the start of the illness (Morrison 299; 302). Just as the women link Sethe's health to her interaction with the larger community, Ella also realizes that Beloved's power threatens not just Sethe, but all of them: "if [the ghost] took on flesh and came in [Ella's] world, well, the shoe was on the other foot. She didn't mind a little communication between the two worlds, but this was an invasion" (302). Ella also convinces the other women that Sethe does not deserve the affliction caused by Beloved because, she explains, "children can't just up and kill the mama," thus restoring child-elder relationships to their proper order in an African American worldview (301).

Most important, the success of the healing depends on restoring a shared commitment to individual health as going hand in hand with community wholeness. Several views combine in the community's identification of the source of harm to Sethe, and it is the balance between these views that enables a successful healing. Some community members believe that "Sethe's dead daughter... had come back to fix her" (Morrison 300) and accordingly arm themselves with plants and objects that will protect them and help Sethe ward off the "fix" (303). This belief in fixing someone to cause illness or even death is part of a complex system of healing and harming called conjure or hoodoo (a practice that is distinct from voodoo). In enslaved communities, conjure served as a way of maintaining social order independently from the control that slaveholders imposed on enslaved people (Fett 107–108). The system explained illness that was untreatable or out of the ordinary as a deliberate "dosing" or "fixing" of one person by another through special materials and rituals known only by conjure doctors. This practice involved not just the afflicted, the conjure doctor, and the afflicted person's enemy, but the whole community. Beloved does cast a spell on Sethe that causes Sethe to grow thin, weak, and so anguished that she can't take care of herself.

The women of the community also believe that "Christian faith—as shield and sword" will heal Sethe (Morrison 303), invoking the faith healings of Baptist and other Evangelical denominations founded by English and European Christians. But most of the thirty women who gather outside 124 Bluestone to heal Sethe brought "a little of both" African American healing ways and Christian faith healing methods (303). A rekindled feeling of solidarity, of sharing a need for protection from the spirits of babies who died because of the violence of slavery, prompts Ella, who passively killed her own baby conceived through rape (305), to lead the healing. The healing ceremony begins with Christian prayers and then ritual singing that blends American and African practices, attracting Sethe to come out of her haunted house. The coincidence of Bodwin appearing in a hat like schoolteacher's prompts Sethe to change her original response to that fear, and instead of murdering Beloved again, she runs toward Bodwin. Now that the community has assembled to help Sethe, however, they take her into their group, "a pile of people out there" (309), which saves her from harming Bodwin and herself. This reclaiming of Sethe by the community makes Beloved disappear. Although she still lurks invisibly around the grounds of the house, she has been effectively expelled from 124 Bluestone by the community.

Even after Beloved leaves 124, Sethe is still ailing; like Baby Suggs in her emotional exhaustion, Sethe has taken to bed and seems to be dying. Paul D is the final piece in healing the massive communal affliction brought on by Beloved's ghost. His own recovery is marked by his ability to feel love again, and that helps him nurse Sethe and save her from a death of despair: he turns the power of Sethe's love for Beloved back to herself (Morrison 322). The novel closes with Sethe grasping at this new way of seeing herself as her own "best thing" and implies that Paul D will stay; their family with Denver will be restored to its promise after the carnival, just before Beloved returned. The ritualistic phrase "You may as well just come on," which has brought both Paul D and Beloved into Sethe's life, is replaced by "It was not a story to pass on" (323–24), effectively reversing the power of Sethe's trauma to return and harm her. In addition, the family is restored within a community that remembers and respects its greatest ancestor, Baby Suggs, holy. From an African and an African American view of healing and universal balance, harmony has been reestablished, and Sethe will return to health.

Beloved as a Political Stand Against the Legacy of Race-Based Affliction

As a narrative of extraordinary suffering due to racial conflict that resolves through a balance of indigenous and adapted healing ways, *Beloved* exemplifies a literary strategy that makes political commentary during the third-wave feminist movement of the late 1970s and early 1980s. Third-wave feminism recognized that the women's liberation movements of earlier eras (before the Civil War and after World War II) often excluded the experience and participation of women of color. Feminist thinkers, such as bell hooks, Paula Gunn Allen, and Gloria Anzaldúa, called attention to the particular effects of racism on African American, Native American, and Chicana women's well-being in mind, spirit, and body. Literary writers who also sought to illustrate these effects alongside *Beloved* include Leslie Marmon Silko with *Ceremony*, Gloria Naylor with *Mama Day*, and Toni Cade Bambara with *The Salt Eaters*. Each of these novels dramatizes internalized racism and sexism as causing an illness affecting mind, spirit, and body that impacts not only the protagonist, but also every member of the community.

In these novels, there are two main strategies for resolving illness caused by sexism and racism: the arrival at a hybridized healing way and a radical return to traditional healing ways. Hybridized healing combines a traditional, indigenous view of illness and healing with views adapted to new conditions caused by conflict with European Americans. Along with the blending of African and American healing ways in Sethe's community, the protagonist of Leslie Marmon Silko's *Ceremony* undergoes a traditional Laguna Pueblo/Navajo healing quest to create a new healing ceremony for his community. Tayo's new ceremony honors ancestral knowledge while adapting its methods to deal with illness induced by twentieth-century oppression, including abusive relationships, alcoholism, and environmental destruction. While Silko's protagonist, Tayo, is male, she balances his quest with female characters, such as Tayo's mother, who suffers and dies from sexual degradation, and a mythical female who guides Tayo to complete his healing quest, reflecting the traditional reverence of femininity in Pueblo religion and social structure.

Other third-wave feminist novels suggest that healing the effects of gender and racial oppression require a radical return to traditional healing ways. *Mama Day* uses a narrative of conjure that takes the life of one protagonist, George, an African American who is alienated from traditional Sea Island African American culture and believes only in science, thus affirming the traditional healing ways of the community healer, Miranda Day. Likewise, in *The Salt Eaters*, the healer Minnie collaborates with a haint and, using a rich mixture of diverse African healing ways, returns the suicidal civil rights reformer Velma to well-being. All of these novels, and *Beloved* in particular, offer us an expanded view of what counts as illness, the ways in which social oppression causes illness, and the rich global approaches to healing that flourish outside of mainstream scientific medicine.

In particular, Morrison's choice to use schoolteacher's racist science as the trigger of a chain of injuries and deaths among the enslaved characters makes a political point about oppression as a social illness. From this perspective, the ways in which the characters adapt an African worldview of health under the constraints of slavery and racism speak pointedly to the mental and physical illnesses caused by dehumanization. At the same time, the novel's scene of healing brings the African worldview back, requiring the rebuilding of community in a specifically American context: survival of the enduring effects of slavery and post-Emancipation racism. Ultimately, *Beloved* invites readers to "come on," to witness the complexity of illness—individual and social—caused by racism and historical slavery. With this strategy, the novel builds a larger community beyond its pages that is ready to recognize healing as a collective undertaking of blended African and American traditions.

Works Cited

Bambara, Toni Cade. *The Salt Eaters*. 1980. New York: Vintage, 1992.

Cartwright, Samuel. "Report on the Diseases and Physical Peculiarities of the Negro Race." *New Orleans Medical and Surgical Journal* 7 (May 1851): 691–715.

Chandler, Genevieve. *Coming Through: Voices of a South Carolina Gullah Community from WPA Oral Histories*. Eds. Kincaid Mills, Genevieve C. Peterkin, & Aaron McCollough. Columbia: U of South Carolina P, 2008.

DeBow, James. Preface. "Diseases and Peculiarities of the Negro Race" By James Cartwright. *DeBow's Review* 11.1 (1851): 64–65. *Making of America*. Web. 4 Feb. 2012.

Fett, Sharla M. *Working Cures: Healing, Health, and Power on Southern Slave Plantations*. Chapel Hill: U of North Carolina, 2002.

Jacobs, Harriet. *Incidents in the Life of a Slave Girl: Written By Herself*. 1861. Ed. Jean Fagan Yellin. Cambridge: Harvard UP, 1987.

Morrison, Toni. *Beloved*. 1987. New York: Vintage, 2004.

Naylor, Gloria. *Mama Day*. 1988. New York: Vintage, 1993.

Nott, Josiah C. and George Gliddon. *Types of Mankind*. Philadelphia: Lippincott, Grambo, 1854. *Internet Archive*. Web. 21 Aug. 2015.

Paris, Peter J. "The *African* in African American Theology." *The Oxford Handbook of African American Theology*. Eds. Katie G. Cannon & Anthony B. Pinn. New York: Oxford UP, 2014. 431-449.

Silko, Leslie Marmon. *Ceremony*. 1977. New York: Penguin, 1986.

"Unspeakable Things Unspoken": Prophetic Utterances in Toni Morrison's *Beloved*_____

Khalilah T. Watson

> There is no place that you or I can go, to think about or not think about, to summon the presences of, or recollect the absences of slaves; nothing that reminds us of the ones who made the journey and of those who did not make it. There is no suitable memorial or wreath or wall or park or sky-scraper lobby. There's no 300-foot tower. There's no small bench by the road.
>
> (Toni Morrison, "Bench by the Road")

The role of the prophet or the notion of prophecy as written in both the Holy Bible and the Holy Qu'ran has been in existence almost since the beginning of the human age. A prophet or messenger of God is born into the world to set matters right or to redirect human creation. In the same way that a biblical prophet is sent to deliver his/her people, the writer that functions as a literary prophet takes on the task, through his/her writing, by critiquing or providing guidance to the society that he/she quietly observes. Like the Biblical and Qu'ranic prophets, the literary prophet considers the historical events of the past in the context of the present, then provides the critique, the warning, and/or the challenge to her or his audience about the deleterious societal conditions and the need for human reformation.

Toni Morrison began to cultivate a heightened sensitivity to unjust societal ills as a result of certain childhood experiences. This further developed while she served as an editor for many up-and-coming black writers. While Toni Morrison did not deliberately or purposefully begin to create fiction with historical and restorative imperatives, eventually all of her works began to revisit the historical implications of black life in America. Her literary prophetic platform bears witness to the challenges of being black in America during times of slavery and all the later periods of social injustice, prejudice, segregation, racism, sexism, and classism; her work tackles the issues of religion and standards of beauty as well.

Like the biblical prophet, the literary prophet fulfills an extraordinary role as an exhortative writer. More specifically, a literary prophetic writer discusses, in contemporary terms, the overall condition that creates disparities in human treatment leading to negative and destructive perspectives of self and others and offers guidance for present and future generations to break the cycle of false hope followed by despair.

Toni Morrison knows that history is bound to repeat itself, unless something significant occurs to disrupt the continuum of past traumatic moments of history. Therefore, like the prophets of the Holy Bible and the Holy Qu'ran—such as Noah, Moses, Abraham, Jesus, and Muhammad, who reinforced the importance of being obedient to God and God's law—Morrison uses her literary platform to provide true and accurate historical representations of the interior lives of blacks in America and stresses the importance of American society not repeating history. In examining Morrison's historical trilogy—*Beloved* (1987), *Jazz* (1992), and *Paradise* (1997)—one discovers that these novels embody the concept that "there is a profound connection between the laws which govern the production of prophecy (which comes from human brains), the laws which govern the process of history, (which also account for the repeating of history), [and] the laws of human behavior and the consequences which flow from human actions" (E. Muhammad 35). Each novel is a prophetic production, derived from the brain of Toni Morrison, based upon her intense study of history. Furthermore, in probing each prophetic production, as manifested in her novels, one discovers that the characters, the narrator, and the overall plot are also governed by insight into real aspects of human behavior and human interaction, which are based upon the narrative of human history.

Hence, the narrative of human history in America is also a theme that Morrison tackles in all of her novels, while also inserting her prophetic utterances, by speaking about societal matters that were once "unspoken." Parallel to such prophetic claims, in the introduction of Carolyn C. Denard's *Toni Morrison: Conversations*, a more recent volume of interviews with Morrison, regarding her works, her role as writer, editor, and beyond, where some comparative and contrasting commentary is provided about these two volumes, Denard asserts that "What is also interesting in these early interviews is the nearly prophetic way that [Morrison's novels] sometimes forecast the future direction of her fiction. When Morrison tells Paula Giddings in 1977 about how important memory is to her work, we can't help but think of *Beloved*, a novel that would not be published until ten years later: "the memory is long, beyond the parameters of cognition. I don't want to sound too mystical about it, but I feel like a conduit, I really do…" (xi). As suggested from these words and her earliest novels, *The Bluest Eye*, presents the story of a little black girl who is trapped in "the house that race built," and in *Song of Solomon*, another story is given about how a black man is in search of his true self and identity. Hence, both novels uncover the function of race and history within each protagonist's life, within his or her family, and within the lives that extend beyond. Similarly, the same level of interrogation about race and history occurs within what can be considered her historical trilogy—*Beloved* (1987), *Jazz* (1992) and *Paradise* (1997)—starting with the first novel.

Beloved demonstrates how Morrison provides a revisionist and prophetic reading of the effects of enslavement and the inevitable racism. In the same vein, she further shows what grows out of the effects of enslavement and inevitable racism, in order to emphasize the importance for contemporary Americans to seek healing from this historically transformative experience. Next, Morrison wants all American readers to face and to learn from the pain of these historical experiences. Lastly, she wants to pay homage to the ancestral spirit that still lives as result of these experiences.

Beloved: Racial History Not To Be Ignored

Beloved represents Morrison's effort to further proclaim the importance of a re-examination of the effects of the Middle Passage and the "interior life" of slavery for Black Americans. She pays homage to the horrific past of slavery, especially to a young female slave mother's riveting story. The fictionalized characters that Morrison creates in this text serve as witnesses, the historical reminders of the experiences of the Middle Passage, the trans-Atlantic slave trade and slavery itself. Morrison creates her characters as historical and psychological representations of how such long-passed traumatic experiences continue to inform contemporary lives. The entire text is like a collective family flashback. However, Morrison uses the actual historical account of Margaret Garner's story as a focal point for this book. According to Morrison,

> [t]he historical Margaret Garner is fascinating, but, to a novelist, confining. Too little imaginative space there for my purposes. So I would invent her thoughts, plumb them for a subtext that was historically true in essence, but not strictly factual in order to relate her history to contemporary issues about freedom, responsibility, and women's place. The heroine would represent the unapologetic acceptance of shame and terror; assume the consequences of choosing infanticide; claim her own freedom. The terrain, slavery, was formidable and pathless. To invite readers (and myself) into a repellant landscape (hidden, but not completely; deliberately buried, but not forgotten) was to pitch a tent in a cemetery inhabited by highly vocal ghosts. (*Beloved* 17)

From the very beginning, the novel is circumscribed by how Sethe's character must strive to fight against a painful past of enslavement. The narrator describes this process in Sethe's life as "working, working, working dough. Nothing better than that to start the days' serious work of beating back the past" (Morrison, *Beloved* 5–6). With every conversation that Sethe has with others, her past as a slave becomes clearer—as she is forced to remember things that she really wants to forget.

Thus, Sethe serves as a manifestation of Toni Morrison's method of "literary archaeology"—Sethe's character is a fictional representation of the experience of a historical female slave: Margaret Garner. As the protagonist of this novel, Sethe often reconnects with her past experiences as a slave, which in part reflects what is known of the real life slave Margaret Garner.

The first chapter of *Beloved* introduces the reader to Sethe's whirlwind of private thoughts, in which all thoughts are connected to or about her life as a slave. Sethe is reminded of the death and the spiritual presence of her mother-in-law: Baby Suggs; the unseen spiteful ancestral presence; images of lynching—bodies hanging from "beautiful" sycamore trees, the chokecherry tree on her back after she is beaten with cowhide, the men that "stole her milk," and finally, to her initial arrival as the only female slave on Sweet Home Plantation, owned by Mr. and Mrs. Garner. All of these moments are the "rememories" of Sethe, an ex-slave. Through these images and the construction of her characters: Baby Suggs, Paul D, Denver, Beloved, and Sethe, Morrison warns America about the lingering emotional and psychological disorders created by experiences of slavery.

The reader is forced to identify with Sethe's pain. Through Sethe's anguish, Morrison represents the interior life of a victimized woman who must try to stop her memories from destroying her. In Sethe's mind, body, and spirit, there is no psychological separation between her present life and her past life at Sweet Home. For example, when Paul D arrives on the porch of 124 Bluestone Road (once a place used like the Underground Railroad for escaped slaves), he and Sethe instantly resume their relationship stories. He picks up right where they left off the last time they saw each other— eighteen years earlier. In one of the most heart-wrenching scenes of this initial reunion, Sethe says:

> "After I left you, those boys came in there and took my milk. That's what they came in there for. Held me down and took it. I told Ms Garner on em. She had that lump and couldn't speak but her eyes rolled out tears...
> Schoolteacher made one open up my back, and when it closed it made a tree. It grows there still."
> "They used cowhide on you?"
> "And they took my milk."
> "They beat you and you was pregnant?"
> "And they took my milk!" (Morrison, *Beloved* 19)

Since the role of the mother is essential to Sethe's existence, when her milk is stolen by a white man and not consumed by her baby, she is unable to restore her own image as a mother. Consequently, she is mentally scarred from this violent act, just as her back is physically scarred from the cowhide whip.

Parallel to this, Marilyn Mobley argues that:

> What also comes back through the stories that Paul D shares are fragments of history. Sethe is unprepared for such as the fact that years ago her husband had witnessed the white boys forcibly take milk from her breasts, but had been powerless to come to her rescue or stop them...perhaps more importantly, these elements comprise the signs of history that punctuate the text and that disrupt the text of the mind, which is both historical and ahistorical at the same time. (23)

Morrison confronts her readers with the horrors of the past that are "too terrible to relate" by allowing the reader to eavesdrop on the private conversations between Sethe and Paul D. Also in this conversation, Morrison offers another rememory of the narrative of black life that is "too terrible to relate"; thus, she "speaks the unspoken."

Another character who represents a significant historical facet of enslavement is the mysterious girl Beloved. Beloved's arrival, however, is described as real, not supernatural: "A fully dressed woman walked out of the water. She barely gained dry bank of the stream before she sat down and leaned against the mulberry tree.... Nobody saw her emerge or came accidentally by. If they had, chances are they would have hesitated before approaching her" (Morrison 60). For Paul D, Sethe, and Denver, Beloved is a mystery; she emerged "one day while Paul D, Sethe, and Denver were coming back from the town carnival, Beloved suddenly appears outside of Sethe and Denver's home, sitting on a tree stump in a wet black dress, wearing a hat and untied ankle boots" (Morrison 60–1). Some critics argue that Beloved's character is the physical embodiment of the crawling-already baby or the ghost of the daughter that Sethe murdered because she did not want her to be enslaved; or she is the one who was introduced to the reader in the beginning of the text as "spiteful[,] [f]ull of baby's venom." But, Elizabeth House argues differently, stating that:

> Such uniform acceptance of this notion [that Beloved is not real but a ghost] is surprising, for evidence throughout the book suggests that the girl is not a supernatural being of any kind but simply a young woman who has herself suffered the horrors of slavery…In large part, Morrison's Pulitzer Prize-winning fifth novel is about the atrocities slavery wrought both upon a mother's need to love and care for her children as well as child's deep need for a family…. (17)

In other words, Beloved is a metaphoric embodiment of all these arguments. Thus, the reader can easily identify Beloved as Sethe's long-lost daughter because of Sethe's sense of guilt, but Beloved also has a strong connection to the general horrors of the Middle Passage, which goes beyond the historical narrative of Sethe's life and is conveyed in the stream-of-consciousness passage near the novel's end. Still, this dark recovery of the horrors of the slave ship can be the kind of racial memory represented by the image of a slave girl who was viciously and sexually abused by her master before he threw her into the river upstream from the place where Sethe lives.

This duality in Beloved's character is necessary to fully grasp the vision of a literary prophet because, as Morrison has said, "until you confront [the past], until you live through it [it] keeps coming back in other forms. The shapes redesign themselves in other constellations, until you get a chance to play it over again" (Caldwell 241). Not only is Sethe's character confronted with actions from her own past, but Beloved's past is also a symbolic representation of a racist past. Only when Sethe confronts her past—as represented in the physical manifestation of Beloved—can she begin to *truly* heal and move beyond her painful personal past.

Beloved's ancestral memory is representative of many of the slaves that experienced the Middle Passage and the trans-Atlantic slave trade; she is the atavistic symbol of those slaves whose stories remained unrecorded or forgotten. Morrison uses the dialog between Beloved and other characters to paint a distinct picture of the historical truths of the past. As depicted in a conversation between Sethe's youngest daughter, Denver and Beloved:

> Beloved closed her eyes. "In the dark my name is Beloved."
> Denver scooted a little closer. "What's it like over there, where you were before? Can you tell me?"
> "Dark," said Beloved. "I'm small in that place. I'm like this here."
> She raised her head off the bed, lay down on her side and curled up.
> Denver covered her lips with her fingers. "Were you cold?"
> Beloved curled tighter and shook her head. "Hot. Nothing to breathe down there and no room to move in."
> "You see anybody?"
> "Heaps. A lot of people is down there. Some is dead."
> "You see Jesus? Baby Suggs?"
> "I don't know. I don't know the names." (Morrison, *Beloved* 88)

Beloved speaks of her experience in "the dark," which is a cryptic description of the foul hold of the slave ship in the Middle Passage experience that brought Africans to America. At the bottom level of these ships, several women, men, and children were piled on top of one another, not often exposed to sunlight. Furthermore, in support of Beloved's narrative words, in the text *The African Experience: A History*, another testimony is given: [o]ther Africans recalled equally terrible scenes: brutal whippings, force feedings, and the smell of death and filth in disease-ridden cargo holds. Hundreds of Africans lay wedged together, bound by chains, and praying that death would come to them, too" (Harley, et al. 41). In this confining space, the slave traders left the Africans to urinate, defecate, regurgitate, and even die on one another.

Morrison further confronts the reader with the horrors of the slave trade by the way Beloved contorted her body and curled up on her side. This physical gesture depicts how closely together captured Africans had to remain on a journey that took days, even months across the Atlantic. To tell the truth, in a section entitled "The Cruelty of the Voyage," a historical account of the slave ship's dimensions are given: "[t]he holds of the most slave ships measured only about 5 feet (1.5 meters) high. But this space was cut in half by a shelf that extended about six feet (1.8 meters). The Africans were chained by the neck and legs to the shelf or to the deck…" (Harley, et al. 41). Despite these details from the slave ship, based on Beloved's apparent age—eighteen years old—and a brief hint that she was dumped into the river, she could not actually have experienced the Middle Passage except as a racial memory that is housed in her subconscious.

Another example of historical racial memory that parallels Beloved's recall of the slave ship occurs in a conversation between Beloved and Sethe:

> Sethe occasionally put to her: "You disremember everything? I never knew my mother neither, but I saw her a couple of times. Did you never see yours? What kind of whites was they? You don't remember none?"
>
> Beloved, scratching the back of her hand, would say she remembered a woman who was hers, and she remembered being snatched away from her. Other than that, the clearest memory she had, the one she repeated, was the bridge—standing on the bridge looking down. And she knew one whiteman. (Morrison, *Beloved* 140)

This dialog between Beloved and Sethe—neither of whom knew their mothers—speaks to the fragmented existence of slave life and how the slave masters regularly separated children from their mothers. Sethe saw her mother only a few times, and Beloved remembers being snatched away from her mother. Sethe also believes that Beloved was captured by some white men, which parallels her painful experience with white men—such as when schoolteacher's nephews stole her milk. Both women have been victimized by white men. Finally, in this scene, Beloved also recalls standing over a bridge; perhaps she, too, escaped from the clutches of the white man that once held her hostage by jumping into the river. Essentially, these two characters force the reader to intimately engage with the interior life of the black female slaves. Parallel to the details given in the true accounts of slavery by legendary figures such as Olaudah Equiano, Frederick Douglass, Harriet Jacobs, and David Walker; Morrison's text continues to "speak the unspoken" and expands the written tradition that documents this aspect of black life that is "too terrible to relate."

Baby Suggs: The Female Prophetic Voice

Morrison also relates her prophetic vision through Baby Suggs, another noteworthy character that is critical to understanding Morrison's novel. As the elder figure in this text and the matriarch of her family, Baby Suggs often reflects a wisdom and grace that not only sustains her family, but also transcends her family. Baby Suggs serves as the *griot*, the seer, and the historical witness to African tribal history and the life of the enslaved. Through Baby Suggs, the novel examines aspects of African mythology, folklore, and storytelling, which are also links to prophetic capabilities, such as serving as a visionary for the community by foretelling what is to come in the future if the past is ignored. As such, Baby Suggs fulfills the role of the speaker prophet, the truthsayer, the historian, and the unofficial record-keeper for her community.

Baby Suggs maintains a profound connection with the past, and she uses her elder wisdom to provide guidance for the present and the future. Her paramount role, however, is to be the religious advisor for the slaves. "Like other preachers, [Baby Suggs] gave the slave community, a context in which it could place itself and in which it could [find] refuge and a source of strength" (Peach 113–4). And the place where Baby Suggs provides former slaves with refuge and sources of strength is in "the Clearing"—"a wide-open place cut deep in the woods nobody knew for what at the end of a path known only to deer and whoever cleared the land in the first place. In the heat of every Saturday afternoon, she sat in the clearing while the people waited among the trees" (Morrison 102). In "the Clearing," Baby Suggs' makes her spiritual ministrations unto the people that come to her, telling them:

> Here...in this here place, we flesh that weeps, laughs; flesh that dances on bare feet in grass. Love it. Love it hard. Yonder they do not love your flesh. They despise it. They don't love your eyes, they'd just as soon pick em out. No more do they love the skin on your back. Yonder they flay it. And O people they do not love your hands! Love

them. Raise them up and kiss them. Touch others with them, pat them together, stroke them on your face 'cause they don't love that either. *You* got to love it, *you*! And no, they ain't in love with your mouth. Yonder, out there, they will see it broken and break it again. What you say out of it they will not heed. What you scream from it they do not hear. What you put into it to nourish your body they will snatch away and give you leavins instead. No they don't love your mouth. *You* got to love it... (Morrison, *Beloved* 103–4, emphasis original)

In this passage, Baby Suggs strives to restore the fragmented existence brought on by slave life. She acknowledges that while they are at "The Clearing," there are still obstructions in their lives—i.e., enslavement—that prevent them from being whole human beings. Chattel bondage notwithstanding, Baby Suggs emphasizes that they must love themselves.

Interestingly, in this role, Baby Suggs functions like Jesus in the New Testament, teaching his followers to love "thy neighbor" as you love thyself. In doing this, she provides her "followers" with the first act of repair, rebirth, and recovery after being severely abused by the institution of slavery and by their oppressors. Since slavery violated the laws of God, Baby Suggs redirects the people who have come to see her, to the Commandments of God by instructing them to love themselves.

Likewise Baby Suggs' prophetic role as described in the passage above can be compared to that of Jesus as a healer. As stated in Matthew 8:7 and the Miracle Stories of Jesus, "Jesus saith unto [them], I will come and heal [them]." Baby Suggs initiates a similar healing process for the many slaves that come to see her in "The Clearing." She encourages them to cherish every aspect of their physical reality—their flesh, their eyes, their skin, their back, their hands, their mouths, and their bodies must be cherished. She provides them with a counter-argument to how every inch of their bodies and their flesh is exploited by the laborious tasks given by their slave-masters. While their slave-masters only see them as property or economic capital, she encourages them to love their bodies.

Baby Suggs preaches that the only means of survival is self-love. In order to enable these fragmented bodies to become truly free and whole, she knows that she has to empower them to take the initial steps in overcoming their present oppressed existence as slaves. While slavery has caused them to engage in self-negation, self-hatred, and self-destruction, Baby Suggs redirects them to see themselves as human and worthy of love. Thus, Baby Suggs' words manifest the spirit of redemption for these slaves, who are being instructed to return back to the true value of themselves.

Through the description of the "The Clearing" as the spatial location where recovery can take place for many slave families, and her portrayal of Baby Suggs as the conduit for this necessary healing process, Morrison uses her text to underscore to American society's need to confront the painful legacy of slavery and its traumatic impact on black life in America. This is in part because America, as a country, has not fully addressed the legacy of slavery, even after four hundred years, and it is still in need of such meaningful healing. Morrison demonstrates the ways in which the human condition continues to be intricately linked to the fragmented and horrific generational past that must be confronted by all—perpetrators and victims.

According to Morrison, as stated in her interview entitled "Bench by the Road," the spirit of those who involuntarily participated in such an unwilling exodus from their native lands deserve such recognition, as depicted in her work. Morrison declares that there is a need for a memorial to honor the history and experiences of black people who live in America today. In addition, she reminds Americans that the horrors of slavery did not end with the Emancipation Proclamation, but will continue in the present and in the future unless a meaningful dialog occurs, followed by a meaningful healing.

Closing

To this end, within the critical literary framework of American literature, Morrison serves her role well as a literary prophetic voice. She accomplishes this visionary task by using various mediums or multiple genres of music, film, and language, to allow her characters to recover the lost history of the American people. For example, on October 22, 1998, after the release of the film adaptation of *Beloved*, in the interview "Things We Find in Language: A Conversation with Toni Morrison," Michael Silverbatt asks Morrison "to talk about the book because it's [his] sense that after the movie hits the public, a book is altered by it and that there are things that we find in language, in the shaping and writing of literature, that a movie cannot touch" (171). In this interview Morrison offers more of her prophetic vision and reflects on how love is a theme at the center of *Beloved*, as well as in her other novels, *Jazz* and *Paradise*. Morrison states:

> This all-consuming love, which is an exaggeration of course of parental love, involved loving in a fierce, unhealthy, distorted way under circumstances that made such a love logical. I mean Sethe's not merely psychotic; she didn't just erupt into the world that way. But I was trying very hard as a writer to put into language the theatrically and the meaning of these kinds of distortions in order to reveal not only their consequences, but what one should be warned against, what we should look out for, what we should be wary of. And I thought Beloved's circumstances, the book circumstances, were not limited in any way to 1873 or 1855. I think for those us who live in 1998, male or female, the problems of trying to love oneself and another human being at the same time is a serious late-twentieth-century problem, a very serious problem. (qtd. in Silverblatt 172)

In this instance, Morrison also acknowledges how the notion of loving in a fierce unhealthy and distorted way—that is not limited to the predicament or traumas associated with slavery or the historical time period of 1855 or 1873—is also relevant to the very serious problems associated with self-love and love of others in 1998: the year of the film adaptation of the novel.

While *Beloved* was published in 1987, the historical reality that informed this novel continued to resonate with Morrison, and eighteen years later, she wrote for the opera, *Margaret Garner*, a stirring libretto revisiting the historical figure at the center of *Beloved*. The opera premiered in 2005 in Detroit, Michigan. In 2008, for the Chicago premiere, the playbill included "A Note from Toni Morrison," which also speaks to her identity as a literary prophetic writer, one called to explain the past in order to affect the future:

> For more than five years I had been in thrall to the material, trying to do justice to the historical characters involved while exercising the license I needed to interrogate the dilemma Margaret both presented and represented…Some ten years later, free from exhaustion following the publication of *Beloved* I realized that there were genres other than novels that could expand and deepen the story…Finally, to the real people who lived this tale, I trust we have done them, their heirs, and the spirits justice. (Morrison, "Note" 12)

Here, once again, Morrison argues that slavery must be acknowledged and examined from various positions and mediums. Free from the exhaustion of her efforts in the past, like the tradition of prophecy, when the message is not heard or understood the first time, another prophetic message is given. Likewise, in this realm, Morrison acknowledges how her literary prophetic voice must reappear to foretell or to warn its readers, viewers, and listeners of the important message once again. Therefore, Morrison is consciously and subconsciously relentless in her role as a conduit, as a witness bearer and as a literary prophetic writer, using her novels, as the platform or the space, to warn her American readers and beyond, of the message or the story that must be heard, or until justice is finally served.

Works Cited

Ali, Maulani Muhammad. *The Holy Qu'ran.* 2nd ed. Ohio: Ahmadiyya Anjuman Isha'at Islam, 2002.

_____. *The Religion of Islam.* 6th ed. Ohio: Ahmadiyya Anjuman Isha' at Islam, 1990. 283–296.

Denard, Carolyn C., ed. *Toni Morrison: Conversations* Jackson: UP of Mississippi, 2008.

Harley, Sharon, et al., eds. *The African American Experience: A History.* Englewood Cliff, NJ: Globe Books, 1992.

House, Elizabeth. "Toni Morrison's Ghost: The Beloved Who is Not Beloved." *Studies in American Fiction.* 18.1(1990): 17–26.

Caldwell, Gail. "Author Toni Morrison Discusses Her Lastest Novel *Beloved*." *Conversations with Toni Morrison*. Ed. Danielle Taylor-Guthrie. Jackson: U of Mississippi P, 1994. 239–245.

Mobley, Marilyn Sanders. "Call and Response: Voice, Community and Dialogic Structures in Toni Morrison's *Song of Solomon*." *New Essays on 'Song of Solomon'*. Ed. Valerie Smith. New York: Cambridge, 1995. 41–68.

Morrison, Toni. *Beloved.* Knopf: New York, NY, 1987.

_____. "A Note from Toni Morrison." *Margaret Garner*. Auditorium Theatre of Roosevelt University. Chicago, 2008.

Muhammad, Elijah. *Message to the Blackman in America.* Chicago: The Final Call Publishing Inc., 1965.

Peach, Linden. *Toni Morrison.* New York: St Martin's Press, 1995.

Silverblatt, Michael. "Things We Find in Language: A Conversation with Toni Morrison." *Toni Morrison: Conversations*. Ed. Carolyn C. Denard. Jackson: U of Mississippi P, 2008. 171–177.

The King James Holy Bible. Thomas Nelson Publishers, 1990.

Watson, Khalilah Tyri, "Literature as Prophecy: Toni Morrison as Prophetic Writer." Dissertation. Georgia State University, 2009. Web. <http://scholarworks.gsu.edu/english_diss/50>.

The Psychological Impact of Slavery and Separation in *Beloved*____

Lynne Simpson

There is a balm in Gilead to make the wounded whole
There is a balm in Gilead to heal the sin sick soul.
(Traditional African American spiritual)

Or is there?

My first attempt at reading *Beloved* was at the age of twenty-two. It took me three trials to get through "the material" to put it in pedagogical terms. On that first read, I could understand, to some extent, the physical pain and humiliation that was experienced by the slaves whose lives were unfolding before me, but I was not ready to comprehend the heartbreak of losing a child due to circumstances both in and out of one's own control. Now, more than twenty years later and with a child of my own, the despair of losing children, parents, siblings, and friends to simply increase another's wealth is beyond my understanding. So, some would question sharing this novel with a high school or college class. Many instructors prefer to rely on the autobiographical slave narratives that were written during that time. And, yes, those narratives are excellent and serve as great instructional tools. These narratives are a valuable "port of entry" for understanding *Beloved* (Greenbaum 83). However, we have more than just nonfiction stories belonging to the slave narrative, such as Hannah Craft's *The Bondwoman's Narrative*, Harriet E. Wilson's *Our Nig*, or Olaudah Equiano's *The Life and Adventures of Olaudah Equiano*; we also have a panoply of stories for students to explore.

Teaching Toni Morrison's *Beloved* to high school or college students in a lower division course, especially those who are not students of literature, poses a unique set of challenges. I have taught only one Toni Morrison novel to college students, *The Bluest Eye*. This novel was chosen in part because of its length (it was one of several novels to be read that semester) and also because the subject matter, the problem of self-perception, is one that may appeal to most college-aged students, especially women. *Beloved*, however, is much longer, but has a depth regarding the American experience that is incomparable to any other novelization of American slavery. *The Bluest Eye* also deals with some classic Morrison themes, such as family and the importance of race to the American experience, so an instructor who is attempting to introduce Morrison's work with a class often chooses this novel.

Some instructors are reluctant to teach *Beloved* to unseasoned students because its themes, such as institutionalized racism, rape, infanticide, economic exploitation, etc., are difficult to discuss in general much less in a classroom. But, it is the novel's frank presentation of these issues that makes it a critical text for teaching about this aspect of American history. This is one of the many reasons why it is important to use *Beloved* in today's integrated classrooms. African American students are increasingly taught about American slavery through a Caucasian viewpoint that often falsely encourages them to think that we are in a "post-race" era. This pretense of color blindness often comes with a minimization of the actual facts surrounding the Atlantic slave trade and the plight of the slave in the United States (Bery 334). This false reality of a post-racial America makes it even more necessary to include an African American voice in the classroom regarding a discussion of slavery and its aftermath.

Nonetheless, there are classics in the young adult classroom that are easier to discuss. Novels such as Margaret Mitchell's *Gone with the Wind* or Harriet Beecher Stowe's *Uncle Tom's Cabin* are regularly used to "teach" students about slavery. But these novels romanticize slavery; so, it is important for the sake of historical truth to share Morrison's voice with students, so as to provide them with a more accurate representation of the real plight of African Americans during this time. Unlike those novels that give the reader the illusion that after slavery everything returned to "normal," *Beloved* allows the reader to see that after the trauma of slavery, there was no such thing as a "normal" to which the now-freed blacks could return. *Beloved* is a story about slavery and the slave trade as interpreted by

Toni Morrison, a black woman, which counters the representation in the fictionalized accounts of white female writers, such as Margaret Mitchell or Harriet Beecher Stowe. *Beloved* provides a more accurate portrayal of the psychological and emotional trauma that was experienced by the slaves both before and after the Civil War. The novel, while fiction, is still one of the most realistic interpretations of the experiences of slavery, because it is based on a historical event. Therefore, it is an ideal text for teaching about one of the darkest chapters in American history.

How to present "the lowest yet" themes in a classroom?

It is estimated that around 12.5 million people were taken from Africa via the Atlantic slave trade and sold into slavery throughout the Americas. That would be the equivalent of the entire populations of Chicago, Houston, Los Angeles, and Philadelphia, four of the five largest cities in America, gone with no hope of return. Of the fifty states in the Union right now, forty-three have less than 12.5 million people, according to the most recent US Census. The sheer number of people involved in slavery is nearly impossible to comprehend; so, it is critical to discuss the fate of the individuals who are a part of this mass. Any historical discussion of *Beloved* must begin with the real-life person of Margaret Garner, upon whom Sethe is based. Margaret Garner herself is an immensely troubling figure in history. Garner, like Sethe, was the mother of four children, two boys and two girls. And, like Sethe, Garner was determined to keep her own children from experiencing the degradation she had experienced under slavery (Yanuck 57). Unlike Garner, who did not remain in Ohio after the murder of her first-born daughter, Sethe does. So, *Beloved* allows the reader a glimpse into what might have happened if Garner had stayed. According to Angelyn Mitchell, Morrison identified early slave narratives as the "site of memory" that she used to expand upon her work in *Beloved* (90). Her novelization of this moment in American history lends itself well to a psychological reading of the stress related to the institution of slavery.

This psychological stress was often tied to the separation of mothers from their children. Baby Suggs' own story of the loss of her children is very telling of the hopelessness of motherhood for the slave woman. After losing her first baby to slavery, she made the conscious choice to not remember any of them because they were not truly hers to love. "…[T]here was no bad luck in the world but white people. They don't know when to stop." (Morrison 104). These are the last words of Baby Suggs who has been rendered nearly catatonic at the end of a life, broken by the forced loss of her children. Save for the memory that one daughter loved the burned part of the bread, she had no memories of any one of her children except for Halle who bought her freedom in an attempt to save her life and then became psychologically lost himself as a result of witnessing what happened to his wife, Sethe. According to Baby Suggs, a person was capable of handling a little bit of trouble, but at some point, there needs to be an understanding of when a person has had too much. With the constant sense of loss that would have been experienced by the slaves, this feeling of trauma would be ongoing. In the *International Handbook of Multigenerational Legacies of Trauma*, the editor has included works related to the Holocaust, Japanese American internment, Australian Aboriginal people, and the Vietnam War. Additionally, there is a chapter by William Cross on Black psychology and slavery. He states that the typical "trauma-transcendence-legacy" that is experienced in other groups does not easily apply to the African American experience with slavery (Cross 387). With the other groups, the periods are shorter, unlike the case of American slavery, which lasted for nearly four hundred years. Additionally, African genocide was not going to benefit the economics of slave holders. On the contrary, the propagation of African slaves was an economic boon to their owners. But this propagation was done at the expense of the slave's psyche. Paul D expresses this psychological effect in the following passage, "Anybody white could take your whole self for anything that came to mind. Not just work, kill, or maim you, but dirty you. Dirty you so bad you couldn't like yourself anymore. Dirty you so bad you forgot who you were…." (Morrison 251).

Beloved focuses more than on just the central character, Sethe, who experiences what some readers may interpret as mental instability. Rather, "the novel features a complex of vignettes recalling the exploitations of black female sexuality, abuses and misuses of motherhood." (Mitchell 90). In these vignettes, we find staggering accounts of women who experience mental crises due to loss. For instance, one of the first women Sethe encounters upon arriving in Ohio is the woman in the bonnet, whose food was always full of tears (Morrison 97). This woman has become mute and perpetually cries over her past and present experiences. The reader is left to wonder when this poor woman's crises began. Ironically, although Sethe kills her own daughter, she sees herself as sane when she thinks of others she has met. In this passage, Sethe describes several of these people who have developed "some permanent craziness like Baby Suggs' friend, a young woman in a bonnet whose food was full of tears. Like Aunt Phyllis, who slept with her eyes wide open. […] All she wanted was to go on" (114).

Paul D also describes the mental illness he witnessed: "He saw a witless colored woman jailed and hanged for stealing ducks she believed were her own babies" (Morrison 66). In this sentence, we are again reminded of the overwhelming loss that black women experienced under slavery. This will give students the opportunity to experience pathos as a universal experience by discovering or understanding the depth of the sufferings of women born into this institution.

Trauma inflicted on a race of people that lasted for four hundred years could not simply be over with a proclamation. The reality of having experienced this ongoing separation of families would exact a heavy toll on all affected by it. To effectively prepare students to understand the psychological impact of bondage as presented in Toni Morrison's text, we must provide students the historical context of the setting of the novel. In 1850, the Fugitive Slave Act was made law. This act gave slave owners the right to take back their slaves from states like Ohio, where they had heretofore found refuge as escapees. It is with this background that we may introduce students to the very real person of Margaret Garner and begin discussion of Sethe. This reality under the Fugitive Slave Act made the Ohio

Sethe entered, which was supposed to be a place of milk and honey, into a land of bitterness.

The Fugitive Slave Act and the vitriol with which the slave owners pursued fugitives like Sethe and other escaped slaves provide another viewpoint of how American slavery affected the mental states of those who were involved in it—the enslaved and those holding them captive. Southern whites were also affected by slavery. D. A. Hartman referred to the white Southerners' habit of justifying what contemporary sensibility would describe as heinous through rationalization (1922). Schoolteacher in *Beloved* embodies the worst characteristics of slave owners. His willingness to watch Sethe be brutalized by his nephews, who pin her down and "stole her milk," or simply watch them beat her with a whip while remaining detached is troubling. Still, in spite of this detachment and that of others like him during the antebellum era, schoolteacher gains from slavery. So, he is not interested in whether or not slavery is justified. Like schoolteacher, Mr. and Mrs. Garner, the husband and wife, who are the original owners of Sweet Home, are just as guilty of the sin of slavery. Although Mrs. Garner was very supportive of her slaves, she did nothing to free them, while Mr. Garner "allowed" Halle to work to purchase his mother's freedom. Even those white men who were not slave owners were willing to assist in the enforcement of the Fugitive Slave Act. "When the four horsemen came—schoolteacher, one nephew, one slave catcher and a sheriff—the house on Bluestone Road was so quiet they thought they were too late" (Morrison 148). Just before the murder of Beloved, this scene depicts this posse sent to retrieve Sethe and her children as the Four Horsemen of the Apocalypse. This re-entry of white men into the text makes them seem supernatural, especially with the apocalyptic overtone of their appearance, which—when one considers the act that their entry precipitates—is quite accurate.

Beth McCoy points out that much of the text is centered on how African Americans function with one another in the absence of white people (44). But, the influence of slavery makes their lives fraught with moral ambiguities. The murder of Sethe's infant daughter is only one. Another important one is the fact that Sethe is ostracized by her community for her daughter's murder even though there are many in the community who understand why she did it. Additionally, at least one of their number, Ella, had allowed her own baby to die because she could not bear to nurse the product of her slave owner.

This ambiguity slips beyond merely the moral significance to the character of Beloved herself (Koolish 171). The reader and the characters are never really sure of what Beloved is or is not. Did she really come back from the grave? The community collectively witnessed her death, but is now left wondering if she has truly returned. The characters in the novel and the reader are all left with the troubling realization that escaping slavery and even its abolition did not truly free the person who had been enslaved. The person who had experienced these atrocities would never be able to move on from the acts that had been committed to her, or in the case of Sethe, by her.

Beloved's return seems almost necessary for the healing process of the witnesses to the murder of the "crawling already" baby. The physical rememory of the baby is needed by more than just Sethe and Denver. Everyone in the community who allowed or witnessed the murder of Beloved needed to participate in her return to some extent, just as Americans are obligated to deal with the very real aftermath of slavery.

The impact of slavery is compounded by Sethe's intense motherly love, which Paul D describes as, "too thick" (Morrison 164). Paul D also offers clarity to Sethe regarding the disappearance of her husband, "You said they stole your milk. I never knew what it was that messed him up. That was it…whatever he saw go on in that barn that day broke him like a twig" (68). While learning from Paul D that Halle had witnessed her milk being stolen in the barn was devastating to Sethe, this was one way for her to reach some kind of closure over the disappearance of her husband, Halle. Paul D's description of Halle is a man who was never previously broken by slavery witnessing his wife's violation and being unable to protect her. Halle, like others, was finally susceptible to the oppressive power of that system. For Sethe, schoolteacher and his boys stole one of the only things she had to give her children, milk. This mother's milk was the one pure thing she could offer her children and now even it had been tainted. Because the children's freedom had been denied even from the moment of their conception, Sethe's act is a desperate attempt to give her children yet another fundamental right, their freedom.

While there are great autobiographical slave narratives written by black men, *Beloved* delves into the emotions of the men who experienced American slavery. Most readers of *Beloved* focus on the plight of women during slavery, but Morrison also pays special attention in her narrative to the unique challenges that enslaved men. For Paul D being chained to more than forty others day after day and reduced to utter brutishness was torture. This treatment rendered him incapable of settling down anywhere for very long until he finds Sethe, who makes him want to finally establish a home of his own. In a moment of introspection with Sethe, he discusses the state of a rooster from Sweet Home, who unlike him, is allowed simply to be a rooster. He realizes that the rooster's circumstance was more normal and affirming than his own status.

The novel also identifies other men like Paul D. We are told of Jackson Till who would only sleep under his bed, but never told why. There is also Stamp Paid, a man who is key to Sethe's freedom. His willingness to sacrifice his nephew's coat or perhaps his own freedom if found helping fugitive blacks made up for a life that began as a slave. He is described as a Renaissance man for his time: "agent, fisherman, boatman, tracker, savior, spy" (Morrison 136). Ironically, his kind action would eventually result in the downfall of Sethe and her family, when he brought her the berries that he had picked with "fingertips so gentle not a single one was bruised." These berries would be the catalyst for a feast that would make the townspeople so jealous that they did not warn Baby Suggs and Sethe of schoolteacher and his crew when they came to take Sethe and her children back into slavery.

Although the town abandoned them for twenty years, the women are ultimately capable of forgiveness. Their shared experience of loss brings salvation to the women and to the residents of 124

Bluestone when they come together to exorcise the "ghost." The women's ability to forgive Sethe is based on their sympathy for her, particularly because as former slave women, many of them felt that death would be a reasonable alternative to a life spent in slavery. Together, they come forward to exorcise Beloved from Sethe's home. Many of these women have dealt with overwhelming loss during slavery. As such, they are capable of stepping into the space left by Baby Suggs.

"I will not lose her again. She is mine" (Morrison 214). Transcendent, deep motherly love is at the center of *Beloved*. In this passage, the very basic instinct of loving and protecting and belonging is presented in a poetic form. The repeated line, "you are mine, you are mine, you are mine…." (216) should encourage deep classroom discussion because, here, students can connect with feelings beyond knowing the history of Margaret Garner, or the Fugitive Slave Act, or any of the indignities that they have come to affiliate with slavery. They are presented with the loss that was part of the life and experiences of African Americans during slavery. Indeed, the repeated language highlights the psychological impact and fear of separation that are so prevalent throughout slave narratives, such as *The Narrative of the Life of Frederick Douglass* and *Incidents in the Life of a Slave Girl*.

Hollywood consistently aims horror films at young adults; through Morrison's *Beloved*, we have an opportunity to experience with students a truly horrific truth about American history: slavery. The "ghost" in *Beloved* is quite corporeal; Sethe's baby girl comes from the bridge fully grown, just as slavery, though over, still manifests its presence in American life. Throughout the text, we are shown how American slavery was made so unique by its pattern of consistently separating children from their mothers, and most importantly, babies from their mothers. According to Frederick Douglass, this practice kept children from ever bonding with their mothers. But clearly, this was not the case when one reads in slave narrative after slave narrative the devastation that was felt by women who had to watch their children taken and sold into slavery. Indeed, this emotional aspect of slavery makes it difficult to teach, which is why so many teachers have come to rely on statistics to teach students about slavery. Consequently, they miss an opportunity to teach real empathy by avoiding or refusing to teach a novel like *Beloved* (Endacott & Pelekanos 2). So, while the reader may interpret, at first approach, Sethe's act as insanity, a close study of the circumstances that confronted her makes it clear that for Sethe, killing her baby may have been one of the sanest acts she could have undertaken given her circumstances. She could not allow her children or herself to be returned to that place of horror known as Sweet Home.

Morrison makes it clear that there is a necessity for remembering slavery's horror (George 116). Whether or not this retelling is digestible will entirely be up to the reader and the teacher who, like Stamp Paid, will need to navigate the waters of the text. The greatest consequence of reading this text is the risk of allowing one's self to confront the reality of the type of desperation that would make it possible to justify the violent infanticide that we witness.

Works Cited

Bery, Sadhana. "Multiculturalism, Teaching Slavery, and White Supremacy." *Equity & Excellence in Education* 47.3 (2014): 334–352. *ERIC*. Web. 24 Aug. 2015.

Cross, William E., Jr. "Black Psychological Functioning and the Legacy of Slavery: Myths and Realities." *International Handbook of Multigenerational Legacies of Trauma.* New York: Plenum Press, 1998. 387–400.

Endacott, Jason L. & Christina Pelekanos. "Slaves, Women, and War! Engaging Middle School Students in Historical Empathy for Enduring Understanding." *Social Studies* 106.1 (2015): 1–7. *ERIC*. Web. 24 Aug. 2015.

George, Sheldon. "Approaching the "Thing" of Slavery: A Lacanian Analysis of Toni Morrison's "Beloved." *African American Review* 45.1/2 (2012): 115–130. *Professional Development Collection.* Web. 24 Aug. 2015.

Greenbaum, Vicky. "Teaching *Beloved*: Images of Transcendence." *English Journal* 91.6 (2002): 83–87. *ERIC*. Web. 24 Aug. 2015.

Hartman, D. A. "The Psychological Point of View in History: Some Phases of the Slavery Struggle." *The Journal of Abnormal Psychology and Social Psychology* 17.3 (1922): 261–73. *ProQuest.* Web. 25 Aug. 2015.

Koolish, Lynda. "To Be Loved and Cry Shame: A Psychological Reading of Toni Morrison's *Beloved.*" *MELUS* 26.4 (2001): 169–195. *Proquest.* Web. 25 Aug. 2015.

Krumholz, Linda. "The Ghosts of Slavery: Historical Recovery in Toni Morrison's Beloved." *African American Review* 26.3 (1992): 395–408. *MLA International Bibliography.* Web. 24 Aug. 2015.

Mitchell, Angelyn. "The Metaphysics of Black Female Identity in Toni Morrison's *Beloved.*" *The Freedom To Remember: Narrative, Slavery, and Gender in Contemporary Black Women's Fiction.* New Brunswick, NJ: Rutgers UP, 2002.

McCoy, Beth A. "Trying Toni Morrison Again." *College English* 68.1 (2005): 43–57. *MLA International Bibliography.* Web. 24 Aug. 2015.

Morrison, Toni. *Beloved.* New York: Knopf, 1987.

US Census Bureau. *Statistical Abstract of the United States: 2012.* 131st ed. Washington, DC: US Census Bureau, 2011. PDF. <http://www.ccnsus.gov/library/publications/2011/compendia/statab/131ed.html>.

Yanuck, Julius. "The Garner Fugitive Slave Case." *Mississippi Valley Historical Review* 40.1 (1953): 47 66. *America: History & Life.* Web. 24 Aug. 2015.

Adoption and Persuasion: Raising and Reckoning with Beloved

Sandy Alexandre

> I will call them my people,
> which were not my people;
> and her beloved,
> which was not beloved.
>
> (Romans 9:25, King James Version)

In the epigraph that ushers readers into the text of Toni Morrison's *Beloved* (1987), we are introduced to a set of strangers (not my people) and an outcast of sorts ([she who] was not beloved). The speaker introducing us to these characters seems to suggest that calling these people the obverse of what they have been called and how they have been treated (or how others, including possibly the speaker, have heretofore related to them) can be transformative in some way. The new names that the speaker plans to confer on them shall somehow magically undo the context in which they came to have the names they had before they were bestowed with these new ones. In speech act theory, this transformative call is what is known as a "performative utterance"; it is an utterance that actually acts upon and changes a social reality—like how the sentence "I do," spoken by the couple during a wedding ceremony, legally weds one human being to another, for example. But the change that the speaker implicitly aspires to, it seems to me, is not summoned merely by a new name for either the strangers or the unbeloved; for the most part, it is also activated by the very endearing and welcoming nature of the terms "my people" and "beloved," respectively. In other words, that change in social reality will constitute an act of incorporation that can only be effectuated through loving and inviting language. Furthermore the would-be-incorporated beloved is not a generic archetype to be understood and assimilated in the abstract; in the context of the world Morrison has created in the novel, the newly

---

beloved is a specific character to whom Morrison intentionally gives the proper name Beloved.

The epigraph—seemingly so straightforward in its announcement of a nominative change to come—implicitly raises a series of questions: What are the implications of incorporating or, indeed, of adopting an erstwhile unbeloved person into our lives? And considering how commonplace it has now become, in the reception history of this novel, to read that now beloved-called person as a metaphor for American slavery, how useful and persuasive is the metaphor of adoption to the desired subsequent mental, social, and political activity of accepting and reckoning with the unsavory and unbeloved parts of our American history? Too often, we hear of individuals who insist that "slavery is over," that we, therefore, need to stop harping on about it; or they attempt to absolve themselves from its structural repercussions by assuring us, through loud pronouncements, that they never owned any slaves themselves or that slavery is strictly the province of black people— as if American history is customizable. Too often, we forget, it seems, that *all* of American history is for *all* Americans. As the novel more succinctly summarizes the issue: "Although [Beloved] has claim, she is not claimed" (Morrison 272). Although Beloved—i.e., the history of slavery—holds sway in America, many Americans are disinclined to claim her by acknowledging its sociopolitical reverberations for all of us. What, then, could be the best strategy to persuade these selective adopters—these recalcitrant adopters— to adopt all of American history? Moreover, what could Morrison possibly be saying about the limits of this persuasive strategy of eventually learning and accepting via familial adoption, especially in light of the unbeloved-cum-Beloved with whom she presents us throughout the novel. Because not only is Beloved what one might rightly diagnose as a "problem child"—she is voracious, possessive, demanding, insatiable, and unpredictable—she is also another kind of problem to the family who takes her in: her uncanny ability to make the family reckon with repressed memories actuates, in each of its members, an existential crisis. So not only is the audience to whom Morrison is pitching historical adoption possibly an uncooperative bunch, but so is the history—that is, so is the would-be adoptee, the unbeloved, whom we are all supposed to welcome with open arms and call Beloved now. Morrison grants that some of our hesitation might indeed be warranted.

The informality of the adoption and the ease with which it so readily happens, in the novel, also constitute a lesson regarding who, perhaps, is more inclined to adopt not only America's checkered past, but also the very people who bear its brunt and scars. To consider the relationship between adopting a child and adopting, along with it, the proverbial bath water of American history is to think about the extent to which adoption works (either as a method or a metaphor) for reconciling with the horrors of the past in a way that not only welcomes that history's "warts and all," but also profoundly changes the adoptive parents—that, in fact, makes them better people. How prepared and equipped are we to be American history's loving and capable adoptive parents? If adoption is a reciprocal event, then what performative work can adoption do besides adding on a new member to a family? *Beloved* asks its readers, first, to watch what transpires after one has verbally agreed to adopt a people, a person, or a person who is a synecdoche for those selfsame people. Then it assures readers that even despite the trials and tribulations that accompany adopting such a figure—such a Beloved (and all she stands for)—the ultimate reward that is worth all the trouble is what the adoption offers or returns, which is a newfound self-consciousness for the adopters and a more informed sense of how to relate to history in a way that neither compromises nor revokes our ability to thrive in the present and future. So while some critics, including Rebecca Ferguson and Dana Heller, argue that *Beloved* is about mending broken family ties—that it is "concerned with the healing of the black American family and the reconstruction of kinship structures," I want to argue that the novel is more inclusive about the makeup of the American family, because it attempts to be (and also succeeds at being) a realistic portrayal of how life would be in an American household that has decided not only to embrace the horrifying history of slavery, but also to grapple courageously with the consequences of that adoption (Heller 107).

The magnanimous gesture of the call ("my people, beloved") is deceiving, because it is no mere act of largesse; there are conditions—one of which requires that those who have been called renounce their origins. To change a name is, in effect, to erase the past or, at the very least, to attempt that erasure. The caller seems to think that the past can yield itself to a cosmetic makeover by way of a simple name change. The caller hopes that these name changes can constitute an act of verbal fiat—that saying it will make it so. However, the sincerity of this call to welcome, incorporate, and adopt must take into account the ways in which the identity of the newly welcomed is constituted of pain and suffering. The caller, as benevolent adopter, completely misses the point if he or she thinks that decreeing, dictating, renaming, or calling the shots, as it were, is all that will be required to actuate a seamless and mutually satisfying incorporation. The caller-cum-adopter must take into account the dialogical nature of adoption. The adoptee has a say, too, and that perspective matters to how well or poorly the course of living in the same household with each other will proceed.

Indeed, one of the main factors to be taken into consideration is that the prehistory of any adoptee is one of abandonment, which can be summarized concisely by the expression "I was left." In her oeuvre, Morrison has consistently demonstrated an interest in the psychological lives of orphaned and adopted children and how they, in turn, affect the lives of those around them. In *The Bluest Eye* (1970), Pecola Breedlove is temporarily adopted by the MacTeers when her family experiences a pretty major setback; the three Deweys are all adoptees in *Sula* (1973); the three main characters in *Jazz* (1992), Dorcas, Violet, and Joe, are all orphaned in one way or another; in her short story "Recitatif" (1983) the narrative begins in an orphanage, and the two protagonists' stint there informs the entire course of their lives; finally, in *A Mercy* (2009) the action that motivates the main protagonist's—Florens's—ardent quest for romantic love is what she perceives as her mother's unceremonious abandonment of her. Orphanhood actuates and sustains the novel's plot. Needless to say, Morrison sees narrative potential and value in the figure of the orphan, whether or not that child is eventually adopted in the course of the storyline. Part of what Morrison seems to understand about the orphan/adoptee is its beautifully complicated humanity, both because of and despite its very special brand of neediness. In becoming incorporated into a new space, the adoptee—Beloved—rightly has her own requirements that need to be met. She, in this particular case, is asking not only for love and sentimental affection from the adopter, but also acknowledgment of her past. She is asking that the adopter be equal to the very transformation being proposed. Otherwise, there will be no true transformation without a confrontation with history.

To demonstrate the various ways in which historical incorporation can go horribly awry, Morrison makes the inhabitants of 124 Bluestone Road suffer the consequences of their generous invitation to Beloved to stay with them. Morrison refuses to allow us to assume that such an undertaking could be anything but grueling and consuming in every sense of the word:

> Then the mood changed and the arguments began. Slowly at first. A complaint from Beloved, an apology from Sethe. A reduction of pleasure at some special effort the older woman made […] She took the best of everything—first. The best chair, the biggest piece, the prettiest plate, the brightest ribbon for her hair, and the more she took, the more Sethe began to talk, explain, describe how much she had suffered, been through, for her children, waving away flies in grape arbors, crawling on her knees to a lean-to. None of which made the impression it was supposed to. Beloved accused her of leaving her behind. Of not being nice to her, not smiling at her. She said they were the same, had the same face, how could she have left her? And Sethe cried, saying she never did, or meant to. (Morrison 240–241)

Beloved effectively takes over the house: running Paul D out, claiming everything for herself, and guilt-tripping Sethe into giving her everything she wants. Further evidence of her greed is demonstrated by the fact of her increasingly growing stomach, which at one point in the novel is described as being fat as a "basket" (Morrison 243) and, later, as big as a "winning watermelon" (250). Beloved is an all-consuming presence. History is not being passively incorporated by the family at all; as a matter of fact, history flips the proverbial script and attempts to do the subsuming itself, countermanding the benevolent incorporation of adoption and replacing it with a terrifying version of incorporation as greedy devouring: "[Sethe] sat in the chair licking her lips like a chastised child while Beloved *ate up her life*, took it, swelled up with it, grew taller on it. And the older woman yielded it up without a murmur" (250; my italics).

Morrison grants us access into the bowels of 124 Bluestone, because that journey into the interior of the house is precisely what it will take to understand fully the implications of Sethe's casual decision to adopt Beloved and treat her as though she were, in fact, her murdered daughter come back from the dead. As Morrison writes in the novel's foreword:

> I wanted the reader to be kidnapped, thrown ruthlessly into an alien environment as the first step into a shared experience with the book's population—just as the characters were snatched from one place to another, from any place to any other, without preparation or defense. (2)

We are meant to feel the various affective charges of the environments Morrison presents to us. The grim goings-on at the house are all Beloved's doing, but they also represent Sethe's comeuppance, not necessarily for her crime of infanticide, but for assuming that adoption would be easy—that her dead daughter's ostensible return, embracing that daughter with open arms, her *mea culpa* to Beloved for the crime of infanticide, and her willingness to do anything to make up for that crime would magically fix everything. Morrison is constantly reminding us that such a serious endeavor is not so simple; in order to understand what the characters literally and figuratively have gotten themselves into, we also need to know about the innards…of houses, character's thoughts, and even tobacco tins.

Perhaps this is one reason why, throughout the novel, Morrison makes it a point to showcase the irony inherent in labels, in names. Names only refer to the surface of a person, place, or thing, after all. What better example than the name of the farm—i.e., slave plantation—from which the novel's protagonist, Sethe, eventually makes her escape? Sweet Home is worthy neither of the descriptor "sweet" nor "home." We hear Sethe's opinion about Sweet Home through the narrator: "although there was not a leaf on that farm that did not make her want to scream, it rolled itself out before her in shameless beauty. It never looked as terrible as it was and it made her wonder if hell was a pretty place too. Fire and brimstone all right, but hidden in lacy groves" (Morrison 6). And, if you will recall, even the word Beloved, engraved on the headstone of Sethe's dead baby, is not actually the baby's name, but half of "every word [Sethe] heard the preacher say at the funeral": Dearly Beloved. Names can be deceiving, and words engraved on a headstone tell only half the story. So while a refusal to name the past might be a deterrent to true transformation, even the ability to name it does not, therefore, prove sufficient to effect that full transformation either. As it turns out, naming and calling are not even half of the battle; in fact, they might not be a part of it at all.

When Sethe takes Beloved in, she joins a long line of black people who welcomed fellow black wayfaring strangers into their homes through the network of the Underground Railroad. Many history books recount the benevolence of courageous black people who sheltered fugitive slaves, especially in Ohio, a major route in the Underground Railroad and where the main part of the novel is set. That impulse to embrace the unbeloved or those who were not kin stems from a keen awareness of the dangers that those fugitive slaves were bound to encounter outside the confines of a designated safe space, however temporary. Sethe demonstrates a clear understanding of Beloved's predicament as a black woman out in the world, particularly in a world that, in the context of the novel's temporal setting (1861–1865), has only recently witnessed the abolition of slavery. As Dennis Child reminds us, "*Beloved* underscores that the terror modalities of chattel slavery have not only survived the putatively static borderline of 1865, but have in fact reached their apogee with […] today's prison industrial complex" (274). Abolition of slavery or not, blacks are just not safe from terror and harm in the United States.

Skeptical about Beloved's motives in accepting Sethe's invitation to stay with them at the house, Paul D voices his concern to Sethe, ultimately revealing that he has a strange feeling about her that he can't quite put his finger on. Sethe immediately snaps back at him in Beloved's defense:

> Well, feel this why don't you? Feel how it feels to have a bed to sleep in and somebody not worrying you to death about what you got to do each day to deserve it. Feel how that feels. And if that don't get it, feel how it feels to be a colored woman roaming the roads with anything God made liable to jump on you. Feel that. (Morrison 67)

"Try a little sympathy," Sethe seems to suggest. This unofficial form of adoption by means of Sethe's sympathy for Beloved as well as her good deed of actually housing Beloved offers up a template—a metaphor—for what it means and possibly what it takes to incorporate the past into our daily milieu.

What does it mean for a scene of intra-racial "adoption" to set the example for how and why we all—irrespective of race—should embrace and reckon with the racial violence of American history? To what extent can a paragon of this particular kind of incorporation (historical incorporation, let's call it) be persuasive enough to encourage us to emulate Sethe's incorporation practice? Does the function of role models work in this instance, and how good a role model is Sethe really? To answer these questions requires that we return to the concept of catharsis. According to Aristotle, who seems to have been the first person to use the term in "both the medical and psychological sense" and to apply it to the theater arts, catharsis occurs when one is able to purge oneself of pity and fear by watching those emotions played out on stage by actors (Aristotle 61). The distance between those who witness as audience members and those who act on the stage allows for the kind of redirection or outsourcing that is necessary to the healing process. What I want to suggest in evoking this concept is that Morrison goes one step further by offering characters who not only live the experience of historical incorporation (however messy that experience is), but who also were once a part of our real life history itself. In other words, Morrison closes the distance between real-life readers and fictional characters and, in so doing, refuses the practice of healing vicariously through the tragedy of others to proffer, instead, the practice of empathizing *with*. Morrison privileges empathy over sympathy, and she visualizes this empathy through the language of geography and location:

> If a house burns down, it's gone, but the place—the picture of it— stays, and not just in my rememory, but out there, in the world [...] Where I was before I came here, that place is real. It's never going away. Even if the whole farm—every tree and grass blade of it dies. The picture is still there and what's more, if you go there—you who never was there—if you go there and stand in the place where it was, it will happen again; it will be there for you, waiting for you. (Morrison 36)

The novel's various settings constitute the places that Morrison requires her readers to go, and these places are meant simultaneously to trigger memories (good and bad) while facilitating empathy for those who lived through the experience of those memories. Rememory sounds apocryphal, like wishful thinking. But it is certainly not farfetched to think that Morrison wants rememory to be a reality for all of us, and the source of this experience of rememory is the novel itself. But the question remains: does it really help to be horrified? In other words, how effective can Morrison's scared-straight tactics ever really be in attempting to convince us to incorporate our own history into our daily lives? I think the end of the novel answers this question for us. Even while we are being told that the story we have just finished reading isn't a story to pass on, the name Beloved (along with all that it references and evokes) literally gets the last word of the novel. In many ways, that last word necessarily returns us to the novel's title page—the very beginning of the story. After all that we have been through as readers, Beloved cannot help but insist herself upon us. She is ever-present now; that is a frightening realization, but it is also true, and what Morrison seems to ask of us is that we reconcile ourselves to the truth so that it doesn't come back to torment us.

In the end, Sethe is neither a negative example nor a paragon of how to do historical incorporation. I assert that she represents our fundamentally human example, our Everyman. She tries and errs, coming out of the trial-and-error experience a stronger person, and, in so doing, introduces us to strengths and capacities for resilience that we may never have imagined. Beloved is a truth and reconciliation commission in novel form; it asks us to confront the truth of America's history of enslaving black people by suggesting that we adopt it, that we live with it, that we allow ourselves the opportunity to survive the very experience, precisely because who we have transformed into by the end of that experience are people capable of recognizing and respecting history's power over us, while coming to terms with our important role in ensuring against its repetition.

Recently, Toni Morrison reviewed Ta-Nehisi Coates's beautifully honest and sobering book *Between the World and Me* (2015); in her blurb for the book, she anointed Coates, not only the natural successor to James Baldwin's intellectual prowess, but also to Baldwin's very ability to intellectually stimulate her. An extraordinary compliment indeed, but I dare say that part of this adoration might also stem from the possibility that Morrison recognizes some of the workings of her own brilliant mind in Coates's book as well because the hope that Morrison expresses for us as would-be history adopters—as incorporaters of history— through *Beloved* is what Coates has himself achieved in reckoning with America's sordid past. He writes, "The greatest reward of this constant interrogation, of confrontation with the brutality of my country, *is that it has freed me from ghosts* and girded me against the sheer terror of disembodiment" (Coates 13; my italics). Morrison asks us to be thus strong-minded; she asks that we wrestle with ghosts; she asks that we acknowledge their existence and formidableness lest they continue, tenaciously, to haunt us in ways that we are, at once, aware and unaware. There is more to American history than our desired, sanitized version of it; if we don't adopt that axiom as the truth of our condition, history will not only come back to bite us, it will—as Beloved tried to do—devour us all.

Works Cited

Aristotle. *Poetics*. Trans. S. H. Butcher. New York: Hill & Wang, 1961. Dramabook Ser.

Austin, J. L. *How To Do Things with Words*. Ed. J. O. Urmson & Marina Sbisá. Cambridge, MA: Harvard UP, 1962.

Childs, Dennis. "'You Ain't Seen Nothin' Yet': *Beloved*, the American Chain Gang, and the Middle Passage Remix." *American Quarterly* 61.2 (2009): 271–297.

Coates, Ta-Nehisi. *Between the World and Me*. New York: Spiegel & Grau, 2015.

Heller, Dana. "Reconstructing Kin: Family, History, and Narrative in Toni Morrison's *Beloved*." *College Literature* 21.2 (1994): 105–117.

Morrison, Toni. *Beloved*. New York: Random House, 1987.

Supernatural Elements in Toni Morrison's *Beloved*

Blessing Diala-Ogamba

Literature in general is full of examples of writers who have used the supernatural in their works as a literary device or as a vehicle to convey certain ideas. The theme of the supernatural relates to anything that cannot be explained scientifically or through observation. Supernatural fiction, however, is the incorporation of characters outside the normal world into a work of literature. This type of work includes literature containing elements of horror, magic, ghosts, and sometimes fantasy. For example, works such as Shakespeare's *Hamlet* (1603), *Macbeth* (1606), Charlotte Perkins Gilman's *The Yellow Wallpaper* (1892), Charles Dickens' *A Christmas Carol* (1843), Henry James' *Turn of the Screw* (1898), Thomas Hardy's *The Withered Arm* (1888), Emily Brönte's *Wuthering Heights* (1847) to mention a few, deal with various forms of the supernatural. There are also supernatural elements found in films and art works depending on what the writer or artist hopes to achieve. According to Edward Norbeck, the supernatural is defined as "all that is not natural, that which is regarded as extraordinary, not of the ordinary world, mysterious or unexplainable in ordinary terms" (11). This definition fits the character of the ghost in Toni Morrison's novel, *Beloved*. In this novel, Toni Morrison uses the ghost of Beloved, which is an element of the supernatural, to explore the evil effects of slavery on the protagonist Sethe, her family, Paul D, and the community. The cohabitation of a ghost with normal human beings violates the natural order of things or life; however, Morrison uses the ghost of Beloved to help the characters relive their slavery experiences, heal from their trauma, and to focus better in their future. This essay seeks to analyze through repeated symbols, images, and actions, the frightening supernatural elements in Toni Morrison's *Beloved*. The essay further explores the characters' suffering as they try to satisfy the voraciousness of Beloved, whom Sethe embraces as the reincarnation of her dead daughter.

Writers use supernatural elements in literature to create suspense and also elicit horror or fear in the readers as seen in the novel. *Beloved* is the story of Sethe, a runaway slave who kills her child out of love and also to avoid her being returned to slavery to suffer the same fate as Sethe. The ghost of this baby returns to haunt the family at 124 Bluestone Road, where she begins to live not only with Sethe and her other children, but also within the community whose members have ostracized Sethe and her family.

The opening page of *Beloved* depicts the effects of the baby ghost of Beloved and frames the structure of this novel. This opening page is frightening and reveals to the reader that something ominous is happening in the text:

> 124 is *spiteful*. Full of baby's *venom*. The women in the house knew it and so did the children. For years each put up with the spite in his own way, but by 1873 Sethe and her daughter Denver were its only *victims*. The grandmother, Baby Suggs, was dead, and the sons, Howard and Buglar, *had run away* by the time they were thirteen years old… (Morrison, *Beloved* 3, emphasis mine)

Buglar does not need any more signal to run away, except "looking in the mirror" (which eventually shatters), and Howard's own sign is, "seeing two tiny hand prints appearing on the cake" (Morrison, *Beloved* 3). These are enough sign to frighten normal human beings, especially children, into fleeing from the house. The boys do not need to see:

> *another kettle of chickpeas smoking in a heap on the floor; soda crackers crumbled and strewn in a line next to the door-sill.* Nor did they wait for one of the relief periods; the weeks, months even when nothing was disturbed. Each one fled at once—the moment the house committed what was for him the insult not to be borne or witnessed a second time. (Morrison, *Beloved* 3, emphasis mine)

Buglar and Howard act on their first instinct by running away from the house without looking back. But these signs are small compared to the chaos and havoc caused by Beloved when she comes back later as an adult.

The arrival of Sethe and her children causes envy from the community because of Baby Suggs' influence and protection of her. The community ignores the fact that Sethe is Baby Suggs' daughter-in-law and fails to alert her about the arrival of schoolteacher and the slave catchers, thus leading her to commit infanticide. The members of the community hope that Sethe will be taken back into slavery, but are disappointed and shocked at her prompt reaction. Sethe is only briefly imprisoned and eventually released. Baby Suggs, the community's spiritual leader, is disappointed at the attitude of the community members towards her and her family; therefore, she decides to stay indoors without any communication with anybody. This incident causes her to withdraw to her room where she concentrates on seeing only colors of *blue and grey* until she dies. Gloria Randle opines that "Baby Suggs' withdrawal to her room signals the renunciation of life of faith and community in order to avoid the pain of living" (295–96). The colors of blue and grey symbolize life and death; therefore, Baby Suggs in her depression, hangs between life and death.

After the funeral of Baby Suggs, the community ostracizes Sethe; no one eats her food, symbolizing the extent of what they see as the crime she has committed and the rejection of such action by the society. When the community eventually finds out that 124 Bluestone is haunted, no one stops by to chat or even to visit Sethe and Denver, who, by this time, are its only inhabitants. The people usually run past 124 Bluestone out of fear: "Outside, a driver whipped his horse into a gallop local people felt necessary when they passed 124" (Morrison, *Beloved* 4). Sethe, for her part, insists that Denver does not touch any other person's food, thus isolating her further from the community. This action indicates that she stands by her decision to commit infanticide in order to save her daughter from the trauma of slavery.

Paul D, one of the slaves at Sweet Home who locates Sethe, senses the presence of the ghost when he is invited to stay. His first notices it when he "tied his shoes together, hung them over his shoulders and followed her through the door straight into *a pool of red and undulating light that locked him where he stood*" (Morrison, *Beloved* 8, emphasis mine). Paul D asks Sethe if she has company and she says "Off and on" (8), without realizing the type of company he is referring to. Still feeling the presence of the ghost, Paul D exclaims, "Good God… What kind of evil you got in here?" Sethe replies: It's not evil, just sad. Come in. Just step through" (8). When Paul D steps in, he notices that "*The red was gone but a kind of weeping clung to the air where it had been*" (10, emphasis mine). For him, this is an eerie feeling, which he does not understand, but he senses danger. The coming of Paul D, however, brings excitement and happiness to 124 Bluestone. However, he eventually finds out that there is something ominous in the house, and being uncomfortable with the environment, he shouts out the baby ghost, breaking a table in the process. This is also how the governess in Henry James' *The Turn of the Screw* screams at the ghost of Jesse to make it disappear, since she is the only person who seems to see the ghost. However, in *Beloved*, the disappearance of the baby ghost makes Denver unhappy, and she dislikes Paul D for monopolizing her mother, since she does not have any friends with whom to play.

The disappearance of the baby ghost does not mean that 124 Bluestone is safe. Rather, it is simply a temporary disappearance because the ghost reappears as an adult, waiting for them in front of their house to return from a carnival in town. Thus, Beloved comes back to the house as an adult woman, who does not know where she is going or from where she comes. Upon Beloved's arrival, Sethe notices that her dog, Here Boy, has disappeared. In some traditions, especially in Africa, dogs are known to sense ghosts and evil spirits more quickly than humans. One can, therefore, conclude that the arrival of Beloved causes the disappearance of Here Boy. Without knowing who the young girl is, Sethe takes her in, believing that she is stranded. Beloved asks for water to drink and gulps down quite a lot. They notice that: "Her skin was flawless except for three vertical scratches on her forehead so fine and thin they seemed at first like hair, baby hair before it bloomed and roped into the masses of black yarn under her hat" (Morrison, *Beloved* 51). Her feet and hands are as soft as a baby's. She sleeps for four days, waking and taking only water. She later starts eating sweets. "She gnawed a cane stick to flax and kept the strings in her mouth long after the syrup had been sucked away" (55). Although her actions are strange, Sethe does not do anything. Beloved is described as: "A young woman, about nineteen or twenty and slender, she moved like a heavier one or an older one, holding on to furniture, resting her head in the palm of her hand as though it was too heavy for a neck alone" (55–6).

Of all three characters, only Paul D notices that Beloved is acting strangely, thus he says: "Something funny 'bout that gal... *Acts sick, sounds sick, but she don't look sick. Good skin, bright eyes and strong as a bull*" (Morrison, *Beloved* 56, emphasis mine). Unlike Sethe, Paul D believes that Beloved is not real, but cannot decipher his feeling. However, Denver who is yearning for a sister and company becomes very protective and intensely devoted to Beloved, just like Sethe. For Sethe, Beloved reminds her of her dead child. Like a child, Beloved follows Sethe everywhere, to the envy of Denver and Paul D. Because Beloved at eighteen wants Sethe to herself, Denver is left feeling lonely. Ironically, through her actions, Beloved manipulates both Denver and Sethe. For instance, Beloved constantly asks Sethe why she killed her, and Sethe tells her that she loved her. Dissatisfied with the answer, Beloved wants to punish Sethe for killing her. Beloved is a sad, vengeful ghost because she may have lived a long, happy life had her mother not been enslaved. Krumholz observes that the arrival of "Beloved forces Sethe to confront her past in her incompatible roles as a slave and a mother" (109). Denver, however, wonders how Beloved knew about the stories she manipulates Sethe to tell her, while Paul D recognizes the way Beloved 'shines' and wonders why Sethe and Denver do not notice the 'shine'. For Paul D, he does not see how an adult can glitter like a new born baby, and no one else observes it.

Beloved continues with her spiteful actions as she becomes envious of Sethe's romantic relationship with Paul D. Realizing that Paul D watches her movements and determined not to allow anything to stop her from achieving her revenge, Beloved forces

Paul D out of the main house into the cold room outside the main house. The reader is told that "SHE MOVED HIM" (Morrison, *Beloved* 114, capitalization original). He finds himself first sleeping all night on the rocking chair, then in Baby Suggs' old room, and finally in the store room. Interestingly, Sethe does nothing about it, since the movement does not change their sexual relationship.

> It went on that way and might have stayed that way except one evening, after supper, after Sethe, he lay on a pallet in the storeroom and didn't want to be there. Then it was the cold house and it was out there, separated from the main part of 124, curled on top of two croaker sacks full of sweet potatoes, staring at the sides of a lard can, that he realized the moving was involuntary. He wasn't being nervous; he was being prevented. (Morrison, *Beloved* 116)

It is while in this storeroom that Beloved mesmerizes Paul D and lures him into a sexual encounter. Morrison writes: "Beloved dropped her skirts as he spoke and looked at him with empty eyes. She took a step he could not hear and stood close behind him" (Morrison, *Beloved* 116). From this point on, Paul D obeys Beloved's instructions. The reader is told that "What he knew was that when he reached the inside part he was saying, 'Red heart. Red heart,' over and over again. Softly and then so loud it woke Denver, then Paul D himself." (117). Beloved seduces Paul D to embarrass him and force him out of the house, so that she can have him herself. This incident disturbs Paul D because he feels he has betrayed Sethe by having sex with her guest and determines to tell Sethe about it. However, the presence of Beloved does not allow him to discuss the incident with Sethe because Beloved dominates the house. Her presence weakens the people in 124 Bluestone and makes them unable to think and act properly, or even say the right things. For example, Beloved's presence hinders Paul D's confession of his sexual relationship with Beloved to Sethe. Although Beloved, a living ghost, manipulates their actions, Paul D leaves the house after Stamp Paid shows him the newspaper article about Sethe's infanticide.

As ghost, Beloved continues to plan her revenge. This is clear later, when she becomes so angry at Sethe that she tries to strangle her at the Clearing, but for Denver's intervention. Beloved is angry because she thinks that Sethe wants to abandon her. Consequently, Beloved begins to dominate Sethe through anger; as a result, Sethe starts to waste away, while Beloved grows bigger, symbolized by her enlarging stomach. But, Denver's attitude reveals that she recognizes Beloved as the baby ghost. Although she is also aware that Beloved has had sex with Paul D and then tried to strangle Sethe at the Clearing, she does not say anything to Sethe because she craves the company of Beloved, preferring her presence in the house to Paul D's. Unlike Denver, Sethe believes that Beloved does not remember anything because she was locked up for a long time by a white man who abused her before she finally escaped. Sethe expresses this opinion:

> Denver neither believed nor commented on Sethe's speculations, and she lowered her eyes and never said a word about the cold house. She was certain that Beloved was the white dress that had knelt with her mother in the keeping room, the true-to-life presence of the baby that had kept her company most of her life. And to be looked at by her, however briefly, kept her grateful for the rest of the time when she was merely the looker. (Morrison, *Beloved* 119)

Being intensely devoted to Beloved, Denver tries to protect her, knowing that Sethe, her mother, once committed a heinous crime of infanticide. However, the more time Beloved and Denver spend together, the more Denver begins to realize that Beloved is physically stronger than she leads them to believe. Denver feels that Beloved would eventually sabotage and destroy her family, as well as the community, unless she speaks out. It is only when she steps out of 124 Bluestone, following the advice of Baby Suggs—whose ghost visits her—that she comes to realize that Sethe committed the crime of infanticide out of love for her children. For Sethe, it is better to kill her children than to leave them in the hands of schoolteacher to suffer the same trauma of slavery that she experienced. This reasoning is why Reginald Watson describes Sethe's action as a "love murder committed by Sethe... (157). But, when Denver leaves the house, she is reintegrated into the society; she gets a job to help out in the house, since Sethe no longer works. Stepping out of the house leads to both personal healing for Denver and the community. Through Denver, the community finds out that the dead baby has reincarnated as Beloved to punish Sethe. This is because Denver realizes that nobody will help her "unless she told it—told all of it" (Morrison, *Beloved* 253). Her telling the story gives her strength and rejuvenates her.

With the help of Ella, one of the women in the community, Beloved is exorcised when the women gather together, sing, and pray in front of 124 Bluestone. When Denver tells Janey, one of the women, about Beloved and about her mother being sick, Janey in turn spreads the news to other women. The community knows that "The news that Janey got hold of spread among the other colored women. Sethe's dead daughter, the one whose throat she cut, had come back to fix her. Sethe was worn down, speckled, dying, spinning, changing shapes, and generally bedeviled" (Morrison, *Beloved* 300). Ella naturally is upset at this news because she understands Sethe's predicament, especially since Sethe is not the first woman to have killed her child. Ella does not want to dwell in the past anymore. *For her, whatever Sethe has done in the past must be forgotten.* She lived through slavery and can relate to Sethe's rash decision. Ella herself spent her teenage years in a house where a white father and his son, whom she calls "lowest yet," shared her (256). Sleeping with father and son, Ella has conceived and "delivered, but would not nurse, a hairy white, fathered by 'the lowest'. It lived five days never making a sound. The idea of that pup coming back to whip her too set her jaw working" (258–59, emphasis mine).

Ella does not want to relive this experience, so she decided to help Sethe free herself by exorcising Beloved out of their lives and from the community. In the end, Sethe, Denver, and the community free themselves from the ghost by banishing it. Clearly, the ghost's arrival in the community brings back the past to torture and alienate them from one another. At the same time, it provides them with an opportunity to remember their pasts, forgive themselves, and move on, thus, they heal themselves. Paul D also has an opportunity to return to 124 Bluestone to begin a family with Sethe and Denver.

When Sethe tells Paul D that she has lost her best thing, he tells her, "You are your best thing" (Morrison, *Beloved* 273). Thus, they are able to recover from their pains. For example, Paul D who has been emasculated by the trauma of slavery and has been careful not to become emotionally involved with anybody, now feels free and man enough to be involved with Sethe.

The appearance of a ghost to the living can represent something positive or negative based on stories one has heard or learned. It is also frightening when a ghost comes to live in a household and interacts with the members of a particular household. For example, the ghost of Baby Suggs appearing to Denver is a positive thing because it helps Denver to summon the courage to seek help and tell people about Sethe's failing health and the torment from the ghost of Beloved. On the other hand, Beloved as a ghost is threatening and represents tragedy and death. Although Sethe's intention is to keep the past experiences of slavery in Sweet Home a secret, the appearance of Beloved as a ghost prevents this. It forces Sethe and the community to reflect on their past in order to purge themselves of the trauma of slavery, so as to heal and move forward.

But, Beloved's possession and manipulation of Sethe, Paul D, and Denver can be seen as the acts of an oppressive superior and indeterminable power. According to Niyi Osundare, such a relationship is threatening. He states that "As grasshoppers to wanton boys, so are we to the gods; they kill us for their sport" (qtd. in Jones 104). Because of this manipulation, the human victims are unhappy as seen in *Beloved*. Similarly, the superior force, here Beloved, is represented as an unhappy being or witch. In his article "The Unhappy Woman in Nigerian Fiction: A Mythic Interpretation of the Archetypes," Charles Nnolim, delineates the archetype of the unhappy woman as "femme fatale or dangerous woman, who either denies a man his manhood or acts as a 'castrating' figure who castrates a man by making him a slave to her beauty" (2). Nnolim also suggests that some cultural beliefs—such as the myth of Ogbanje or evil spirit, the changeling, the witch, and all kinds of supernatural divinations—are used to create the unhappy women who are regarded as flawless. Like the women Nnolim describes, Beloved, whose skin is represented as flawless, also seduces Paul D into a sexual act in order to emasculate him. Similarly, she manipulates Sethe to tell her story, which she never planned to divulge, by blurring Sethe's senses, making it difficult for her to shout away Beloved, as both Paul D and the governess in James' *The Turn of the Screw* did.

These archetypes and supernatural horrors are seen in Renaissance and early Victorian writings. For example, in Shakespeare's *Hamlet*, the ghost of King Hamlet, seeking revenge, appears to both the castle guards and to his son. The appearance of the ghost is what sets the plot in motion. In *Macbeth*, not only does the ghost of Banquo appear, but a floating dagger and witches are seen. The forest even moves. The appearances of these ghosts and the movement of the forest symbolize something dangerous and ominous. They suggest that an atrocity has been committed about which the people do not know; therefore, the ghost, in this case, comes to torment the culprit or the killer, just as in *Beloved*. The ghost of Beloved comes back to life as a baby ghost, but she is easily shouted out by Paul D. However, the ghost returns as an adult to torment Sethe because, as a fully materialized figure, she becomes more difficult to expel. Besides, she has more power to control her environment. In the process of this torment, and with the help of the community, Sethe is eventually freed after the exorcism is completed.

Just as in Charles Dickens' *A Christmas Carol*, the ghostly visitors lead the miserly protagonist, Ebenezer Scrooge, on a tour of his past, thus helping him to get a second chance at life. Beloved also helps Sethe get a second chance at life by making Sethe relive her past experiences of slavery. Going back to his pitiable past, his solitary boyhood, where he grieves for his dead sister, Ebenezer Scrooge, recovers his humanity. Through supernatural contact with the settings, experiences, and inanimate objects—from bedposts to buildings—of his former life, Scrooge is made to relive his boyhood and the poverty-stricken life he wants to forget. Similarly, Beloved forces Sethe to relive her slavery days. Scrooge is transformed as an individual and realizes the importance of gift-giving and generosity. Likewise, Sethe is transformed after confronting her past, and this helps in her healing process. The sexual relationship between Beloved and Paul D helps him prove that he is a man. He begins to feel guilty for sleeping with Beloved and thus his real emotions, which he had bottled up in a tin, return.

As in *Beloved*, the activities of ghosts and other supernatural elements are present in a number of works, such as Emily Brönte's *Wuthering Heights* (1847), Wilkie Collins' *The Woman in White* (1859), Daphne Du Maurier's *Rebecca* (1938), John Milton's *Paradise Lost* (1667), and Horace Walpole's *The Castle of Otranto* (1764). The activities of the water spirits, gods, and other ominous creatures are also seen in some African texts such as Elechi Amadi's *The Great Ponds* where the god, Ogbunabali, kills families out of treachery and in *The Slave* where Aleru's death is blamed on the gods. Flora Nwapa also portrays Efuru, her main character in *Efuru*, as flawless because she is the worshipper of Uhamiri, the blue lake goddess. Uhamiri endows Efuru with very good qualities; however, Uhamiri makes her childless, so that Efuru is forced to give up something. Onuorah Nzekwu in *Wand of Noble Wood*, also endows Nneka with beauty and good qualities, but entrusts her to the hands of the deity, Iyi ocha, which tragically ends her life.

The theme of the supernatural is not new in literature. It is found in different types of fiction, drama and also in Children's fantasy. The kind of supernatural elements a writer chooses to use depends on the writer and the message of the work. The delineation of symbols, images and the actions of the ghost in *Beloved* as discussed is evidence that certain unnatural events are beyond human comprehension. The ghost is unnatural and should not cohabitate with the living. Hence, through incantations and exorcism, the ghost is expelled from the realm of the living. At the same time, Sethe's feeling of guilt as well as her confrontation of her past and the horrors of slavery serve collectively to cleanse her and help her heal.

The novel *Beloved* starts in medias res, indicating that Sethe has a lot to remember in her past, but the presence of Beloved stops her from doing so. Beloved makes her relive her painful past and through this, Sethe is able to cleanse herself and become whole again. As Sethe invites Paul D to eat with her and Denver, Sethe tells him:

> I got a tree on my back and a haint in my house, and nothing in between but the daughter I am holding in my arms. No more running… from nothing. I will never run from another thing on this earth. I took one journey and I paid for the ticket, but let me tell you something, Paul D Garner: it cost too much! Do you hear me? It cost too much. Now sit down and eat with us or leave us be. (Morrison, *Beloved* 15)

Paul D, on the other hand, is psychologically damaged, thus he lacks manhood. He is very insecure and constantly questions himself and if he is truly a man. Moreover, his slavery experiences have dehumanized him, and he does not want to remember them. He also experiences anxiety and tremors when he thinks of his past life as a slave before his escape. Consequently, he avoids loving people to keep himself from getting hurt and does not live at a place for too long. However, once he meets Sethe, he stops his wandering life.

Although Beloved manipulates Denver and Sethe by pretending to be fragile, Morrison uses her return as a ghost as a device to make the characters relive their past experiences as slaves, so that they can heal and become whole again. Thus, the character Beloved serves as a symbol of the voiceless victims of slavery, who help to keep the memories of slavery alive in the minds of the ex-slaves. In *Beloved*, the community members remember their experiences because it is important for them to keep the memory of their past alive in order to properly navigate the future. Therefore, the novel serves to make people aware of how slavery not only affected people individually, but also the community as a whole.

Works Cited

Amadi, Elechi. *The Concubine*. London: Heinemann, 1966.

_____. *The Slave*. London: Heinemann, 1978.

_____. *The Great Ponds*. London: Heinemann, 1970.

Brönte, Emily. *Wuthering Heights*. 1848. New York: Barnes & Noble Classics, 2005.

Collins, Wilkie. *The Woman in White*. 1859. New York: Barnes & Noble Classics, 2005.

Dickens, Charles. *A Christmas Carol*. 1843. *The Longman Anthology of British Literature*. New York: Longman, 2002.

Du Maurier, Daphne. *Rebecca*. 1938. New York: Barnes & Noble, 1994.

Gilman, Charlotte Perkins. *The Yellow Wallpaper*. 1892. New York: The Feminist, 1999.

Hardy, Thomas. *The Withered Arm*. 1888. *The Longman Anthology of British Literature*. Ed. David Damrosch. New York: Longman, 2002.

Homer. *The Odyssey*. New York: Penguin, 1991.

James, Henry. *The Turn of the Screw*. London: Macmillan, 1898.

Jones, Eldred Durosimi, ed. *African Literature Today* 11. London: Heinemann, 1980. 104–118.

Krumholz, Linda. "The Ghosts of Slavery: Historical Recovery in Toni Morrison's Beloved." *Toni Morrison's 'Beloved': A Casebook*. Eds. William L. Andrews & Nellie Y. Mckay. New York: Oxford UP, 1999.

Milton, John. *Paradise Lost*. 1667. New York: Barnes & Noble Classics, 2004.

Morrison, Toni. *Beloved*. New York: Knopf, 1987.

Nnolim, Charles. "Mythology of the Unhappy Woman in Nigerian Fiction." *The Critical Theory of African Literature*. Ed. Ernest Emenyonu. Ibadan, Nigeria: Heinemann, 1987 2–18.

Norbeck, Edward. *Religion in Primitive Society*. New York: Harper, 1961.

Nwapa, Flora. *Efuru*. London: Heinemann, 1966.

_____. *Idu*. London: Heinemann, 1970.

Nzekwu, Onuora. *Wand of the Noble Wood*. London: Heinemann, 1971.

Osundare, Niyi. "As Grasshoppers to Wanton Boys: The Role of the Gods in the Noels of Elechi Amadi."*African Literature Today* 11. Ed. Eldred Durosimi Jones. London: Heinemann, 1980. 104–118.

Poe, Edgar Alan. "The Tell-Tale Heart." *Literature: An Introduction to Fiction, Poetry and Drama*. Eds. X. J. Kennedy & Dana Gioia. 1843. New York: Longman, 2002.

Randle, Gloria. "Knowing When to Stop: Loving and Living Small in the Slave World of *Beloved*." *CLA Journal* 41.3 (1998): 290–299.

Shakespeare, William. *Hamlet*. 1603. New York: Signet Classic, 1986.

_____. *Macbeth*. 1606. New York: Norton, 2003.

Walpole, Horace. *The Castle of Otranto*. 1764. Oxford, UK: Oxford World's Classic, 1998.

Watson, Reginald. "The Power of the Milk and Motherhood: Images of Deconstruction And Reconstruction in Toni Morrison's *Beloved* and Alice Walker's *The Third Life of Grande Copeland*." *CLA Journal* 47.2 (2004): 155–162.

Exploring the LIST Paradigm: Reading and Teaching *Beloved*_____

Durthy A. Washington

> One writes out of one thing only—one's own experience. Everything depends on how relentlessly one forces from this experience the last drop, sweet or bitter, it can possibly give. This is the only real concern of the artist, to recreate out of the disorder of life that order which is art.
>
> (James Baldwin)

> One writes out of one thing only, one's own experience as understood and ordered through one's knowledge of self, culture, and literature.
>
> (Ralph Ellison)

The Power of Stories

In February 2001, shortly after accepting a teaching assignment at the US Air Force Academy (USAFA), I was asked to coordinate a Black History Month event for the Academy community. I decided to focus on Black literature. Consequently, I worked with a small group of cadets and prepared them to present dramatic readings of poems or excerpts from longer works by authors such as Langston Hughes, Zora Neale Hurston, Countee Cullen, Paul Laurence Dunbar, and, of course, Toni Morrison. We titled our presentation "Stories That Can Save Us."

Last year I was reminded of that theme when I read the horrific story of fifteen-year old Cassidy Stay who witnessed the murders of her parents and siblings, ages four to thirteen, in their Texas home. In her first interview, Cassidy quotes J. K. Rowling's *Harry Potter and the Prisoner of Azkaban*: "Happiness can be found even in the darkest times, if one only remembers to turn on the light" (qtd. in Bothelo).

John Edgar Wideman contends that "[A] story is a formula for extracting meaning from chaos, a handful of water we scoop up to recall an ocean" (Wideman 58). Clearly, stories *can* save us, if only by enhancing our awareness of the world. But how can we get students immersed in a world of technology and social media to read poems, short stories, and novels? Admittedly, few would choose to read *Beloved* on their own. But most have seen one or more of the recent films about slavery, such as *12 Years a Slave*, Lee Daniel's *The Butler*, *Belle*, and *Django Unchained*. Similarly, few may have read John Ehle's *Trail of Tears* or Homer's *Odyssey*, but most have seen films such as *Avatar* and the *Star Wars* trilogy, whose themes of colonization and the hero's journey, respectively, were inspired by these texts. Moreover, countless music fans enjoyed Lauryn Hill's album *The Mis-Education of Lauryn Hill*, although few, if any, recognized the artist's homage to Carter G. Woodson's *The Mis-Education of the Negro*.

I would argue that if we can help students analyze various modes of popular media they already enjoy—movies, music, video games, graphic novels, etc.—and connect them to literary works, we can help them learn to enjoy the novels we know can enhance, enrich, and transform their lives. The LIST Paradigm provides students with the tools to make that connection.

Asking Significant Questions: Exploring the LIST Paradigm

The LIST Paradigm explores four "keys to culture"—Language, Identity, Space, and Time—that can "unlock" a text for deeper learning. Drawing on James Baldwin's observation that, "The purpose of all art is to lay bare the questions that have been hidden by the answers," it focuses on *critical inquiry*, prompting students to *ask significant questions* designed to foster critical reading from multiple perspectives:

- *Language*: "How does the author contextualize linguistic signs and symbols?"
- *Identity*: "Who are these people and what do they want?"
- *Space*: "How do characters navigate the text's physical, psychological, and cultural landscapes?"
- *Time*: "How does the author manipulate time?"

By incorporating race, culture, and ethnicity into the conventional study of literature, the LIST Paradigm offers a culturally responsive approach to critical reading that combines aspects of both *literary analysis* (exploring the elements of fiction, such as plot, setting, and character) and *literary criticism* (analyzing texts from various perspectives, such as historical, psychological, and archetypal). By helping readers *access* literary works and *analyze* them from multiple perspectives, the LIST Paradigm also prompts them to examine the process of *knowledge construction*. Consequently, by encouraging students to consider unique aspects of multicultural literatures often dismissed or devalued by Western scholars and critics, the LIST Paradigm prompts students to cultivate an awareness of literary styles and narrative structures, which ultimately leads them to write more creative, insightful papers.

In "How Toni Morrison's *Beloved* is Taught in the Schools," Anna Clark lists several reasons teachers cite for assigning the novel. She concludes that, "At best, teaching *Beloved* provokes a reckoning with literary complexity and the deranged American relationship with race. At worst, it's set up for students to decode symbols and extract moral certainties from a novel that refuses it" (Clark).

Clearly, the reader's role is not to "extract moral certainties" from a novel. However, those who seek to understand a text's "literary complexity" must work to "decode [its] symbols," a process that lies at the heart of literary analysis. In fact, ignoring this process is tantamount to teaching *The Wasteland* without exploring Eliot's "Objective Correlative;" teaching *The Odyssey* without discussing the Homeric simile; teaching *A Farewell to Arms* without acknowledging Hemingway's "Code Hero;" or teaching *Macbeth* without noting Shakespeare's use of puns, extended metaphors, and inverted sentence structure. Similarly, teaching *Beloved* without exploring its motifs of flight and fragmentation, its focus on healing rites and rituals, or its emphasis on Black music and Black vernacular would be to discount the novel's cultural roots and dismiss Morrison's goal "to give nourishment" to the Black community.

As illustrated in the following pages, the LIST Paradigm encourages readers to not only "decode [the] symbols" in literary works, but to connect with texts from multiple perspectives.

Introducing the Novel

Having taught *Beloved* at the US Air Force Academy (USAFA) over the past sixteen years as part of my "Introduction to Literature" course, I have learned that the best way to prompt students to engage with the text is to provide them with some background and context for the novel, alert them to some of its challenges—such as its complex themes, fragmented narrative structure, and graphic depictions of sex and violence—and then encourage them to make their own discoveries through close reading. Consequently, I introduce some major contexts for *Beloved*, such as African and African American folktales, rites, and rituals; the Middle Passage; slave narratives; African American music; the Bible; the Western literary canon; cultural myths (e.g., the Hamitic Myth, the Myth of White Supremacy), and, of course, the "peculiar institution" of slavery.

We also note that the novel raises several *significant questions*, which provide a basis for our critical reading:

- What is history? Whom do we entrust to document our history?
- What is the relationship between history and memory? Between Afrocentric and Eurocentric worldviews?
- How do people subjected to bestial treatment maintain their inherent humanity?
- How do survivors of traumatic experiences negotiate the recovery process?
- What is "the legacy of slavery"?

By the time they encounter *Beloved*, my students have already been introduced to the LIST Paradigm. They have also read several poems and short stories, including Dudley Randall's "Roses and Revolution," Flannery O'Connor's "A Good Man Is Hard to Find," Alice Walker's "Everyday Use," and James Baldwin's "Sonny's

Blues." Therefore, they have been exposed to concepts such as color symbolism, biblical allusions, the power of music, the legacy of slavery, and the quilt as a metaphor for African American culture. They have also been exposed to war literature, such as Brian Turner's *Here, Bullet* and Tim O'Brien's *The Things They Carried*, which feature graphic scenes of violence and portray soldiers struggling to cope with trauma and survival, themes that resonate throughout *Beloved*. Linking *Beloved* (generally defined as a historical novel) to war literature also underscores an important point: Even though the novel is set in the post-Civil War era, its characters remain embroiled in a Race War that continues to this day.

To begin our exploration of *Beloved*, we preview the novel, discuss it as Morrison's monument to enslaved Africans, and note its connection to the Margaret Garner story. We also watch the trailer from the film and, if time permits, a short clip from *12 Years a Slave*. I then give students time to read *Beloved* outside of class in preparation for a close re-reading in class, guided by the LIST Paradigm.

As illustrated in the following pages, the components of the LIST Paradigm often overlap. I discuss them as separate "keys to culture" to emphasize the significance of each component as a contributing factor to the overall concept of culture.[14]

LANGUAGE: "How does the author contextualize linguistic signs and symbols?"

Language creates our reality and shapes our ability to construct myths and images that reframe the past, transform the present, and help us envision the future. Generally defined as an organized pattern of signs and symbols we use to communicate with one another, language comprises the basis of culture, be it feminist culture, military culture, prison culture, youth culture, GLBTQ culture, or Black culture. Within these contexts, we can speak of body language, sign language, or racist language. Similarly, we can discuss the language of music, the language of violence, the language of humor, and the language of love. We can also identify stylistic elements that characterize an author's writing style, such as diction, syntax, dialogue, dialect, repetition, and literal vs. figurative language (symbols, metaphors, irony, etc.).

According to Morrison, "The most valuable point of entry into the question of cultural (or racial) distinction… is its language—its unpoliced, seditious, confrontational, manipulative, inventive, disruptive, masked and unmasking language." ("Unspeakable Things Unspoken" 35). She reiterates this point in her *Paris Review* interview, when she asserts that black writers writing in a world dominated by white culture must "alter language… to free it up… [and] Blast its racist straitjacket" (372).

To begin our exploration of language in *Beloved*, we discuss the motifs of flight and fragmentation. We also highlight the language of music, a recurring motif threaded throughout the novel. (Examples include allusions to Psalm 124, Sethe's lullabies, and Hi Man's song, as well as frequent references to the Blues, spirituals, and work songs.)

We then focus on stylistic elements such as the following:

Color Symbolism: In commenting on the use of color in *Beloved*, Morrison states, "The painterly language of *Song of Solomon* was not useful to me in *Beloved*. There is practically no color whatsoever in its pages…" (33). Even so, color symbolism plays a critical role in the novel. *Song of Solomon* opens with a dramatic scene enacted against a canvas of red, white, and blue, which forms a backdrop for the novel and establishes it as a uniquely American story. Although the opening scene of *Beloved* is much more subdued, astute readers will recognize a similar canvas created by "the pool of red undulating light" and the "white stairs" in the house on *Blue*stone Road. Other examples of color symbolism include various plays on black and white, red, green, orange, and pink.

Nature Imagery: The most prominent example of nature imagery in *Beloved* is the tree which, from a traditional perspective, is "a symbol of immortality." But in the novel, the narrator focuses on the "tree" on Sethe's back. Consequently, the tree emerges not as "a symbol of immortality," but as a scar and a site for lynchings. By thus upsetting the "natural" order of the universe, Morrison offers a scathing indictment of the "natural" institution of slavery. She also introduces the recurring image of the scars and marks used to identify enslaved Africans, from the slavemaster's brand ("the hot thing") to the "stain of blackness" that marks them as "inferior."

Signifying: Generally defined as the art of indirect discourse, signifying enables the powerless to wield the power of language. As Ashraf Rushdy points out, "Through Beloved [Morrison] signifies on history by resurrecting one of its anonymous victims" (47). She also signifies on the Margaret Garner story by portraying Sethe as a fictionalized version of Margaret and by using the Garner name to identify the "benevolent" slave holders at Sweet Home.

Code Switching: Like signifying, *code switching*—redefining terms and concepts or switching back and forth between two languages or modes of discourse—challenges and undermines the hegemony of dominant power structures. Morrison uses code switching primarily to demolish racist stereotypes. For example, she portrays Sixo, "the wild African" not as an uncivilized "black savage," but as the most intelligent and compassionate of the Sweet Home men. She also portrays Lady Jones not as a "tragic mulatto" who yearns to be white, but as a strong, independent black woman who despises her "gray eyes and yellow woolly hair" and embraces her African heritage by marrying "the blackest man she could find, [having] five rainbow-colored children and [sending] them all to Wilberforce, after teaching them all she knew right along with the others who sat in her parlor" (Morrison, *Beloved* 291).

Racist Language (Calibanic Discourse): In their book *Racism & Psychiatry*, Alexander Thomas and Samuel Sillen note that the stereotype of blacks as "uniquely fitted for bondage" was so deeply ingrained in whites that runaway slaves were often diagnosed with *drapetomania*, the flight-from-home madness, while slaves who refused to submit to their "masters" were said to suffer from *dysaesthesia Aethiopica*, a disease "which caused them to pay no attention to the rights of property...slight their work...[and] raise disturbances with their overseers" (Stampp 1956, qtd. in *Racism and Psychiatry* 2)

In *Black Male Fiction and the Legacy of Caliban,* James W. Coleman defines this racist rhetoric as "Calibanic discourse," an allusion to Shakespeare's Caliban, "the untamed force of natural man." As he explains:

> Calibanic discourse is the perceived history and story of the black male in Western culture that has its genesis and tradition in language and nonlinguistic signs. It denotes slavery, proscribed freedom, proscribed sexuality, inferior character, and inferior voice. In summary, the black male is the slave or servant who is the antithesis of the reason, civilized development, entitlement, freedom, and power of white men, and he never learns the civilized use of language. His voice is unreliable; his words fail to signify his humanity. He also preys on civilization and represents bestial, contaminating sexuality. (3)

In *Beloved*, this "bestial, contaminating sexuality" is attributed to schoolteacher's nephews, thereby reversing the racist stereotype of "savage" blacks and "civilized" whites. But schoolteacher's contempt for the Sweet Home men best exemplifies the dehumanizing violence of racist language. As Paul D recalls:

> It was schoolteacher who taught them… [that] they were only Sweet Home men at Sweet Home. One step off that ground and they were trespassers among the human race. Watchdogs without teeth; steer bulls without horns; gelded workhorses whose neigh and whinny could not be translated into a language responsible humans spoke. (Morrison, *Beloved* 147–48)

Sermonic Language: Dolan Hubbard defines sermonic language as "spiritually and emotionally charged symbolic language…molded by the black experience—one whose central impulse is survival and resistance" (6). As he points out, in the Black community, it is the preacher who helps people "assert their rights to a genuine existence" and "gives them a sense of being at home in the universe" (11). Morrison illustrates the power of sermonic language through Baby Suggs's sermon in the Clearing, during which she rejects Christianity's justification for slavery and its promise of a better life in the "hereafter." Instead, she urges her congregation to "Love your heart. For this is the prize" (104).

Language Validation: One of Morrison's most powerful statements concerns the validation of a speaker's native language. She illustrates this concept through Sixo, whom the narrator describes as "speaking another language." However, instead of devaluing or degrading Sixo's language by "translating" it into dialect or "broken" English, the narrator recounts events at Sweet Home as they relate to Sixo's language. For example, Paul D recalls sitting under the trees "with Sixo, who was gentle then and still speaking English" (Morrison, *Beloved* 25) and we learn that Sixo [danced] among trees at night... before he stopped speaking English because there was no future in it" (30). In this way, Morrison not only validates Sixo's native language, but also privileges it over English. By emphasizing Sixo's refusal to renounce his African culture and become "civilized," she also signifies on the racist notion of blacks "reverting to type."

IDENTITY: "Who are these people and what do they want?"

With the current emphasis on a multicultural society, American identity has undergone countless permutations, especially for "hyphenated" Americans (Mexican-American, Jewish-American, African-American, etc.) who often struggle to validate their status as "American," while maintaining their cultural and historical roots. In many respects, the focus on fluid, shifting, or multiple identities has complicated the issue of identity construction, deconstruction, and reintegration. A focus on identity also enables students to examine how issues such as race, gender, and ethnicity impact identity and self-image, and to explore the power of *literary archetypes* (the ancestor, the classic hero, the Trickster) and *cultural stereotypes* (Uncle Tom, the "bad nigger," the tragic mulatto).

To open our discussion of Identity in *Beloved*, we reflect on Morrison's observation concerning the psychological damage inflicted by the loss of names:

If you come from Africa, your name is gone. It is particularly problematic because it is not just your name but your family, your

---

tribe. When you die, how can you connect with your ancestors if you have lost your name? That's a huge psychological scar. (LeClair 126)

Beloved's experience exemplifies this dilemma. As the narrator explains at the end of the novel, "Everybody knew what she was called, but nobody anywhere knew her name. Disremembered and unaccounted for, she cannot be lost because no one is looking for her, and even if they were, how can they call her if they don't know her name?" (Morrison, *Beloved* 323)

We also consider Valerie Smith's comment concerning Morrison's characters who, she claims, "achieve autonomy and a sense of identity only to the extent that they can understand and name themselves in relation to a social unit, be it family, neighborhood, or town" (122).

We note that this Afrocentric focus on community contradicts the Eurocentric focus on the independence of the individual. Consequently, instead of identifying with Descartes's assertion, "I think, therefore I am," Morrison's characters identify with the philosophy of African historian John Mbiti: "I am because we are, and since we are, therefore I am" (qtd. in Hord & Lee, 14).

To further illustrate this concept, we focus on characters such as the following:

Sixo: When we first encounter Sixo, we may picture him as the "Wild African Savage" exhibited at the circus. We may be amused by his outlandish behavior, see him as a caricature, and dismiss him as "almost cartoonishly heroic" (David 117). But as we observe his actions and his interactions with Halle, Sethe, Paul D, and Patsy, his "30-mile woman," we begin to see him as a man who refuses to compromise his dignity and humanity by adapting to his brutal environment. Ultimately, Sixo, who sacrifices himself for his friends and family, emerges as a composite character who embodies traits of the Black folk hero (such as High John the Conqueror and Stagolee) as well as the Trickster (often portrayed in black folktales as Br'er Rabbit). But Sixo is also Nat Turner, the rebel slave, and Madison Jefferson, the protagonist of Frederick Douglass's *The Heroic Slave,* as well as shaman/healer, griot/storyteller, and spiritual guide.

Significantly, just as Sixo's name (6-0) links him to the "Sixty Million and more" victims of the Middle Passage, his "flame-red tongue"(Morrison, *Beloved* 25) links him to Stamp Paid's "red ribbon," Paul D's "red heart," and the "pool of red undulating light" that is Beloved.

Schoolteacher: Schoolteacher personifies scientific racism, which launched the myth of white supremacy and its devastating impact on blacks who internalized its dehumanizing message. As Carter G. Woodson points out in *The Mis-Education of the Negro*, "When you control a man's thinking, you do not have to worry about his actions" (xiii). In "A Talk to Teachers," James Baldwin echoes Woodson's statement, noting that "any Negro who is born in this country and undergoes the American educational system runs the risk of becoming schizophrenic" (326). Ultimately, it is schoolteacher's recording of the "human" and "animal" traits of Sethe's children in his notebook that prompts Sethe's escape.

Mr. Garner: Mr. Garner, who refers to his male slaves as "men," represents the humane slavemaster who evokes the myth of enslaved Africans treated "like one of the family." Morrison highlights the absurdity of this myth as well as the god-like power wielded by whites over blacks when Mr. Garner dies and the Sweet Home men become schoolteacher's "property."

In his parody of the slave narrative, *Flight to Canada*, Ishmael Reed signifies on the notion of the kind slavemaster with his depiction of Mr. Davis. As his trickster protagonist, Raven Quickskill, points out:

> Davis' slaves are the only ones I know of who take mineral baths. And when hooped skirts became popular he gave some to the slave women, and when this made it awkward for them to move through the rows of cotton, he widened the rows. (24)

SPACE: "How do characters navigate the text's physical, psychological, and cultural landscapes?"

How characters interact with physical and psychological space can help reveal or conceal their identities. Do they have "room to bloom" or are they locked out or hemmed in? Do they assertively claim their space, or are they somehow constrained or limited by it?

Exploring the concept of Space focuses on issues such as the process of creating and transforming physical/psychological as well as personal/public space, examining the role of the "Outsider" in literature, and exploring the concept of *cultural landscapes* (the virtual spaces occupied by people who share a common history).

We begin our exploration of Space in *Beloved* with a map of the US showing "free states" and "slave states." We note, however, that for blacks, the definition of "free states" was meaningless, as demonstrated in the Dred Scott Case (1857) when the Supreme Court ruled that even though Scott lived in the free state of Illinois, he had to be returned to the slave state of Missouri after his "master" died. When Scott tried to file an appeal, the Court denied it, declaring that blacks "are so far inferior that they have no rights a white man is bound to respect" (qtd. in Mullane 132).

We also note physical spaces that have special meanings for characters, such as Sweet Home, the house at 124 Bluestone Road, the Clearing, the Arbor, the cornfield, and the prison yard.

In his essay, "The Psychological Reactions of Oppressed People," Richard Wright contemplates the psychological space between Blacks and their white oppressors by drawing on Nietzsche's notion of "Frog Perspectives" used "to describe someone looking from below upward…who feels himself lower than others" (6). In *Beloved*, Paul D experiences this sensation for the first time after he is recaptured by schoolteacher and learns his true "worth." However, Morrison provides us with one of the most powerful examples of psychological space in her introduction to the stream-of-consciousness chapters [20 through 23] that culminate in the trio of voices that merge with the voices of their drowned ancestors: "When Sethe locked the door, the women inside were *free at last* [my emphasis] to be what they liked, see whatever they saw and say whatever was on their minds" (*Beloved* 235).

TIME: "How does the author manipulate time?"

Beloved challenges the Western, Eurocentric view of history as a linear profession of "significant" events marked by wars and leading towards "progress." Instead, it presents an Eastern, Afrocentric view of history as a continuous cycle of events marked by the experiences of individuals. From this perspective, history is not dead; it is alive in the present and provides a vital key to the future. The late South African singer Miriam Makeba summarizes these perspectives as follows:

> When a Westerner is born, he or she enters a stream of time that is always flowing. When a point in life is passed, it is finished. When a Westerner dies, he leaves the stream, which flows on without him. But for us, birth plunges us into a pool in which the waters of past, present, and future swirl around together. Things happen and are done with, but they are not dead. After we splash about a bit in life, our mortal beings leave the pool, but our spirits remain. (380)

Exploring the concept of Time focuses on issues such as exploring "history" within the context of culture; exploring the relationships between real time and narrative time; and exploring rhetorical devices such as flashbacks, foreshadowing, and stream-of-consciousness, as well as allusions to songs, stories, or films that evoke a certain era, or references to notes and letters, dreams and visions, or memories of significant events.

To address the issue of Time in *Beloved*, we begin with the opening words of Morrison's Nobel Lecture: "Once upon a time." After reflecting on the imagery associated with these words and their origin in fairytales—stories traditionally set in a world beyond time—we are better able to grasp Morrison's assertion that:

> [In *Beloved* there is] No compound of houses, no neighborhood, no sculpture, no paint, *no time* [my emphasis] especially no time because memory, pre-historic memory, has no time. There is just a little music, each other and the urgency of what is at stake. Which is all they had. ("Unspeakable Things" 33)

With this in mind, we can help students understand the novel's complex narrative structure, which consists primarily of a fragmented and disjointed chronology.[5] After exploring this structure with my students, I encourage them to construct a timeline of key events in the novel. Through this exercise, we discover that the actual events in *Beloved*, which focus primarily on Sethe's life, span approximately two years, from Paul D's arrival at 124 Bluestone Road in the summer of 1873 to Beloved's exorcism in the summer of 1875. But Sethe's life is only part of the story. Through several flashbacks to the Middle Passage and to events such as Sethe's arrival at Sweet Home, her marriage to Halle, the birth of their children, and Beloved's death, the novel also chronicles the history of blacks in America, thus providing global and historical perspectives of the origins and cultures of African peoples.

Carter G. Woodson contends that, "If a race has no history, it has no worthwhile tradition. It becomes a negligible factor in the thought of the world and it stands in danger of being exterminated" (*BrainyQuote*). In *Beloved*, Morrison reconstructs the history of slavery in the United States. She also invites readers to participate in the process of knowledge construction by reconstructing significant events excluded from history, a process that can be viewed as a literary parallel to the historical period of "Reconstruction" (1867–1877). For example, the scene in which Paul D, Sethe, and Denver see the "Wild African Savage" on display at the circus may seem outrageous. But it alludes to the case of "a young African named Ota Benga—a so-called 'pygmy'—exhibited in an iron monkey house cage" at the Bronx Zoo during September 1906. (Newkirk). Similarly, one could argue that Paul D's horrific experience in the prison camp in Alfred, Georgia, mirrors Ma'am's experience on the slaveship during the Middle Passage. Consequently, we realize that though the setting has changed, the brutality towards blacks continues.

We also note that when Paul D reflects on his friendship with Sixo, he recalls that "Time never worked the way Sixo thought, so of course he never got it right" (Morrison, *Beloved* 25). However, when Sixo develops his plan for the escape from Sweet Home, he shrewdly calculates the time required for the plan to succeed. It fails not because he miscalculates the time, but because Paul A and Paul F waste precious time wondering whether they are willing to assume the risks involved.

In summarizing the novel, we discuss how Morrison weaves together the various strands of the narrative to trace the history of Sethe's family through four generations. We also note that through her characters, Morrison provides a voice for the thousands of enslaved Africans who could not speak for themselves.

Conclusion: Changing Lives through Literature

One of the most gratifying aspects of teaching literature through the LIST Paradigm is the positive feedback I receive from my students on their reading experiences. In fact, even students who generally do not read or who merely skim texts to retrieve enough information to discuss the plot and characters become actively engaged in the reading process.

Ultimately, teaching *Beloved* alongside texts such as Euripides's *Medea*, Shakespeare's *Othello*, and Junot Díaz's *The Brief Wondrous Life of Oscar Wao* offers students an opportunity to explore a complex and powerful work that engages both historical and contemporary themes and concepts through the lens of culture. Consequently, it compels them to expand their perspective of literary genres, explore the process of knowledge construction, and write more thoughtful, insightful papers.

In describing her experience of reading *Beloved*, *Poets & Writers* editor Mary Gannon recalls:

> When I reached the final chapter... I read it out loud slowly, savoring each word, my voice breaking along the way... the power of the story, its moral complexity—and Morrison's beautiful writing—had transported me beyond myself. I felt like I had lived it, and when it was over, that *I had been changed by it...* [my emphasis](6)

Ultimately, this is the kind of reading experience we desire for our students. By providing them with four "keys to culture" that can help them "unlock" complex literary works through the LIST Paradigm, we can bring them one step closer to that ideal.

Notes

1. Within the context of this paper, I focus on Wade Noble's definition of culture as "A vast structure of language, customs, knowledge, ideas, and values, which provide a people with a general design for living and patterns for interpreting reality. I also cite Anil Ramdas's statement that "Culture is the observation of the outsider." Implicit in this definition is that "when you live inside it, you do not see a culture, but only a chaos of styles."

2. My research incorporates Geneva Gay's definition of culturally responsive teaching: "Using the cultural knowledge, prior experiences, frames of reference, and performance styles of ethnically diverse students to make learning encounters more relevant and effective for them."

3. James Banks cites "five dimensions" of multiculturalism: (1) Content integration, (2) Knowledge construction; (3) Equity pedagogy, (4) Prejudice reduction, and (5) Empowering school culture & school structure. The LIST Paradigm focuses primarily on two of these dimensions: Knowledge construction and Equity pedagogy.

4. For more information on the LIST Paradigm, see "Teaching Ernest Gaines's *A Lesson Before Dying. Academic Exchange Quarterly.* Summer, 2008: 238–244, and "Teaching *Song of Solomon*: Exploring the LIST Paradigm." *The Fiction of Toni Morrison: Reading and Writing on Race, Culture, and Identity.* Ed. Jami L. Carlacio. Urbana, IL: National Council of Teachers of English, 2007. 55–64.

5. For more information on narrative structure, see Diane Lefer's "Breaking the 'Rules' of Story Structure." *The Best Writing on Writing.* Ed. Jack Heffron. Cincinnati: Story Press, 1994. 11–19.

Works Cited

Baker, Houston A., Jr. "Black Folklore and the Black American Literary Tradition." *Long Black Song.* 1972. Charlottesville: U of Virginia P, 1990. 18–41.

Baldwin, James. "A Talk to Teachers." 1963. *The Price of the Ticket: Collected Non-fiction 1948–1985*. New York: St. Martin's, 1985. 325–332.

Bothelo, Greg. "Sole survivor in Texas shooting looks for hope amid her horror." *CNN*. Cable News Network/Turner Broadcasting, 14 July 2014. Web. 26 Oct. 2015. <http://www.cnn.com/2014/07/12/justice/texas-shooting/>.

Clark, Anna. "How Toni Morrison's *Beloved* Is Taught in Schools." *The Daily Beast*. The Daily Beast Company LLC, 4 Oct. 2012. Web. 26 Oct. 2015. <http://www.thedailybeast.com/articles/2012/10/04/how-toni-morrison-s-beloved-is-taught-in-schools.html>.

Coleman, James W. *Black Male Fiction and the Legacy of Caliban*. Lexington: UP of Kentucky, 2001.

David, Ron. *Toni Morrison Explained*. New York: Random House, 2000.

Douglass, Frederick. "The Heroic Slave." 1853. *Three Classic African American Novels*. Ed. William L. Andrews. New York: Penguin, 1990. 23–69.

Gannon, Mary. "Editor's Note: Summer Reading." *Poets & Writers*. (July/August 2006): 6.

Harris, Middleton A. *The Black Book*. New York: Random House, 1974.

Hord, Fred Lee & Jonathan Scott Lee, Eds. *I Am Because We Are: Readings in Black Philosophy*. Amherst: U of Massachusetts P, 1995.

Hubbard, Dolan. *The Sermon and the African American Literary Imagination*. Columbia: U of Missouri P, 1994.

Krumholz, Linda. "The Ghosts of Slavery: Historical Recovery in Toni Morrison's *Beloved*." *African American Review* 26.3 (Fall 1992): 79–95.

LeClair, Thomas. "The Language Must Not Sweat: A Conversation with Toni Morrison." *Conversations with Toni Morrison*. Ed. Danille Taylor-Guthrie. Jackson: UP of Mississippi, 1994. 119–128.

Makeba, Miriam. "Spirit." *My Soul Looks Back, 'Less I Forget: A Collection of Quotations by People of Color*. Ed. Dorothy Winbush Riley. New York: HarperCollins, 1991. 380.

Morrison, Toni. "The Art of Fiction." 1993. *'The Paris Review' Interviews, Vol. II*. New York: Picador, 2007. 355–394.

_____. *Beloved*. 1987. New York: Vintage, 2004.

_____. "Nobel Lecture." *NobelPrize.org*. Nobel Media AB, 7 Dec.1993. Web. 26 Oct. 2015. <http://www.nobelprize.org/nobel_prizes/literature/laureates/1993/morrison-lecture.html>.

_____. "The Site of Memory." *Inventing the Truth: The Art and Craft of Memoir*. Ed. William Zinsser. New York: Houghton Mifflin, 1998. 183–200.

_____. "Unspeakable Things Unspoken: The Afro-American Presence in American Literature." *Michigan Quarterly Review* (Winter 1989): 1–34.

Mullane, Deirdre, ed. "The Case of Dred Scott." *Crossing the Danger Water: Three Hundred Years of African American Writing*. New York: Doubleday, 1993. 132–33.

Newkirk, Pamela. "When the Bronx Zoo Exhibited a Man in an Iron Cage." *CNN*. Cable News Network/Turner Broadcasting, 3 Jun. 2015. Web. 26 Oct. 2015. <http://www.cnn.com/2015/06/03/opinions/newkirk-bronx-zoo-man-cage/>.

Reed, Ishmael. *Flight to Canada*. New York: Atheneum, 1989.

Roberts, John W. *From Trickster to Badman: The Black Folk Hero in Slavery and Freedom*. Philadelphia: U of Pennsylvania P, 1990.

Rushdy, Ashraf H.A. "Daughters Signifyin(g) History: The Example of Toni Morrison's *Beloved*." *Toni Morrison's Beloved: A Casebook*. Ed. William L. Andrews & Nellie Y. McKay. New York: Oxford UP, 1999. 37–66.

Smith, Valerie. "Toni Morrison's Narratives of Community." *Self-Discovery and Authenticity in Afro-American Narrative*. Cambridge: Harvard UP, 1987. 122–153.

Thomas, Alexander & Samuel Sillen. *Racism & Psychiatry*. Secaucus, NJ: Citadel Press, 1976.

Wideman, John. "Writers' Forum: Language and the Writer." *Ousmane Sembéne: Dialogues with Critics and Writers*. Ed. Samba Gadjigo, et al. Amherst: U of Massachusetts P, 1993. 45–80.

Woodson, Carter G. *The Mis-Education of the Negro*. 1933. Trenton, NJ: Africa World Press, 1990.

_____. "Carter G. Woodson." *BrainyQuote.com*. Xplore Inc, 2015. Web. 23 Sept. 2015. <http://www.brainyquote.com/quotes/quotes/c/cartergwo230679.html>.

Wright, Richard. "The Psychological Reactions of Oppressed People."
    White Man, Listen! 1957. New York: Harper Perennial, 1995. 1–43.

Literary Analysis of Toni Morrison's *Beloved*: An Introduction for Students_____

Nicole M. Coonradt

Literary analysis can be anxious for students who may wonder, "What can I possibly say about this text that will be interesting to readers other than me... and that hasn't already been said by those far more capable than I?" Yet the smallest insight can be affective for students and their peers once they are better equipped to share their thoughts in writing. Learning the ropes is mostly about entering the ongoing conversations that make texts more relevant to readers, and the opportune moment to dive in is when a reader feels invested intellectually and emotionally. Literary analysis is about entering a discourse community—with all of its linguistic and rhetorical strategies—and becoming aware of the requisite forms and formats. As Graff and Birkenstein explore in their valuable *They Say/I Say* (Norton 2014), once students realize that they are more capable of academic writing than they previously feared—given the right strategies—not only is the process less intimidating, it is actually enjoyable. What is more, students already have great ideas when they read texts, especially one as profoundly affective as Toni Morrison's *Beloved*. Indeed, one cannot really read *Beloved* without being deeply moved. At issue for students are the lack of tools and self-assurance to articulate their ideas more fully. This essay seeks to use literary analysis to get students thinking critically about Morrison's *Beloved*. Morrison's text provides canonically fertile ground for what I like to call budding literary detectives, but will likewise challenge every reader. *Beloved* not only stays with readers, but also yields up new insights with every additional reading. It is little wonder it received the Pulitzer Prize for Fiction in 1988, just as Morrison's *corpus*, the body of her work, subsequently received the Nobel Prize for Literature in 1993.

Because students are learning how to make their way into various discourse communities in the academy—each with its own specific requirements—literary analysis is a good way to practice joining academic discussions, and Morrison's richly meaningful *Beloved* is an ideal proving ground. Literary analysis of any work must be based on the text. In essence, what one does in literary analysis is say, "I have read this text, and I think it can mean X" or, "This is one way of understanding based on the text." Students should be aware that even if a reading seems very obvious to them, it may be less so to others. Their job is to share their findings in an attempt to help other readers see their analysis as plausible. The best way to do this is to take readers directly to the text, "Here's what I think and here's why." Whenever students can do that, they stand on solid ground and are ready to contribute to the conversation.

In a similar fashion, students should temper their language with qualifiers in order to avoid absolutes, which, to most readers, are off-putting: may *vs.* must, might *vs.* should, perhaps *vs.* undoubtedly, sometimes *vs.* always, many *vs.* all. Due to their rarity, absolutes can damage one's ethos: outside of science or mathematics, rarely is something true *all* of the time and in *every* circumstance. Additionally, since each thesis, by definition, is an argument, one has to keep in mind that others may think differently. *Suggesting* a way of interpreting a text seems better than offering one's ideas as the sole interpretation. It is a polite way of entering the conversation with respect and deference to one's audience. If one does an adequate job providing and explaining the evidence to support the claim, the audience will be far more likely to accept that interpretation as viable. Before one can do any of this, however, one must have something relevant to say. One must "invent" the claim, which is perhaps the aspect of literary analysis that makes students most anxious.

"Invention" is the chief canon among the traditional Five Canons of Rhetoric—rhetoric being the practice of using language persuasively. From the Latin "*invenire*," meaning "to find," invention is finding the "what" that will be argued (the other four canons are about "how" the argument is made). This is also known as the thesis. A good way to find one's thesis is to begin with a strategy known as asking interpretive questions. Students should ask a question about how to interpret a specific element in the text: "What might this mean?" or, "How can this particular image or scene be understood?" When one *answers* the interpretive question, one is offering a way of comprehending something significant about the text, something that offers readers a deeper understanding of the text. To ask interpretive questions, one must first pay close attention to the language and specific images the author presents. This is part of what is known as close reading or critical thinking. This is when students get to play literary detective, collecting clues as they read. Like individual pieces of a puzzle, each part contributes to the greater whole.

To begin, students can annotate their texts—reading with pencil in hand to note any and all words or passages that particularly interest them. "Interest" may be positive or negative. One may react to the *beauty* of the writing with awe (positive), just as one may also react to the *horror* of a scene with repulsion (negative). Morrison gives readers plenty of both in *Beloved*. Annotation promotes active reading "with a visible record of the thoughts that emerge while making sense of the reading" (Porter-O'Donnell 82). When readers annotate texts, they engage with them in important ways that allow them to participate in the generation of meaning. Readers also remember what they have annotated better than readers who do not annotate. Many readers are very visually oriented, and the act of note taking can even help readers to picture the text after the fact. For instance, readers might recall marking a passage on a left-facing page in a specific place—say near the top or the middle of the page. This facilitates finding particular notes later, which helps students write about the text. If, for whatever reason, students cannot mark the text directly, keeping a separate reading journal is a good alternative. They also might find it useful to do a combination of both.

To annotate, if this is a novelty, readers should also be alert to any repeated terms or images—what we call motif (discussed shortly)—since repetition is often crucial to a text's deeper meaning. Students should also note words or expressions that seem to be used in unique ways along with any allusions (discussed below) to other texts or events.

Because annotation can cover a wide range of things, students may wish to devise a personal system of markings that are meaningful to them. Underlining (straight or wavy), circling, and using marks such as stars, asterisks, checks, brackets, and the like can be useful. There are also handy adhesive pads ("sticky notes") that come in various sizes and colors with which one may tab important information with space for notes (Porter-O'Donnell 85). These are a good alternative to writing in a borrowed text or one in which a reader may for some other reason wish to keep the pages clean. Many students like to use highlighter pens, but these are less beneficial than pencils. The problem with highlighting lies in its limited function. As Porter-O'Donnell reflects on her own experience using a highlighter, "The yellow marks in my college textbooks, which left little of the page in its original color, did not help me to learn very much" (82). Clearly, one can get carried away with highlighting, which makes it difficult later to distinguish why the text was marked in the first place if every other word or line is highlighted.

While students read a text the first time they should not become too preoccupied with specifics—such as worrying about what every word means. Instead, trying to determine meaning based on *context* is a better initial strategy. Then, when one finishes a passage, section, or chapter, if meanings still perplex the reader, one might take the time to consult a dictionary to learn the denotations of any unfamiliar words. For example, one might know a word based on its generally accepted usage, but in a particular passage, it is clearly being used in a different way because the accepted denotation does not make sense in that circumstance. In such cases, it is helpful to consider how the context seems to alter the meaning. This is the difference between the details and the big picture. Sometimes, like an impressionist painting, the meaning is not clear when one is too close. Greater distance—by which the viewer can take in the whole painting—brings a sharper focus to its individual elements. Often, however, Morrison uses such a unique vocabulary—with words like "rememory," which functions as both noun and verb—that even a dictionary may not help. At other times, one may need to learn the *etymology*, or the origins, of a word. Perhaps the author is using what may be a lesser-known definition or an "archaic" meaning, which is a technical way of saying that the meaning is no longer current.

Annotation is a good first step in the process of literary analysis. One might also jot personal reactions to the text in the margins or list questions one has while reading. Even something like, "Who is this character?" or, "What does this mean?" could become valuable interpretive questions that guide the reader in later analysis. At any rate, notes allow one to go back to the text—often again and again—to revisit these moments and probe them more earnestly. Annotation also makes it easier to notice important patterns, and this brings me to motif.

A motif is a repeated image—a thing—that contributes to a larger theme—a concept. For example, in Homer's *Odyssey*, birds are a recurring image, thus a motif, that contributes to a larger theme about prophecy. A motif cannot really be a theme. One could ask students while they are learning this concept: Can "bird" be a theme? No, because "bird" is a thing and not a concept. In Shakespeare's *Hamlet*, poison is a motif that contributes to the larger theme of corruption. Color can be a motif. In *Beloved*, besides the obviousness of black and white, students might notice that color plays an important role. The fact that Baby Suggs spends the end of her life purposely meditating on color is significant. Color is a distinguishing feature of existence, but for the black population in the novel—and the white girl, Amy Denver—it is a luxury, the notice and scrutiny of which, their existence does not allow.

When Baby Suggs retires to the keeping room to spend the rest of her days contemplating color, this must mean something. Sethe says about this odd resignation, "She never had time to see it, let alone enjoy it before" (Morrison, *Beloved* 237). As Perez-Torres notes, "Color becomes a metonym for the richness of life… The concept [of hue] undergoes a literary transformation whereby color serves as a metonym for luxuriousness, comfort, pleasure" (694). A metonym is a word that is substituted for something else. For example "Lansing" can be a metonym for the State government in

Michigan. When one pays close attention to repetition, this is a first step in detecting motif and understanding how it guides readers to interpret the text on deeper levels.

Let us consider the repetition of the color red in *Beloved*. If readers were to mark its occurrence among their annotations, they would notice that Morrison uses red frequently—about thirty times. Incidentally, with the technological access to full-texts online, it is easy to run searches for words (and phrases) in order to catalog more precisely their use and occurrence, which is a nice reinforcement for the printed text and students' notes. The next step would be to ask what the motif might mean. In this case: How is the color red used? When it appears, is the context negative or positive? With which characters is it most often associated? What does the pattern tell us? To what larger theme can it be connected? Are there any exceptions to its use?

In tracking the motif, students will perceive that Morrison uses red primarily as a negative image—with bloodshed as its worst depiction. Sethe observes that Baby Suggs "was well into pink when she died. I don't believe she wanted to get to red and I understand why because me and Beloved outdid ourselves with it. Matter of fact, that and [Beloved's] pinkish headstone was the last color I recall" (237). Of course here, "outdid ourselves" refers to the blood shed during Sethe's sanguinary act of infanticide when she all but severs the head from her "crawling already?" baby, who is later Christened "Beloved" at the murdered infant's funeral.

That said, not every occurrence of the word red is necessarily negative or part of the motif. It is important when dealing with motif to not simply lump every instance of a word into the same category, tempting as that may be. For example, Sixo's "flame-red tongue" is mentioned twice (Morrison, *Beloved* 25, 26) but is not part of the word's negative usage, nor, is Garner's face going "red with laughter" (167). Some uses of a word may not be part of the motif. It is up to the reader to be discerning. One must read with care to test each instance of the word. If one is careless and makes the claim that all of the thirty occurrences of the word red are part of the negative motif, this would not be entirely accurate. Such a careless claim would also damage one's credibility as a writer and could even call one's ethics into question depending on the circumstances if the writer claims what is not quite true. Accuracy matters.

Red, as a negative color, is transformed by the white girl, Amy, when she insists on calling it something else: "Carmine. That means red but when you talk about velvet you got to say 'carmine'" (Morrison, *Beloved* 41). In another instance, while it still is not entirely positive, Amy also uses language to transform the red on Sethe's flayed back when she says: "It's a tree, Lu. A chokecherry tree. See, here's the trunk—it's red and split wide open, full of sap, and this here's the parting for the branches" (93). Perrez-Torres explains that "the marks of slavery inscribed on the one [Sethe] are transformed by the other [Amy] into signs signifying an image of fruition instead of oppression, [as] Amy gives back to Sethe her identity as a nurturing source" (697). Based on other discussions about language in the novel, which Morrison tells us is normally controlled by "the definers," such as schoolteacher, and not by "the defined," we see how subjugated characters appropriate language for their own purposes—humanizing, dignifying purposes. Thus, Amy's "carmine" velvet—which is red, but linguistically and connotatively better than red—and her tender narrative of the tree on Sethe's back provide additional aspects of the color that help readers make sense of and follow the motif.

Allusion, another important literary device, is when an author makes a reference to some other known text, event, or historical figure. Allusion can offer further insight for readers. Take the "Garners," for example. As the Masters of "Sweet Home"—the ironically named place where many of the main characters in *Beloved* were enslaved, "It wasn't sweet and it sure wasn't home" (Morrison, *Beloved* 16)—the last name alludes to Margaret Garner, the historical slave woman whose own act of infanticide to spare her child from the atrocities of slavery is, on some levels, the inspiration for Sethe. As Morrison says in her "Foreword" to the Vintage edition of the novel:

The historical Margaret Garner is fascinating, but, to a novelist, confining. Too little imaginative space there for my purposes. So

I would invent her thoughts, plumb them for a subtext that was historically true in essence, but not strictly factual in order to relate her history to contemporary issues about freedom, responsibility, and women's "place." The heroine would represent the unapologetic acceptance of shame and terror; assume the consequences of choosing infanticide; claim her own freedom. (xvii)

Preceding the "Foreword," but following the dedication, Morrison uses a direct biblical citation from Paul's *Epistle to the Romans*. At first glance, it is somewhat cryptic, but can be seen as another kind of allusion to the greater narrative to which the passage refers: Paul's prophecy of God's acceptance of the Gentiles. Morrison quotes, "I will call them my people, / which are not my people; / and her beloved, / which was not beloved" (Romans 9:25). If the reader took that passage alone, at face value, without knowledge of what follows, it might not seem to be a very hopeful one. The literary detective, however, can go to the Bible to locate the verse and read what follows. The passage concludes, "And it shall come to pass / in the place where it was said to them, / 'You are not My people,' / there they shall be called / children of the living God" (Romans 9:26). Knowing this makes all the difference for it is integral to Morrison's message. The Africans were taken as slaves to North America where they were told that, not only were they not God's people, they also were subhuman. Schoolteacher has his pupils draw and record the "characteristics" of the Sweet Home slaves. One is detailing Sethe, and she is appalled to overhear schoolteacher scold the pupil, "No, no. That's not the way. I told you to put her human characteristics on the left; her animal ones on the right" (Morrison, *Beloved* 228). Yet *all* are "Children of the living God." Other moments in the novel support this as when Morrison describes Bodwin, the abolitionist, whose father taught him "one clear directive: human life is holy, all of it" (*Beloved* 307).

Ultimately, humanity connects characters in the narrative. Besides general meanings of words, names are often highly significant in novels. As discussed above, the last name "Garner" is noteworthy for its allusion to Margaret Garner. Readers may sense that Sethe is like "seethe," synonymous with "boil," "fume," and "rage" in reference to anger, and this is one aspect of her complex character. Denver is the name of the daughter who was delivered on the banks of the Ohio River as Sethe fled slavery for safety in the North. Denver, initially a helpless character, becomes one of hope. Her namesake is Amy Denver, the humane white girl who saved Sethe and her baby, helping to deliver Denver. Amy herself was a runaway indentured girl, and there was no material gain for her in aiding Sethe; rather, she put her own flight in jeopardy by abetting a runaway slave. Without Amy, there would be no story to tell. Sethe thought about "how unlikely it was that she made it. And if it hadn't been for that girl looking for velvet, she never would have" noting to Paul D how "[a] whitegirl helped me," to which he replies, "Then she helped herself too, God bless her" (Morrison, *Beloved* 9). Besides the white girl's last name, "Denver," what, if anything, might be significant about the first name "Amy"?

Sometimes insight can be random and one can scarcely account for how it happens. Here I will note my own experience as a new graduate student pursuing a Master of Arts degree in language and literature. I was in my first seminar of my first semester and had to write the required paper at the end of the term. Of all the texts we read during those sixteen weeks—most dealing with supernatural phenomenon and persecuted people—I knew I wanted to write about *Beloved*. More than the other books assigned in an impressive list, the novel so affected me that I did not just want to write about it; I knew I *needed* to. But, as with the idea of the daunting task of literary analysis with which this chapter began, I, too, felt lost, with no idea where to begin, until I landed on the name "Amy," which also *means* "beloved." In observing this, I sensed that Morrison, by eponymously naming not one, but two of the characters in the novel "Beloved," may well have meant for readers to pay attention to that fact because Amy is among countless beloveds.

My interpretive questions about this included: "Now why would Morrison do that? Why would she, in essence, name another character Beloved by using a different, commonplace name that means "beloved"? Perhaps more importantly, why, in a novel about the African slave experience, would Morrison name a *white* girl

Beloved, too?" And it was almost as if it might be taboo to notice this—that to write about the white girl was somehow wrong, since whites were the antagonists. The more I re-read the text, however, I became convinced that her whiteness was part of the key to understanding her pivotal role in the novel—and its greater cultural significance beyond the text, which is the final point about literary analysis with which, shortly, I will conclude. However black-and-white the issue of racism may be, it takes *both* sides to work things out, and they need each other.

Contemplating these issues forced me to rethink a lot in the novel, such as how Sethe's own community rebukes her and Baby Suggs for what they perceive as excessive pride when they fail to warn them about the arrival of the four horsemen at 124 Bluestone Road. Later, they ostracize Sethe more entirely in reaction to her infanticide. Even Paul D, Sethe's friend and lover, judges her by equating her with animals, "You got two feet, Sethe, not four" (Morrison, *Beloved* 194), when he learns she murdered her baby. Although the slave-owning Garners and even the abolitionist Bodwins, for the most part are presented as sympathetic characters, they are still part of the problem. They are not actually good people. Amy, however, is outside of that fallow white status quo. Amy is different. Thus, Amy became the subject of my seminar paper in which I examine her as a far more significant figure in the novel than anyone had previously acknowledged.

As I started doing research on Amy initially, I found that there was little published material discussing her and not one critical study devoted exclusively to her. My essay noted that "she is often mentioned only in passing—in one instance as a parenthetical aside (Krumholtz 399) as if she is too insignificant even to warrant dismissal in the first place. Indeed how can one dismiss what has not been noticed?" (Coonradt 169). Critics who have discussed Amy include Homi K. Bhabha, who writes movingly about Sethe's infanticide; Doreatha Drummond Mbalia, who focuses on class consciousness; Rafael Perez-Torres, who traces the novel's postmodern narrative; and Ashraf H. A. Rushdy, who explores "rememory" among other concepts in Morrison's work. I argue, however, that more was necessary. As a character, Amy is only mentioned directly in about fifteen pages of the novel, but there are other more subtle references to her throughout, as if to remind us of her important presence. I was fixated on the idea that Amy is "integral to the very telling of the story, for without her there would likely be no story" (Coonradt169).

As I reread the novel in preparation for writing this essay, I was struck again by Amy's importance, but also by how easy it probably is for everyone to ignore her in the first place. Given the sickening intensity of the atrocities and injustices revealed in the novel, it is hard to focus on anything else. In the fractured narrative, Morrison describes the heinous, unconscionable nature of slavery that caused a young mother to murder her own baby with a handsaw out of "too-thick love" (*Beloved* 193, 94) in order to protect her, ironically to *save* her—and would have done it to her three other children as well had she not been stopped. In light of such trauma, what else can possibly matter? And yet, if Sethe and the hopeful Denver had died on the riverbank, the infanticide never would have happened; there would be no story "to pass on," or at least there would be a different story. It would not have been Sethe's story.

One can read the final pages of the novel with Amy in mind—along with Beloved and the other beloved characters the name represents, the staggering "Sixty million and more" of the dedication—in a more direct way. In my essay, I note that the opening lines of the last two pages recall Amy, as I analyze linguistic cues and the imagery, diction, and repetitions that link to earlier passages in the novel that are pointedly about Amy, but I also think of her as I read, "Disremembered and unaccounted for, she cannot be lost because no one is looking for her, and even if they were, how can they call her if they don't know her name?" (Morrison, *Beloved* 323). Sethe met Amy wandering the same hillside, fleeing servitude and abuse, lost and alone. It is hard to find "Amy" beloved if you do not know that this is what her name means. As the novel begins with Romans 9:25, "I will call her beloved / which was not beloved," by extension we realize that we are *all* beloved, each one of us. Given the final word of the novel, which is also "Beloved," as both a noun and verb, the word seems to be the whole point. Plenty of other biblical quotes come to mind, especially from the fourth chapter of John.

To close, the other thing that literary analysis does, perhaps the most important thing, is to ask the crucial "So what?"—meaning, what does this matter to us, to society, to posterity? Why should we care about it? As a scholar, I have to think in a very conscious way, "If I am correct in my analysis of Amy's importance to the novel, what does this matter?" Students have to ask these questions, too. My essay explores the wherefore of Amy as vital to the novel, which is not in spite of her whiteness but because of it. She is exceptional and serves as the model, for white and black, which Morrison hopes readers will emulate:

> Through Amy and Sethe's encounter, Morrison hopes to show the possibility of mutual understanding and love... By contrasting Amy's tenderness with the evil of the 'schoolteachers' of the world, we realize exactly what Morrison wants us to understand: Christian charity is colorblind [sic], and in the love that is charity [caritas], hope resides. (Coonradt 183)

Students who read with a personally original innocence will always find interesting new meanings, and Morrison's *Beloved* is a good place for this. Asking interpretive questions can help students engage with this Pulitzer Prize-winning text.

Works Cited

Bhabha, Homi K. *The Location of Culture*. London: Routledge, 1994.

Bible (KJV). The Official King James Bible Online. 2015. Web. 25 Aug. 2015.

Coonradt, Nicole. "To Be Loved: Amy Denver and Human Need Bridges to Understanding in Toni Morrison's *Beloved*." *College Literature* 32.4 (2005): 168–87.

Graff, Gerald & Cathy Birkenstein. *They Say/I Say: The Moves That Matter in Academic Writing*. 3rd ed. New York: Norton, 2014.

Krumholz, Linda. "The Ghosts of Slavery: Historical Recovery in Toni Morrison's *Beloved*." *African American Review* 33.3 (1992): 313–24.

Mbalia, Doreatha Drummond. *Toni Morrison's Developing Class Consciousness*. Toronto: Associated UP, 1991.

Morrison, Toni. *Beloved.* New York: Vintage, 2004.

Perez-Torres, Rafael. "Knitting and Knotting the Narrative Thread *Beloved* as Postmodern Novel." *Modern Fiction Studies* 39.3–4 (1993): 689–707. *Project Muse.* Web. 25 Aug. 2015.

Porter-O'Donnell, Carol. "Beyond the Yellow Highlighter: Teaching Annotation Skills to Improve Reading Comprehension." *The English Journal* 93.5 (2004): 82–89. *JSTOR.* Web. 25 Aug. 2015.

Rushdy, Ashraf H. A. "'Rememory': Primary Scenes and Constructions in Toni Morrison's Novels." *Contemporary Literature* 31.3 (1990): 300–23.

RESOURCES

Chronology of Toni Morrison's Life_____

1931	Toni Morrison is born Chloe (Anthony) Wofford on February 18 in Lorain, OH, to George and Ella Ramah Wofford. She adopted the middle name "Anthony" at age 12 when she became a Catholic.
1949	Graduates from Lorain High School.
1953	Graduates from Howard University with BA in English and minor in classics.
1955	Graduates with MA from Cornell University. She writes a thesis: *The Treatment of the Alienated in Virginia Woolf and William Faulkner.*
1955-1957	Teaches at Texas Southern University.
1957	Returns to Howard University to teach.
1958	Marries Jamaican-born architect, Harold Morrison.
1963	Joins Howard writers' group; moves to New York as senior editor with Random House.
1965	Moves to work as senior editor with L.W. Singer in Syracuse, New York (Textbook subsidiary of Random House).
1970	*The Bluest Eye*, her first novel, about a young black girl who wishes to have blue eyes so that she could be loved, is published.
1973	*Sula*, a novel about kinship and a wide range of social kinship in a small all-black fictional town in Ohio, is published.

1974	*Sula* is nominated for the American Book Award; *Sula* receives Ohioana Book Award.
1977	*Song of Solomon*, a book about a young man's journey through the Midwest in search of his identity, is published. The book is chosen as a Book of the Month Club Selection, the first by an African American author since Richard Wright's *Native Son*.
1978	Morrison receives the National Book Critics' Circle Award and the American Academy and Institute of Arts and Letters Award for *Song of Solomon*. She is named distinguished writer by the American Academy of Arts and Letters. *Song of Solomon* earns Morrison the Oscar Micheaux Award, Friends of Writers Award, and the Cleveland Arts Prize for Literature.
1980	Appointed to National Council of the Arts.
1981	*Tar Baby*, a book about African diaspora connections using a Caribbean folktale of the tar baby as its source, is published. Morrison is elected to the American Academy and Institute of Arts and Letters. Morrison appears on the cover of the March issue of *Newsweek Magazine*.
1983	Morrison's short story "Recitatif," appears in *Confirmations: An Anthology of African American Women Writers*, edited by Amiri Baraka and Amina Baraka. Morrison resigns from Random House after eighteen years.
1984	Named the Albert Schweitzer Professor of the Humanities, College of the Humanities and Fine Arts, State University of New York, Albany.

1986	*Dreaming Emmett*, an unpublished play about Emmett Till, is directed by Gilbert Moses and performed at the Marketplace Capitol Repertory Theater of Albany. Play is commissioned by the New York State Writers Institute and wins New York State Governor's Award.
1987	*Beloved*, novel based on the Margaret Garner case, is published; receives Anisfield-Wolf Book Award.
1988	Receives several awards for *Beloved*—Pulitzer, Melcher Book Award, Elmer Holmes Bobst Award for Fiction, Robert F. Kennedy Book Award; delivers Robert C. Tanner Lecture at the University of Michigan; receives City of New York Mayor's Award of Honor for Art and Culture; receives State of Ohio, Ohioana Career Medal Award; inducted into the American Academy of Arts and Letters.
1989	Appointed to the Robert F. Goheen Chair in the Council of the Humanities at Princeton University; receives the Modern Language Association of America Commonwealth Award in Literature; receives Sara Lee Corporation Front Runner Award in the Arts.
1990	Delivers several lectures, including: Massey Lectures at Harvard University; the First Chazen Lecture at the University of Wisconsin; Charter Lecture at the University of Georgia; Clark Lectures, Trinity College Cambridge, England; Awarded Chianti Ruffino Antico Fattore International Literary Prize; receives Chubb Fellowship, Yale University.
1992	*Playing in the Dark: Essays on Whiteness and the Literary Imagination* (critical essays on American Literature) is published; *Jazz*, a novel about blacks in Harlem during the Jazz Age, is published.

Edited *Race-ing Justice, En-Gendering Power: Essay on Anita Hill, Clarence Thomas, and the Construction of Social Reality.*

1993	Awarded Nobel Prize for Literature (the first African American to win a Nobel Prize for Literature); awarded Commander of the Order of Arts and Letters (Paris); *Honey and Rue*, (lyrics) a cycle of six songs commissioned by Carnegie Hall for soprano Kathleen Battle, is released.
1994	Receives several awards: Pearl Buck Award, Pearl Buck Foundation; Premio Internazionale "Citta dello Stretto," Rhegium Julii, Reggio Calabria, Italy; Condorcet Medal; Awarded International Condorcet Chair, École Normale Supérieure and Collège de France; Delivered Condorcet Lecture, Collège de France.
1996	Named Jefferson Lecturer in the Humanities by the National Endowment for the Humanities; awarded the National Book Foundation Medal for Distinguished Contribution to American Letters; *The Dancing Mind*; National Book Foundation Lecture published by Knopf.
1997	*Birth of a Nation'hood: Gaze, Script, Script, and Spectacle in the O.J. Simpson Case*, a collection of essays on the O. J. Simpson Case, is released; "Sweet Talk" (composed by Richard Danielpour; performed by Jessye Norman at Carnegie Hall) is released.
1998	*Paradise*, novel exploring racial and gender tensions and violence in Ruby, OK, is released; "Spirits in the Well" (composed by Richard Danielpour; performed by Jessye Norman at Avery Fisher Hall) is released; receives Medal of Honor for Literature, National Arts

Club, New York; named A. D. White Professor-At-Large, Cornell University; delivers Moffitt Lecture Princeton University; delivers Berliner Lektionen Theater, Berlin; *Beloved*, the movie, starring Oprah Winfrey and directed by Jonathan Demme, is released; receives Grammy nomination for Best Spoken Word Album for *Beloved*.

1999	Receives Ohioana Book Award for Fiction; Oklahoma Book Award, Oklahoma City; named *Ladies Home Journal* Woman of the Year; nominated for Orange Prize, London; *The Big Box*, (children's book), coauthored with son, Slade, is released.
2000	Awarded the National Humanities Medal. Writes lyrics for *Woman,Mind.Song*, performed by Jessye Norman.
2001	Receives several awards: Pell Award for Lifetime Achievement in the Arts, Providence, RI; Jean Kennedy Smith NYU Creative Writing Award, New York; Enoch Pratt Free Library Lifetime Literary Achievement Award, Baltimore, MD; Cavore Prize, Turrin, Italy; Fête du Livre, Cité du Livre, Les Écritures Croisées, Aix-en-Provence, France.
2002	Delivers University of Toronto Alexander Lecture; delivers United Nations Secretary General's Lecture Series; *Margaret Garner* (libretto), opera composed by Richard Danielpour is released and co-commissioned by Michigan Opera Theatre, Cincinnati Opera, and Opera Company of Philadelphia; *The Book of Mean People*, with Slade Morrison, is released.
2003	*Love*, a story about a dead hotel owner and the people (women) around him, is published; receives Docteur Honoris Causa, Ecole Normale Superieure, Paris.

2004	*Remember: The Journey to School Integration* is published by Houghton Mifflin; delivers Amnesty International Lecture, Edinburgh, Scotland; receives Academy of Culture, "Arts and Communities" Award, Paris. Receives the NAACP Image Award.
2005	Receives Coretta Scott King Award, American Library Association; World Premier of the Opera *Margaret Garner* (Detroit); Cincinnati Premier of the opera, *Margaret Garner*; awarded Doctor of Letters Degree, Oxford University, England; delivers Leon Forrest Lecture, Northwestern University, Evanston, IL.
2006	*Margaret Garner* opera premiers in Philadelphia, then Charlotte; awarded Honorary Doctorate of Letters, the Sorbonne, Paris; *New York Times* names *Beloved* one of the best works of American fiction in the last twenty-five years; retires from Princeton after seventeen years; curates "A Foreigner's Home" exhibit at the Louvre Museum, Paris.
2007	Curates "Art is Otherwise" Humanities Programs in New York City, sponsored by the French Alliance; receives the Ellie Charles Artist Award from African Voices at Columbia University; named Radcliffe Medalist by the Radcliffe Institute at Harvard; New York Premiere of *Margaret Garner*, New York City Opera; receives Lifetime Achievement Award and named one of twenty-one "Women of the Year" by *Glamour* magazine.
2009	Receives the Norman Mailer Prize for Lifetime Achievement.

2010	Appears on PEN World Voices in conversation with Marlene van Nierk and Kwame Anthony Appiah in a conversation about South African literature.
2011	Receives an Honorable Doctor of Letters Degree from Rutgers University.
2012	Receives the Presidential Medal of Freedom; establishes residency in Oberlin College; *Desdemona* with Peter Sellars and Rokia Traoré.
2013	Receives the Nichols-Chancellor's Medal from Vanderbilt University.
2014	Receives National Book Critics Circle Ivan Sandrof Lifetime Achievement Award.
2015	*God Help the Child*, Morrison's latest novel about childhood trauma, is published; "I Regret Everything" NPR podcast is released (a *Fresh Air* interview with Terry Gross).

Information for Toni Morrison's chronology has been culled from various literary and electronic sources, including the Toni Morrison Society webpage: www.tonimorrisonsociety.org; *The Encyclopedia Britannica*: www.britannica.com; and the Nobel Prize webpage: http://www. nobelprize.org.

Works by Toni Morrison

Fiction

The Bluest Eye (1970)

Sula (1973)

Song of Solomon (1977)

Tar Baby (1981)

Beloved (1987)

Jazz (1992)

Paradise (1997)

Woman.Life.Song (2000), with Judith Weir, Maya Angelou, & Clarissa Pinkola Estés

Margaret Garner: An Opera in Two Acts (2002), with Richard Danielpour

Love: A Novel (2003)

A Mercy (2008)

Peeny Butter Fudge (2009), with Slade Morrison & Joe Cepeda (illustrator)

Little Cloud and Lady Wind (2010), with Slade Morrison, Sean Qualls (illustrator), & Aesop

The Tortoise or the Hare (2010), with Slade Morrison, Joe Cepeda (illustrator), & Aesop

Desdemona (2011), with Peter Sellars & Rokia Traoré

God Help the Child (2015)

Other

"Recitatif." *Confirmations: An Anthology of African American Women Writers* (1983)

"Rootedness: The Ancestor as Foundation." *Black Women Writers (1950–1980): A Critical Evaluation* (1984)

"The Site of Memory." *Invented the Truth: The Art and Craft of Memoir* (1987)

"Unspeakable Things Unspoken." *Michigan Quarterly Review* (1989)

Playing in the Dark: Whiteness and the Literary Imagination (1992)

Race-ing Justice, En-Gendering Power: Essays on Anita Hill, Clarence Thomas, and the Construction of Social Reality (1992)

"The Nobel Lecture in Literature." *From Nobel Lectures, 1991–1995* (1993)

The Dancing Mind. National Book Foundation Lecture (1996)

*Birth of a Nation'hood: Gaze, Script, Script, and Spectacle in the O.J. Simpson Case (*1997), with Claudia Brodsky Lacour

"Home." *The House That Race Built* (1997)

"A Slow Walk of Trees (as Grandmother Would Say), Hopeless (as Grandfather Would Say)." *Toni Morrison: What Moves at the Margin* (2008)

"On the Back of Blacks." *Toni Morrison: What Moves at the Margin* (2008)

Burn This Book: PEN Writers Speak out on the Power of the Word (2009, 2012)

To Die for the People: The Writings of Huey P. Newton (2009), with Huey P. Newton

"Peril." *Burn This Book: Notes on Literature & Engagement* (2009, 2012)

"'I Regret Everything:' Toni Morrison Looks Back on Her Personal Life" (2015), radio interview

Bibliography

Adell, Sandra. *Toni Morrison.* Detroit: Gale, 2002.

Alexandre, Sandy. "From the same tree: Gender and Iconography in Representations of Violence in *Beloved.*" *Signs* 36.4 (2011): 915–940.

Anderson, Melanie R. *Spectrality in the Novels of Toni Morrison.* Knoxville: U of Tennessee P, 2013.

Andrews, William L. & Nellie Y. McKay. *Toni Morrison's 'Beloved': A Casebook.* New York: Oxford UP, 1999.

Anker, Elizabeth S. "The 'scent of Ink': Toni Morrison's *Beloved* and the Semiotics of Rights." *Critical Quarterly* 56.4 (Dec. 2014): 29–45. Web.

Baillie, Justine. *Toni Morrison and Literary Tradition: The Invention of an Aesthetic.* London, UK: Bloomsbury, 2013.

Balon, Rebecca. "Kinless or Queer: The Unthinkable Queer Slave in Toni Morrison's *Beloved* and Robert O'Hara's *Insurrection: Holding History.*" *African American Review* 48.1–2 (Spring/Summer 2015): 141, 155, 223. Web.

Byrne, Dara. "'Yonder They Do Not Love Your Flesh.' Community in Toni Morrison's *Beloved*: The Limitations of Citizenship and Property in the American Public Sphere." *Canadian Review of American Studies* 29.2 (1999): 25–60. Web.

Conner, Marc C. *The Aesthetics of Toni Morrison: Speaking the Unspeakable.* Jackson: UP of Mississippi, 2000.

"Conversation with David McCullough; Conversation with Toni Morrison; Conversation with Kazuo Ishiguro." *The Charlie Rose Show.* PBS. KQED, Northern California, 10 Sept. 2015. Television.

"Conversation with Sherrilyn Ifill; Conversation with Toya Graham and Michael Singleton; Conversation with Toni Morrison." *The Charlie Rose Show.* PBS. KQED, Northern California, 1 May 2015. Television.

Cutter, MJ. "The story must go on and on: The Fantastic, Narration, and Intertextuality in Toni Morrison's *Beloved* and *Jazz.*" *African American Review.* 34.1 (Spring 2000): 61–75.

Denard, Carolyn C., ed. *Toni Morrison: What Moves at the Margin.* Jackson: UP of Mississippi, 2008.

Dubek, Laura. "'Pass it on!' Legacy and the Freedom Struggle in Toni Morrison's *Song of Solomon.*" *The Southern Quarterly* 52.2 (Winter 2015): 90, 109, 196. Web.

Eke, Maureen N. "Performing Africa in the American Midwest: Memories of Africa in Toni Morrison's *Beloved* and *Song of Solomon.*" *Critical Insights: Midwestern Literature.* Amenia, NY: Salem, 2013. 109–23.

Eyerman, Ron. *Cultural Trauma: Slavery and the Formation of African American Identity.* Cambridge, UK: Cambridge UP, 2001.

George, Sheldon. "Approaching the Thing of Slavery: A Lacanian Analysis of Toni Morrison's *Beloved.*" *African American Review* 45.1–2 (2012): 115–30. Web.

Goulimari, Pelagia. *Toni Morrison.* New York: Routledge, 2011.

Greenbaum, Vicky. "Teaching *Beloved*: Images of Transcendence." *The English Journal* 91.6 (Jul. 2002): 83. Web.

Grewal, Gurleen. *Circles of Sorrow, Lines of Struggle: The Novels of Toni Morrison.* Baton Rouge: Louisiana State UP, 1998.

Griesinger, E. "Why Baby Suggs, Holy, Quit Preaching the Word: Redemption and Holiness in Toni Morrison's *Beloved.*" *Christianity and Literature* 50.4 (Summer 2001): 689–702. Web.

Hichri, Asma. "Hunger 'Beyond Appetite': Nurture Dialectics in Toni Morrison's *Beloved.*" *ARIEL: A Review of International English Literature* 44.2–3 (Apr.–Jul. 2013): 195–220.

Hoby, Hermione. "Toni Morrison: 'I'm Writing for Black People ... I Don't have to Apologise.'" *The Guardian.* The Guardian News and Media Limited, 25 Apr. 2015. Web. 1 May 2015. <http://www.theguardian.com/books/2015/apr/25/toni-morrison-books-interview-god-help-the-child>.

Holland-Toll, Linda J. & Angela R. Mullis. "(En)Lightening The Dark Vision: Redemption Through Storytelling In Toni Morrison's *Beloved.*" *Teaching African American Women's Writing.* Basingstoke, UK: Palgrave Macmillan, 2010. 102–120.

Jennings, La Vinia Delois. *Toni Morrison and the Idea of Africa.* Cambridge, UK: Cambridge UP, 2008.

Jesser, Nancy. "Violence, Home, and Community in Toni Morrison's *Beloved.*" *African American Review* 33.2 (Summer 1999): 325. Web.

King, Lovalerie. "Property and American Identity in Toni Morrison's *Beloved*." *Toni Morrison: Memory and Meaning*. Ed. Adrienne Lanier Seward, Justine Tally, & Carolyn C. Denard. Jackson: U Mississippi Press, 2014. 159–71.

Kitts, Lenore. "Toni Morrison and 'Sis Joe': The Musical Heritage of Paul D." *MFS Modern Fiction Studies* 52.2 (Summer 2006): 495–523. Web.

Koolish, Lynda. "Fictive Strategies and Cinematic Representations in Toni Morrison's *Beloved*: Postcolonial Theory/Postcolonial Text." *African American Review* 29.3 (Autumn 1995): 421–438.

Krumholz, Linda. "The Ghosts of Slavery: Historical Recovery in Toni Morrison's *Beloved*." *African American Review* 26.3 (Autumn 1992): 395–408. Web.

Ledbetter, Mark. "An Apocalypse of Race and Gender: Body Violence and Forming Identity in Toni Morrison's *Beloved*." *Victims and the Postmodern Narrative or Doing Violence to the Body: An Ethic of Reading and Writing*. New York: Palgrave McMillan, 1996. 37–55.

Lillvis, Kristen. "Becoming Self and Mother: Posthuman Liminality in Toni Morrison's *Beloved*." *Critique: Studies in Contemporary Fiction* 54.4 (2013): 452–464.

Magill, D. E. "Hypermasculinities in the Contemporary Novel: Cormac McCarthy, Toni Morrison, and James Baldwin." *Choice* 52.7 (2015): 1142.

Middleton, Joyce Irene. "'Both Print And Oral' And 'Talking About Race': Transforming Toni Morrison's Language Issues Into Teaching Issues." *African American Rhetoric(s): Interdisciplinary Perspectives*. Carbondale, IL: Southern Illinois UP, 2004. 242–258.

Mitchell, Angelyn. *The Freedom to Remember: Narrative, Slavery, and Gender in Contemporary Black Women's Fiction*. New Brunswick, NJ: Rutgers UP, 2002.

Moglen, Helene. "Redeeming History: Toni Morrison's *Beloved*." *Cultural Critique* 24 (Spring 1993): 17–40.

Montgomery, Maxine L. *Contested Boundaries: New Critical Essays on the Fiction of Toni Morrison*. Newcastle upon Tyne, UK: Cambridge Scholars, 2013.

Morrison, Toni & Danille Kathleen Taylor-Guthrie. *Conversations with Toni Morrison*. Jackson: UP of Mississippi, 1994.

Murphy, S. "'Not a Story to Pass On': Sexual Violence and Ethical Act in Toni Morrison's *Beloved.*" *Studies in Law, Politics, and Society* 36 (Jul. 2005): 103–123.

Nweke, Ob. "Mother/Daughter Relationship: Psychological Implication of Love in Toni Morrison's *Beloved.*" *Lwati: A Journal of Contemporary Research* 6.2 (2009): n.p. Web.

Parker, E. "A New Hystery: History and Hysteria in Toni Morrison's *Beloved.*" *Twentieth Century Literature* 47.1 (2001): 1–19.

Perez, Richard. "The Debt of Memory: Reparations, Imagination, and History in Toni Morrison's *Beloved.*" *WSQ: Women's Studies Quarterly* 42.1–2 (2014): 190–198.

Raynaud, Claudine. "*Beloved* or the Shifting Shapes of Memory." *The Cambridge Companion to Toni Morrison.* Ed. Justine Tally. Cambridge, UK: Cambridge UP, 2007. 43–58. PDF.

Rody, Caroline. "Toni Morrison's *Beloved*: History, 'Rememory,' and a 'Clamor for a Kiss.'" *American Literary History* 7.1 (1995): 92–119.

Roynon, Tessa. *Toni Morrison and the Classical Tradition: Transforming American Culture.* Oxford, UK: Oxford UP, 2013.

Rushdy, Ashraf H. A. "Daughters Signifyin(g) History: The Example of Toni Morrison's *Beloved.*" *American Literature* 64.3 (Sept. 1992): 567–597. Web.

Scarpa, Giulia. "Narrative Possibilities at Play in Toni Morrison's *Beloved.*" *MELUS* 17.4 (Winter 1991/92): 91.

Schreiber, Evelyn Jaffe. *Race, Trauma, and Home in the Novels of Toni Morrison.* Baton Rouge: Louisiana State UP, 2011. Southern Literary Studies Ser.

Seward, Adrienne Lanier & Justine Tally, eds. *Toni Morrison: Memory and Meaning.* Jackson: UP of Mississippi, 2015.

Sheriff, Karen M. "Metonymical Re-membering and Signifyin(g) in Toni Morrison's *Beloved.*" *Semiotics* (1996): 290–300. Web.

Smith, Valerie. *Toni Morrison: Writing the Moral Imagination.* Chichester, West Sussex: Wiley, 2012.

Stone, Rebecca. "Can the Breast Feed the Mother Too? Tracing Maternal Subjectivity in Toni Morrison's *Beloved.*" *British Journal of Psychotherapy* 31.3 (Jul. 2015): 298–310.

Terry, Jennifer. "'Breathing the Air of a World So New': Rewriting the Landscape of America in Toni Morrison's A Mercy." *Journal of American Studies* 48.1 (Feb. 2014): 127–45.

Webb, Barbara J. "'Unspeakable Things Unspoken': Reflections On Teaching *Beloved*." *WSQ: Women's Studies Quarterly* 42.1–2 (Spring/Summer 2014): 199–204.

Weisenburger, Steven. *Modern Medea: A Family Story of Slavery and Child-Murder from the Old South*. New York: Hill & Wang, 1998.

White, Jeanna Fuston. "Two Vashtis: Morrison's *Beloved* and the Book of Esther." *The Explicator* 71.3 (2013): 188–90.

Wyatt, Jean. "Giving Body to the Word: The Maternal Symbolic in Toni Morrison's *Beloved*." *PMLA* 108.3 (May 1993): 474–488.

Yanuck, Julius. "The Garner Fugitive Slave Case." *The Mississippi Valley Historical Review* 40.1 (1953): 47.

Zamalin, Alex. "Beloved Citizens: Toni Morrison's *Beloved*, Racial Inequality, and American Public Policy." *WSQ: Women's Studies Quarterly* 42.1–2 (Spring/Summer 2014): 205–211.

Zauditu-Selassie, K. *African Spiritual Traditions in the Novels of Toni Morrison*. Gainesville, FL: UP of Florida, 2014.

About the Editor

Maureen N. Eke is professor of English at Central Michigan University, where she teaches courses in African diaspora literatures, postcolonial literatures and theory, world literature, women writers, and the literary dimensions of film. She is the past president of the African Literature Association, USA (ALA). Eke has served as an editor of the African Literature Association's s *Annual Series*. Her publications include several coedited volumes and special collections of essays: *Cross-Rhythms* (1989); *African Images: Recent Studies and Texts in Cinema* (2000); *Gender and Sexuality in African Literature and Film* (2007); *Emerging Perspectives on Nawal El Saadawi* (2010); *Literature, the Visual Arts and Globalization in Africa and its Diaspora* (2011); and a special collection of essays in *Research in African Literatures* (RAL) on "Memory/History, Violence, and Reconciliation." She has published numerous articles on African American Literature, as well as African Literature and cinema. Her articles have appeared in *African Literature Today, Callaloo, Critical Insights: Midwestern Literature, Research in African Literatures, South African Theatre Journal*, and *Visual Anthropology*. She is an associate editor of *African Literature Today* and serves on the editorial boards of several international publications, including *Critical Arts, Journal of African Cinema*, and *African Literature Today*. Eke is also the convener of the biennial international conference on Human Rights, Literature, the Arts, and Social Science at Central Michigan University.

Contributors_____

Sandy Alexandre is associate professor of literature at MIT. Her research spans the late nineteenth-century to present-day black American literature and culture. Her first book, *The Properties of Violence: Claims to Ownership in Representations of Lynching* (Mississippi UP, 2012), uses the history of American lynching violence as a framework to understand matters concerning displacement, property ownership, and the American pastoral ideology in a literary context. She is currently writing a second book, *Up From Chattels: Thinghood in an Ethics of Black Curation*, which will take as its point of departure the premise that the former, enforced condition of black Americans as fungible merchandise can haunt, inform, and morally energize their own relationships to material objects. She has published articles in *Mississippi Quarterly*, *Signs: Journal of Women in Culture & Society*, *Modern Drama*, *The Journal of American Drama and Theatre*, and *Criticism*.

Herman Beavers is associate professor of English and Africana Studies and the graduate and undergraduate chair in the Department of Africana Studies at the University of Pennsylvania, where he teaches courses in twentieth-century and contemporary African American literature and creative writing. He has published essays on the works of Charles Johnson, Toni Morrison, August Wilson, Richard Wright, Ralph Ellison, and Michael S. Harper. His poems have appeared in *The Langston Hughes Colloquy*, *MELUS*, and *Versadelphia, Cleaver Magazine*, and the *American Arts Quarterly*. His poem "The Relative of Fear" appears in the anthology, *Obsession: Sestinas in the Twenty First Century*. His publications include a recently completed scholarly monograph titled *Changing the Order of Things: Geography and the Political Imaginary in the Fiction of Toni Morrison* and his first book *Wrestling Angels into Song: The Fictions of Ernest J. Gaines and James A. McPherson*. He is currently working on a project titled, *Uncertain Blackness: African American Literature and the Poetics of Cultural Turbulence, 1940–2007*, which utilizes chaos theory to read canonical texts in African American literature. He serves as an advisory editor for *The African American Review*, *Modern Fiction Studies*, and *The Black Scholar*.

Sarah L. Berry is an assistant professor of biomedical humanities in the Center for Literature and Medicine at Hiram College and has served as a curricular diversity consultant at the University of Rochester Medical College. She teaches courses in multicultural medicine, health and social justice, literature and illness, and narrative bioethics. She is the author of several articles on race, gender, medicine, and ethics, including, most recently, "Paradoxical Worsening of Empathy: Ambassadorial Science Journalism and *The Immortal Life of Henrietta Lacks*" and "'No doctor but my master:' Health Reform and Antislavery Rhetoric in Harriet Jacobs's *Incidents in the Life of a Slave Girl*." Her learning module "A Medicine of Their Own: The Stories of American Women Healers" appears online in the National Library of Medicine's *Changing the Face of Medicine* page and offers lesson plans for teaching about women and African Americans entering the medical profession in the nineteenth century: (http://www.nlm.nih.gov/changingthefaceofmedicine/resources/highereducation.html). She is currently at work a book, *Patient Revolutions: Alternative Medicine and Civil Reform, 1840–1975*.

Nicole M. Coonradt is an independent scholar and poet. After earning her doctorate at the University of Denver in 2012, she returned with her three sons to Michigan where her teaching career began in 1996. She currently teaches literature and writing at various institutions. Combining passions for social justice and teaching, she recently pursued work in a prison, which both humbles and inspires her.

Blessing Diala-Ogamba is a professor in the Department of Humanities at Coppin State University, Baltimore, MD. She is the coordinator of world literature and also teaches English composition, African and British literature. She teaches face-to-face, hybrid, and online courses. Her articles have appeared in scholarly journals and chapters in books. She is a coeditor of *Literary Crossroads: An International Exploration of Women, Gender, and Otherhood*. She is currently working on a book about the representation of women in the African novel. Diala-Ogamba is a Quality Matters Peer Reviewer and holds a Sloan-C Certificate in Online Design and Delivery 2013. Her current research interests include world literature, immigration, and women issues.

Anne Herbert is a lecturer in English at Bradley University, Peoria, IL. She holds a BA from Bradley University and an MA from Northwestern University, specializing in British Victorian studies and postcolonial literatures. Additional pedagogical and research interests include approaches to teaching African American literature, black classicism, and race, class, gender, and sexuality in 3-D virtual worlds.

Touria Khannous is associate professor in the Department of Foreign Languages and the International Studies Program at Louisiana State University. Her research interests include African and black diaspora studies, postcolonial studies, women studies, and film. She has published articles on African literature and film, race in Arabic literature, as well as a manuscript on African women's literature, film, and Internet discourse. She is currently working on a book that deals with the Black diaspora in the Arab world.

Joseph McLaren is professor of English at Hofstra University in New York. A specialist in African, Caribbean, and African American literatures, his publications include numerous articles on literary and cultural subjects. He is the author of *Langston Hughes: Folk Dramatist in the Protest Tradition, 1921–1943* (1997). In addition, he coedited *Pan-Africanism Updated* (1999) and *African Visions* (2000) and edited two volumes of the *Collected Works of Langston Hughes: The Big Sea* (2002) and *I Wonder As I Wander* (2002). He is coauthor, with legendary jazz saxophonist-composer Jimmy Heath, of Heath's autobiography, *I Walked with Giants* (2010).

Lynne Simpson is an associate professor at Oklahoma State University and is the interim head of the Veterinary Medicine Library. She also serves as an adjunct professor at the University of North Texas College of Information. Before her current position at Oklahoma State University, she worked in information centers at Georgia-Pacific Corp. and the Jet Propulsion Laboratory of NASA. She has held positions at Langston University and Emory University. She is currently a board member of the Toni Morrison Society Bench by the Road Project.

Durthy A. Washington has taught literature and academic writing at several colleges and universities, including the US Air Force Academy, the Colorado College, and St. Petersburg State University, Russia. Her publications include articles, essays, and book reviews, as well as literary study guides (*Cliffs Notes*) on the works of Toni Morrison, Harriett Jacobs, Ralph Ellison, and Ernest Gaines. Durthy served as facilitator for two "Language Matters" workshops cosponsored by the Toni Morrison Society and the National Endowment for the Humanities. She is currently working on a textbook based on the LIST Paradigm© and on building her seminar business, LitUnlocked.

Khalilah T. Watson is assistant professor in the Department of English, Literature and Reading at Olive-Harvey College, one of the City Colleges of Chicago. Her PhD areas of specialization are twentieth-century African American fiction and literary theory and Toni Morrison. Aside from her teaching responsibilities, she has presented at a few national literary conferences, and she has written and published a few articles for University of Chicago's Court Theatre and one article for its *Center for Classical Theatre Review*. In addition, she has written several articles for the *Final Call* Newspaper and is also a member of Toni Morrison Society, College Language Association, the International Writing Across the Curriculum Network (INWAC), and Lambda Iota Tau, an international literature honor society.

Kristine Yohe is associate professor of English at Northern Kentucky University, where she has taught since 1997, just after receiving her PhD from UNC-Chapel Hill. Her teaching and scholarship focus on African American literature, especially Toni Morrison and Frank X Walker, as well as Afro-Caribbean literature, especially Jean-Robert Cadet. In 2005, Kris served as director for the Toni Morrison Society Fourth Biennial Conference, which took place in greater Cincinnati and at NKU, in conjunction with Morrison's *Margaret Garner* opera. Recent publications include an essay on teaching Morrison's *Love* in an edited book from the National Council of Teachers of English, and a chapter in a 2013 collection about *Margaret Garner*, published by the University of Illinois Press.

Kokahvah Zauditu-Selassie is professor of English in the Humanities Department at Coppin State University. She is the author of "I Got a Home in Dat Rock: Memory, Orisa, and Yoruba Spiritual Identity in African American Literature" in *Orisa: Yoruba Gods and Spiritual Identity in Africa and the Diaspora,* as well as several journal articles including, "Step and Fetch It: The Reclamation of African Ontology in Zora Neale Hurston's *Their Eyes Were Watching God*," "Women Who Know Things: African Epistemologies, Ecocriticism, and Female Spiritual Authority in the Novels of Toni Morrison," and "Every Goodbye Ain't Gone: Using Adinkra Symbols to Frame Critical Agenda in African Diasporic Literature." She is also the author of *African Spiritual Traditions in the Novels of Toni Morrison* (2009), which won the Toni Morrison Society's 2010 award for the best single-authored book. Her latest publication is a collection of short stories titled, *At the End of Daybreak,* published by Middle-Passage Press. Her novel, *The Second Line*, is forthcoming.

Index

Clifton, Lucille 18
Coates, Ta-Nehisi 111, 181
code switching 203
Coffin, Levi 29
Collins, Patricia 55
Collins, Wilkie 193
confrontation 85, 107, 176, 181,
    193
conjure 141, 144
cosmology 59, 112, 131, 134
Craft, Ellen 5
Craft, William 5
culturally responsive teaching 212
cultural semiotics vii, 59, 66, 67
cultural studies 44

Danielpour, Richard 21, 33, 42,
    234, 235
Davies, Carole Boyce 53
Davis, Kimberly 47, 48
Day, Miranda 144
Dead, Milkman 19
DeCrow, Karen 18
dehumanization 97, 104
Demetrakopoulos, Stephanie 103
Demme, Jonathan 21, 43, 235
Denard, Carolyn C. 23, 41, 148,
    160
Denver, Amy 35, 54, 96, 97, 220,
    224, 227
Deslondes, Charles 14
Dickens, Charles 183, 192
diegesis 61
Dikenga dia Kongo 125
divine revelation 132, 133
Douglass, Frederick 4, 5, 9, 11,
    35, 41, 91, 92, 96, 100, 127,
    154, 169, 206
drapetomania 203
Dumas, Henry 18, 111

Du Maurier, Daphne 193
dysaesthesia aethiopis 135

earth/mother goddess 59, 75
Ehle, John 198
Eisgruber, Christopher L. 22
Eke, Maureen N. vii, 3, 17, 247
Ellison, Ralph 197, 249, 252
Emancipation Proclamation 157
embodiment 38, 84, 112, 123,
    124, 151, 152
Equiano, Olaudah 5, 154, 161
Euro-American canon 46
Euro-American literary tradition
    44
Evans, Mari 52, 76
exorcism 39, 192, 193, 210

Fabre, Genevieve 124
Faulkner, William 18, 44, 51, 57,
    231
feminism and gender studies 44
feminist writing/theory 43
Ferguson, Rebecca 174
Fett, Sharla 132
Forrest, Leon 18, 236
Fugitive Slave Act 5, 91, 95, 98,
    165, 166, 169

Gaines, Archibald K. 97
Garcia Marquez, Gabriel 51
Garner, Lillian 99
Garner, Margaret vii, viii, 3, 4, 5,
    7, 8, 9, 12, 14, 15, 20, 21,
    169, 201, 203, 222, 223,
    233, 235, 236, 239, 252
Garner, Mr. viii, 52, 80, 81, 82,
    83, 84, 87, 91, 92, 96, 97,
    99, 100, 104, 105, 166, 207